*Temples
of
South India*

Temples
of
South India

AMBUJAM ANANTHARAMAN

EastWest Books (Madras) Pvt. Ltd.
• Chennai • Bangalore • Hyderabad • New Delhi

EastWest Books (Madras) Pvt. Ltd.
571, Poonammalle High Road, Aminjikarai, Chennai - 600 029.
3-5-1108, Maruti Complex, II Floor, Narayanaguda, Hyderabad - 500 029
Praja Bhavan, I Floor, 53/2, Bull Temple Road, Basavangudi, Bangalore - 560 019
A-10, Lower Ground Floor, Lajpat Nagar III, New Delhi - 110 024

Copyright 2006 © Ambujam Anantharaman
All rights reserved

ISBN : 81-88661-42-2

· Price : Rs. 350

Cover design :
J Menon, www.grantha.com

Printed at
Sri Venkatesa Printing House
Chennai 600 026.
e.mail : saiprints@saimail.com

Published by
EastWest Books (Madras) Pvt. Ltd.
571, Poonammalle High Road, Aminjikarai, Chennai - 600 029.

CONTENTS

Acknowledgements v
Introduction vii

Temples of Tamil Nadu
Sriperumbudur – birthplace of Sri Ramanuja 1
Temples of Anjaneya — the symbol of courage, strength and "bhakthi" ... 8
Ashtalakshmi Temple on the beach 17
The great temple of Tiruvannamalai 21
The Nava Tirupathis praised by Nammazhwar 31
Thirunangur — Town of temples 41
Union of art and spirituality in Thanjavur Big Temple 47
The God who eats no salt : Uppiliappan; Kumbakonam 54
The powerful deity of Palani 59
Bestowing all good — Karpaga Vinayaka of Pillayarpatti 64
Pilgrimage to Rameswaram 69
Twin temples at Mamallapuram and Kadalmallai 75
Lord Venkateshwara at Gunaseelam 80
The grand temple of Mylapore 85
Kumariamman at Kanyakumari 95
Meenakshi Amman at Madurai 99
The cosmic dance of Siva : Chidambaram 107
A beautiful boar! : Tiruvidanthai 115
The famed Parthasarathy temple of Chennai 118
Divine deliberations on riverbank : Pazhayaseevaram 125
Lord Ranganatha of Srirangam 129
Uchi Pillayar temple on Rock Fort 139

The temple town of Kanchipuram	146
The fairest Azhwar of them all : Srivilliputhur	156
Rama the Saviour : Madurantakam	162

Temples of Karnataka

Belur, Halebid and Somnathpur – marvels of architecture	167
Sree Chamundeeswari of Mysore	175
Hilly abode of Narayana : Melkote	181
The unimaginable wonder that is Hampi	185
Mookambiga at Kollur: Trishakthi	199
Serenity in Srirangapatnam	204
Sri Saradambal of Sringeri	208
Lord Krishna: ever benevolent to his devotees : Udipi	215
Sandy "darshan" at Talakad	221

Temples of Kerala

Sree Ananthapadmanabha Swamy of Thiruvananthapuram	225
Temples of Ayyappa — the universal deity	232
The glory of Guruvayurappa; Guruvayur	236
Lord Janardhana at Varkala	243
Vadakkunatha Temple in Thrissur	249
Kaladi – birthplace of Adi Sankara	254

Temples of Andhra Pradesh

Raghavendra — the saint of Mantralayam	259
The true devotion of Bhadrachala Ramdas	266
The spider, the serpent and the elephant – Srikalahasthi	273
Lord Srinivasa of Tirumala	279
The unique idol of Varaha Narasimha : Simhachalam	293
Panchanarasimha sthala – Yadagirigutta	299

Temples of Pondicherry

Propitiating Lord Saneeswara at Tirunallar	302
Manarkula Vinayaka in Pondicherry	306
Cautions	310
Bibliography	313

ACKNOWLEDGEMENTS

The deep urge to express the devotion I feel to God in all manifestations whether as the omnipresent Ganapathi, omniscient Vishnu or the omnipotent Goddess is what prompted me to write this book. What started as a series of articles crystallised into a venture that could be useful to the devotee, the tourist and the researcher, thanks to the guidance and encouragement of the publisher Mr. K.S.Padmanabhan, Managing Director of EastWest Books (Madras), Chennai. In the first place this book would not have been possible but for the sustained help and support given by my husband, S.Anantharaman, despite his full time duties as a railway officer and the consideration shown by my children Manisha and Harsha. I also owe a lot to the encouragement given by my mother Mrs. Shilu Ranganathan, my father-in-law Mr. A.Sampathkumar, my mother-in-law Mrs. Kalyani Sampathkumar and my sister Sumitra. Thanks are due to my extended family and colleagues who have chivvied me on at various points. A deep debt of gratitude is owed to Mr.S.Muthiah, author and historian who first taught me the skills of observation and reporting.

Particular thanks are due to my editor Shobha Menon with whom I worked over the nitty gritty of the text. My gratitude abounds to the original publisher of the articles some of which have been used in a modified form in the book – *www.chennaionline.com* & *www.saranam.com* Part of the text was also prepared as material for Tamil Nadu Tourism Department and I am grateful to them for permitting me to use it as well as their collection of photographs. Photographs have also been contributed by the Regional Tourist Office, Government of India, Tamil Nadu, Chennai. Thanks are also due to Tourism Departments of Karnataka, Andhra Pradesh and Pondicherry. For source material I am indebted first to the scholars who have documented the rich history and culture of India, institutions like Archeological Survey of India who have made available the documents and texts and numerous officials and others associated with temple administration.

I hope readers will find it interesting as well as evocative to read this maiden effort of mine.

—Ambujam Anantharaman

INTRODUCTION

The human mind ever needs to fix itself on some object, material or immaterial, for the satisfaction of its physical, mental and spiritual needs. In the early years of mankind, people prayed to forms of nature like the tree or the sun, inanimate objects like stones and rivers, and lesser beings like animals and birds. It did not take Man much longer to search for something more to look up to, to find something that he could fashion with his own hands and worship. He made rough figurines of mud and stone, coloured with them with natural powders, and decorated them with flowers and leaves. These figurines invariably took on the shapes that he was accustomed to seeing everyday – the hill that he could spot in the distance, the elephant he avoided while hunting or the boy with the fine features who lived next door.

Man recognized from the very beginning that these figurines or objects were distinct from himself. In some process difficult to explain, he endowed them with powers. Perhaps, one day, prayer to a figurine in the form of a lion brought him good hunting spoils, or worshipping a river brought rains that his crops desperately needed. At some point, he began to feel that if he, in turn, made some offerings to what had now become his deities or Gods, they would look more kindly upon him. So, he offered them fruits and vegetables, raw flesh and cooked flesh. When his wishes came true, he organised elaborate thanksgiving to the deities, involving the local people. He even built crude structures to protect them from the very elements he thought they represented!

Such must have been the evolution of the temple. Of course, it is an enormous gap from what early man thought and did, to the marvellous constructions conceived and executed by later 'civilizations'. But, essentially, it was this sixth sense given to Man that led him on this quest for something outside himself. Temples are manifestations of the soul's desire to look and find something that is larger than itself. This is why fanes, whether they be Mosques, Churches, *Viharas* or Temples, are common to all religions.

Divisions over idol worship, customs and practices, differing concepts of mortality and immortality, sin and salvation, these are all of later origin. What came first was the need to have something different from oneself to supplicate to, and this need has persisted and outlasted all other needs of mankind.

Coming to Hinduism, this philosophy tells us that all human endeavour should be aimed at overcoming the trials and tribulations of earthly life through means such as *bhakti* and surrender, and thereby attain *moksha* or salvation. In this state, the mortal comes closest to the immortal. Hinduism says that the crucial distinction between the human and the divine is that the former, caught in *samsara* (worldly affairs), is torn between the poles of pain and pleasure, misery and ecstasy, while God is in a state of eternal bliss or *Ananda*. Salvation frees one from the cycle of rebirths that Hinduism believes in.

The soul and its union with the Divine have always been subjects for introspection among the scholarly and the simple. Who is God? What do his manifestations stand for? What is the relationship of Man to God? In most of us, these questions remain in the back of the mind, while in some they lead to the study of the scriptures. In a rare and brilliant few, the enquiring mind is wrought to such an extreme that there is a process of intense agitation leading to enlightenment and outpouring of joy. In the not so enquiring too, at some point in day-to-day life the question assails us — should I not give up the material and the mundane to pursue spirituality and godliness and achieve freedom from rebirth?

Ascetics do just this when they renounce the material world and become *sanyasins*. Obviously, for 99% of mankind, this is not possible. So, it is to the temple that he turns, to satiate his inclination for the spiritual.

This thesis does not intend to denigrate or even reduce the great importance the temple has played in the social fabric of our country, or the socio-cultural role it continues to play. Temples have always been places for kings to bestow favours to poets and philosophers while getting honours themselves, for people to congregate and exchange ideas, for elders to plan welfare schemes for the common folk. There may be no more kings, but this custom still continues.

For that matter, temples of the past were built mainly by kings or their vassals. To rulers, temples were first a symbol of their sovereignty. God reigned inside the temple, but the king reigned in the land where the temple stood! The grander the temple, the more respect the ruler got from his subjects. Second, temples were built as a measure of thanks for victory in war or martial campaigns. In this case, the temple usually had as the presiding deity, the *kula deivam* or family deity of that royal line. Third, fortunately for us, Indian rulers have been of an aesthetic bent of mind. Temples were the best way for them to exercise this penchant and organise the building of fantastic works of art. Whether it be sculpture on huge pillars of granite or minute idols of metal, whether it be painting of massive murals on temple walls or intricate paintings on palm leaves, whether it be huge canopies of hand-worked cloth or small golden robes for the idols of gods and goddesses, the best of Indian art has been associated with the temple.

In South India, various dynasties contributed to temple construction and embellishment. Most often, the antiquity of a temple and those who built it have been established with the help of numerous epigraphic inscriptions in the temples themselves. Sometimes, references to certain temples in ancient literature like the Tamil Sangam classics, have proved helpful. There are many instances where the dating of a temple has not been proved conclusively.

Tamil Nadu became a land of temples thanks to the Pallavas, the Pandyas and the Cholas. The Pallavas built both rock-cut and structural temples from the 4th century A D to the 9th century A D. An outstanding example is Mamallapuram. The Pandya (7th – 16th century A D) temples predominate the southern parts of Tamil Nadu and adjoining Kerala. The most magnificent temple builders were the Cholas, who lavished wealth on temple construction from the 9th to 13th centuries A D. What better example than the Thanjavur Brihadeeswara temple? After the fall of the Cholas, the Vijayanagaras (14th – 17th century A D) and the Nayaks continued the tradition. Once the East India Company entered the scene, these activities diminished.

The Vijayanagaras dominated neighbouring Karnataka and Andhra Pradesh too, whether amazing Hampi in Karnataka or astounding Lepakshi in Andhra Pradesh. Before their advent, the Western Gangas (3rd – 11th century A D), Western Chalukyas (6th to 8th century A D) and the Hoysalas (11th – 14th century A D) — the master architects of Belur and Halebid — fashioned great temples in the Karnataka region. In fact, Hoysala influence can be seen as far down south as Tiruvannamalai in Tamil Nadu.

In the Andhra Pradesh region, the Eastern Chalukyas (7th – 11th century A D) and the Eastern Gangas (11th to 15th century A D) built many grand temples like Simhachalam.

In Kerala, the Chera influence was strong till the rulers of Venad, Travancore, Cochin and other princely states from the 14th to the 19th century A D evolved the unique style of Kerala temple architecture with sloping roofs, intricate wooden sculptures and panels, use of tiles and brass ornamentation.

Talking of architectural styles, while the Kerala type is suited to the rainy terrain, the Hoysalas preferred soapstone as it lent itself to the most elaborate and intricate sculpture and carving. It was also locally available. Their style is also marked by a central shrine with manifold smaller shrines around. The Cholas liked the grandeur of granite and tall towers, while the Vijayanagaras combined all these elements to reach near perfection.

In all these cases, there was adherence to the *Shastras* – codified traditions. These related to *Vastu* (location), *Shilpa* (structure) and *Agama* (ritual). There was also selection of temple style based on the *shikara* (roof over the sanctum sanctorum). The three styles, in brief, are the *nagara* – four sided, *dravida* – hexagon or octagon and the *vesara* – circular, apsidal or ellipse. Barring some rare Chola temples, the *shikara* (*vimanam*) would invariably be smaller than the temple tower or the *gopuram*. Further variations involved how many *mandapams* or ornate halls the temple had.

Proceeding now to the legends that are an integral part of the Indian psyche. Gods, goddesses, the *vahanas* (vehicles) they travel on, the demons they fight and overcome, the stories of their weddings and the stories of their marital disputes, their periodic 'visits' to Earth for some festival or the other, these are as real to the Indian mind as they may be alien to the Western mind. There is no fun visiting a temple without finding out the legend behind its construction. As Indian children are told these stories by their mothers and grandmothers right from childhood, a visitor to a temple, even when adult, would first tend to ask why Lord Krishna was in a particular pose in a particular temple, rather than ask which school of architecture the temple belonged to! The serious student, of course, would undoubtedly ask the latter question, along with queries on antiquity, history and combination of architectural styles.

This book has attempted to describe History and Antiquity, Art and Architecture, Legend and Lore, Customs and Culture, to the best extent possible. In the around 50 temples covered, every one of these aspects may not have been covered, for want of information. This is not for lack of trying. While most of the temples described are in worship, some not in worship such as Hampi, Belur, Halebid and Somnathpur, have been included for the benefit of those interested in architecture and for foreign tourists. Temples which have come up around the *samadhis* of saints, such as Mantralayam in Andhra Pradesh, have also been included as saints like Raghavendra and Adi Sankara have a large following. This writer has visited all the temples, which have been written about, except Sabarimala in Kerala. For this temple, accounts of those who have been there have been relied on.

The number of temples selected for each state is in proportion to the number of important temples in that state. Therefore the temples included from Tamil Nadu are more in number than those in Karnataka, Andhra Pradesh or Kerala. At the same time, there are many more temples which should have been written about, but have not, either because this writer has not been there or because of space constraints.

In addition, at the end of each piece, exhaustive travel information has been provided with regard to access, accommodation, nearby attractions and other details. At the end of the text, there is a section on precautions, which all potential visitors should read.

But the overriding strand which runs through every piece is devotion, since, ultimately, the temple is a standing symbol of devotion to God.

—*Ambujam Anantharaman*

Tiruvannamalai

Temples of
TAMIL NADU

Brihadeeswara Temple, Thanjavur

Tirunageswaram

Mahamaham Tank

Swamimalai

Tirupparankundram

Meenakshi Amman - Madurai

Mariamman Teppakulam - Madurai

Jayamkondacholapuram

Kanjanur Sukran

Pillayarpatti

Mamallapuram - Arjuna's Penance

Kundrakudi

Navabashanam - Sea Temple

Kuttralanathar Temple

Marudar Malai

Tiruchendur

Alangudi Guru Temple

Sri Rangam

Tirunelveli

Rameswaram

Thiruthani

Tirunallar

Trichy Rock Fort

Tiruvengadu

SRIPERUMBUDUR
the birthplace of Sri Ramanuja

The temple of Sri Adhikesavaperumal in the township of Sriperumbudur, 60 km to the southwest of Chennai, is one of the ancient shrines in the neighbourhood of the metropolis. The township is famous as the *avatara sthala* (birthplace) of Saint Ramanuja, the great philosopher of Vaishnavism. You can see the newly painted *rajagopuram* (temple tower) even from the highway, which is easily accessed from Chennai through the Poonamallee High Road.

It was the presence of Mahavishnu in the form of Adhikeshavaperumal and the beautiful setting of the village, which prompted Asuri Kesavacharya, the father of Ramanuja, to settle at this spot. Ramanuja incarnated in the year 1017 AD on the 12th day of the Chitrai month under the star Tiruvadirai. Every year his birth is celebrated with a grand festival including a car procession.

In the shrine of the main deity, Sri Adhikesavaperumal of the smiling visage, with his consorts Sreedevi and Bhoodevi, bestows his abundant grace on his devotees. To the right of the main shrine is the sanctum sanctorum of Sri Ramanuja and to the left is Sree Yatirajanathavallithayar, her name denoting that she is the consort of the master of the king of saints, Yathiraja or Ramanuja. This is a rare instance where Goddess Lakshmi has a name attributed to a devotee of the Lord, and here she is believed to be a *Varaprasadi*, or 'Granter of all wishes'.

The temple is in the south Indian style of temple architecture with features of both Chola and Vijayanagara periods. It was constructed in the later Chola and Vijayanagara period. There is an inscription dated 1572, which mentions Srirangaraya I of the Vijayanagara period. Vijayanagara sources mention that in 1556 during the reign of Rama Raya, a gift of 31 villages was made at the request of one Sadasiva to maintain this temple.

The temple's golden *vimanam* (tower over the sanctum sanctorum) with Sri Ramanuja's image etched on it, was erected in the year 1912. It is believed to be the first golden *vimanam* in south India. A copper plate commemorating the event can be seen fixed on the temple floor, at a point from where you can look up and see the great devotee seated on the *vimanam*.

During the *Chitrai* festival, the *utsava murthy* (festival idol) of Sri Ramanuja is placed in the garden adjacent to the place of his birth. It is said that Ramanuja was so impressed with its likeness to him that he hugged it, thereby passing on all his powers to it. It is therefore called '*than ugandha thirumeni*' ('the body touched by him'). Two events support this belief. When the *stapathi* (sculptor) opened the eye of the *vigraham* (idol) with the chisel, blood came out of the eyes of the teacher, then residing at Srirangam. When asked for the reason, the preceptor replied that the idol was himself. Secondly, when the *vigraham* was sanctified, Ramanuja gradually became weaker and shuffled off his mortal coils within a fortnight. This has been interpreted as his *prana* (life force) coming to abide in the *vigraham* at Sriperumbudur. Therefore this idol is believed to be very powerful, and worshipping here is believed to confer all benefits including *moksham* (salvation). In Sriperumbudur, Ramanuja is addressed as '*Swamy*' (Lord).

On the festival day, the idol is bejewelled, dressed in glittering robes and carrying a sword, indicating Ramanuja's status as the 'King of Saints'. The idol is brought to the garden after the ride in the temple car in the morning. Before the *thirumanjanam* (ritual bath), the jewels and robes are removed and the idol can be seen in all its original glory. It is difficult to find words to describe the visage and form of the great saint. His back is shaped like a hooded serpent, flared and vibrant. This is because he is considered an incarnation of Adi Sesha, the 1000-headed serpent on which Lord Vishnu is recumbent. People eagerly wait to see the *thirumanjanam* and the *pushpa pallakku* (palanquin decked with flowers) that follows. Devotees from all over come to see the Lord. The locals exude warmth and hospitality even to strangers.

The legends behind the construction of the Sri Adhikesava temple are astounding. In the main forecourt of the Sri Adhikesavaperumal shrine, four huge pillars support the high roof, over 25 feet in circumference, with *yalis* (a mythical beast sculpted on pillars) carved on them. They are so gigantic that one wonders how mere human effort could have hoisted them without the help of high capacity lifting equipment!

Legend has it that the builders of the temple tried to erect the pillars, but owing to their excessive size and weight they failed and gave up the endeavour at nightfall. The next morning, to their utter surprise, they found the pillars duly installed. The people concluded that only giants or *bhootas* could have accomplished this. This is why the place came to be called Sri-perum-budur! (great town of giants). Little wonder that the saint who was born in such a place wrought miracles at various planes of life — physical, temporal and spiritual.

It is a general opinion that the life of a saint is one of peaceful renunciation. But this calm veneer also hides a ferment of thought and action aimed at the realization of truth and performance of good. Few lives exemplify this more than that of the Saint of Sriperumbudur, Ramanujacharya.

Once, a *Brahmarakshasa* (demon) possessed the princess of Kanchipuram and no amount of exorcism could cure her. Finally, it was Ramanuja who cured the princess. When Ramanuja asked the demon to go away, the fiend is said to have requested the saint to keep his feet on his head and bless him. The saint said that he would do so if the demon showed proof of his departure. And no sooner had Ramanuja placed his feet on the princess' head than the demon left, breaking the topmost branch of a nearby tree!

Performance of temporal duties for the good of human beings is an ordained responsibility of a pontiff. Ramanuja exemplified this too, in the course of his life. During his stay near Mysore in Thirunarayanapuram (Melkote), Ramanuja constructed a huge tank at Thondanur and restored the grand temple of Chelvapillai and Sampathkumara in the hilly abode of Melkote.

While a potentate is content with merely providing the material well being of his subjects, the saint goes beyond and works for their spiritual salvation as well. The Thirukkottiyur Puranam can best illustrate this aspect of Saint Ramanuja's life. Mahapurna, who was the *guru* (teacher) of Ramanuja at Srirangam advised him to seek the knowledge of the *Vaishanava mantra* from Goshtipurna, a great teacher, who was residing in Thirukottiyur. Ramanuja made 18 trips to Goshtipurna and each time he was turned back by the latter. Ramanuja was so distraught that he wondered whether he was suffering from some impurity, which was making Goshtipurna consider him unworthy to hear the great *mantra* that could save a being from the repeated birth and death cycle.

Tradition says that one of the priests of the Ranganatha temple at Srirangam told Goshtipurna, at the behest of the Lord himself, to impart the *mantra* to Ramanuja. To this he is said to have replied, "Oh my Lord, you have made the law that this is never to be spoken to one who is devoid of austerity or devotion, nor to one who does not render service, nor to one who cavils at thee". At this the reply came "You do not know Ramanuja's purity. He is the saviour of humanity".

After some time, moved by pity for the grieving saint and his relentless quest, Goshtipurna imparted the sacred eight syllable *mantra* with its mystic meaning and said "None but Sri Vishnu is aware of its glory. Whoever hears this will attain liberation and go to *Vaikunta* (the abode of Vishnu) after his death. So do not give it to anyone else".

Upon hearing the mantra *'Om Namo Narayanaya'*, Ramanuja felt blessed and a powerful feeling arose in him to share it with the people who were suffering, so that they could attain peace and strength. He proceeded forth to gather people from far and near and when a substantial number had gathered, he climbed to the top of the temple tower at Thirukkotiyur and imparted the *mantra* to the huge congregation. Records of certain writers say that at that point of time the people were so joyous that Thirukottiyur itself appeared like *Vaikunta*!

When Goshtipurna heard of this, he was outraged. And when Ramanuja approached him to worship at his feet, he called him 'a heinous sinner' and cursed that he would rot in hell. A calm Ramanuja is believed to have said, "My Lord, I don't mind rotting in hell if so many suffering thousands can reach *Vaikunta*". His compassion moved Goshtipurana, who at once realised his grave folly and fell at the feet of Ramanuja.

Ramanuja lived up to the age of 120 and shuffled off his mortal coils at Srirangam. He left behind a priceless legacy of *Visishtadvaita* for countless generations to lead their lives in the path of virtue and goodness. *Visishtadvaita,* which states that it is the goal of life for the *Atman* (soul) to reach the *Brahman* (godhead), gives hope of salvation to every being.

FAST FACTS

How to reach

Air	:	The nearest airport, Chennai, is 65 km away.
Rail	:	The nearest railhead, Kanchipuram, is 29 km away.
Road	:	Sriperumbudur is connected to Chennai by an excellent highway, as it is on the way to Bangalore and Tirupati. It can also be reached from Kanchipuram. Public buses are available from Chennai.
Local Transport	:	Walking is recommended.
Season	:	Throughout the year.
Clothing	:	Tropical, light cottons.
Languages spoken	:	English and Tamil.
Accommodation	:	It is best to visit the temple from Chennai. Alternatively Kanchipuram can be the base.

Kanchipuram

	Tariff (INR)	Phone
MM Hotel	300-800+tax	954112-230023
TM Hotel	550-1000+tax	04112-225250
Shelter Resorts	1450-1900	04114-272424

For Chennai hotels see article on Sri Kapaleeswarar Temple.

PLACES OF INTEREST NEARBY

Kanchipuram: This temple town of Tamil Nadu can be accessed via Sriperumbudur from Chennai. There are over a hundred beautiful temples to visit.

Narasingapuram: An ancient Lakshmi Narasimha temple, which is 5 km from Sriperumbudur. The consort is Maragathavalli. There is another ancient temple at Manimangalam, 20 km east of Sriperumbudur, with a shrine for Sri Rajagopala, in the company of Sreedevi and Bhoodevi.

Kshetropasana: An ashram founded by the renowned exponent of Hinduism, Prof. Prema Pandurang.

Rajiv Gandhi Memorial: The site where Rajiv Gandhi, former Prime Minister of India, was killed in a bomb blast. A memorial with a circular formation of towering pillars has been created here.

Irungattukottai: A modern track for motorbike and car racing. A number of events are held here.

TEMPLES OF ANJANEYA
the symbol of courage, strength and bhakthi

Anjaneya, the *bhakta* or devotee *non-pareil*, God himself and a pathway to the Gods too. In times of distress and conflict a virtual pillar of strength and a symbol of hope, his very presence on earth offers direction in the path of spiritual progress.

Worship of Anjaneya, the great devotee of Lord Rama, has grown immensely in the last two decades. Hanuman, Vayuputra, Maruti, and Bajrangbali are his various names. What sets him apart is his unequalled devotion to Lord Rama. When Rama offered him *moksha* (salvation) he is said to have refused, saying he wanted to stay on earth as long as the *Rama Nama* (the name of Rama) was uttered. Hanuman's idol is found in all Vishnu and Rama temples. The Ramayana pictures him as an erudite, cultured and divine person. He is as strong as he is wise, and as devoted as he is strong — a rare combination.

Anjaneya, the son of Vayu, has two main forms, *bhakta* and *veera*. Both forms are beneficent. 'Bhakta Anjaneya' stresses the devotional aspect while 'Veera Anjaneya' underlines the importance of valour and fearlessness. It is believed that Lord Siva himself incarnated as Anjaneya to assist Lord Rama in overcoming the demon Ravana, as Rama could not exercise his divine powers in that *avatar* (incarnation) of Lord Vishnu.

During the battle in Lanka, Rama and Lakshmana were grievously wounded and unconscious. The physician of the monkey army, Sushena, called for the Sanjeevini herb from a mountain in the distant Himalayas. Hanuman, who took on the impossible task, used his inimitable presence of mind to uproot the whole mountain when he could not identify the herb. For all the help he rendered, Rama blessed him with immortality. In other words, He made Hanuman a *Chiranjeevi*.

Anjaneya is represented in two postures. In the company of Rama, Sita and Lakshmana, he is shown standing humbly at a distance with folded hands or kneeling devoutly at the feet of Sri Rama. In temples specially devoted to him, he is awe-inspiring, usually carrying the mace in his left hand and the Sanjeevini Mountain on his right hand. Earlier, there were few temples devoted exclusively to Anjaneya, but now more temples with Anjaneya as the principal deity have been consecrated.

The leaves of the *tulsi* (basil) plant are dear to Lord Anjaneya, as are betel leaves. His idols are most often decorated with these garlands.

Let us look at three Anjaneya temples in Chennai. Perhaps the oldest among the many Anjaneya temples in Chennai is the one at Luz.

Luz Anjaneya: The Sree Sundaravinayagar and Sree Selvavinayagar Anjaneya Devasthanam is on Royapettah High Road near Luz. Here, only the profile of Anjaneya can be seen. Facing south, he seems to be essaying a trip to Lanka. The right hand is the *abhaya hastam* (hand which protects) and the left hand is placed on the thigh.

This temple was founded by the Salivahana Chettiars, potters by profession, who migrated to Mylapore from Mysore. It is sited on land that was granted to them by the Nawab of Arcot, whose suppliers the Chettiars were. They established two temples for Lord Vinayaka and while digging a well found the *swayambhu* (self-manifested) *vigraham* of

Anjaneya. The temple celebrated the 200th year of its founding in 2000.

In the beginning, the Salivahanas performed *pujas*, and later Vaishnavite priests were appointed. A view was expressed that since Anjaneya was a *bhaktha* of Lord Vishnu, he would be happy only when temple offerings were first given to the Lord. Accordingly, a copper *vigraham* of Sri Venugopala was installed in the sanctum sanctorum. On festival days except *Sri Rama Navami*, the idol of Sri Venugopala is taken on a procession in the temple neighbourhood. A separate shrine for Sri Rama was built in 1954.

An interesting story about Anjaneya goes thus. One among the five Pandavas, Bhima, the great wrestler who vanquished the evil Kichaka, was justifiably proud of his physical might. Once during the period of the Pandavas' exile, he was asked by Draupadi to fetch her a fragrant flower from the forest. Bhima, the chivalrous husband ever eager to please, set out following the trail of fragrance. After quite a distance, Bhima tracked the source of the pleasant smell and sighted the flower. As he proceeded ahead, he found a small simian blocking his path. Bhima bade the monkey to move and leave way for the Pandava. The small monkey said he was too old and weak and hence could not move. Would Bhima kindly lift his tail and proceed? Outraged by this audacious suggestion, an angry Bhima lifted his mace and in one swift movement attempted to flick the tail of the monkey. What a rude surprise to the proud Bhima, for he could not move the slender tail even an inch! Clever Bhima immediately realised that this was no ordinary monkey and humbly requested the animal to reveal its identity. Thereupon, the monkey stood up and said it was none other than Hanuman, the elder brother of Bhima, both being the sons of Vayu. A delighted Bhima requested that he be shown the massive form that Anjaneya assumed to cross the ocean and frighten the demons in Lanka. Anjaneya obliged his brother and hugged him in order to pass on all his strength to his brother and blessed him with victory in the coming battle of Kurukshetra. Such was Anjaneya's love for his brother and such is the aspect that he exhibits in this temple.

The temple is open both mornings and evenings and one should not miss the grace of the *Varaprasadi*, the granter of boons, residing here. Devotees throng this temple to offer Lord Anjaneya a garland of *ulundu vadais*, (a savoury made of pulses, known popularly as *Hanumar vadas*). The significance of this offering is that *ulundu* has a cooling property and is therefore supposed to reduce Anjaneya's *ugra* (ferocity) and make him beneficent to his devotees. Also, this *vadai* has ingredients that will please Saneeswara, Rahu and Ketu (three of the 9 planets or *navagrahas*, part of Hindu lore). It is believed that planetary positions do not affect devotees of Anjaneya. On Saturdays, the day most auspicious for Saneeswara, devotees offer *vadamalas* (a garland strung with 108 *vadais*) to the Lord.

It was to this temple that the first Governor General of free India, C Rajagopalachari, brought the completed manuscript of his *Ramayana* for Anjaneya's blessings. In 1998, the *mahasamprokshanam* (purification according to Vaishnavite traditions) of this shrine was performed after a gap of 35 years. Recent renovations include marble flooring, better kitchen facilities, and a wedding hall constructed in the temple precincts.

Nanganallur Anjaneya : At Nanganallur in Chennai, a 32-foot idol of Sri Adhivyathi Hara Bhakta Anjaneya stands majestically. Despite a towering presence, He is full of *kaarunya* (compassion). The idol was sculpted from one large block of granite, installed in 1989 and consecrated in 1995.The significance of large idols is that they depict the power of good as superior to the forces of evil.

That the valorous Anjaneya was full of compassion too, is best delineated in the *Sundara Kanda* of the *Valmiki Ramayana*. To him fell the opportunity of bringing good tidings to the suffering Sita at Ashoka Vanam (the place where Sita was incarcerated in Ceylon), and later to Sri Rama, that his wife was alive and awaiting rescue by the Lord. Reading the *Sundara Kanda*, which describes Anjaneya's journey to Lanka, his meeting with Sita, their ensuing conversations and so on, is believed to be a cure for any problem – physical, mental or spiritual. This reading is to be followed by reading a chapter in the *Ramayana* devoted to the coronation of Lord Rama.

Anjaneya epitomises courage, and therefore relieves the devotee from fear. He stands for strength, and thus bestows good health. He is the most loyal among all beings, showing the path in today's self-serving world. Most important, he exemplifies *Bhakthi* (devotion), guiding the devotee on the path to God. All these aspects are highlighted in the Nanganallur Anjaneya temple. Of these, his quality of giving relief from illness is exemplified here, with his very name meaning 'Destroyer of the original illness'.

During the *Sri Rama Navami* festival, the whole of Nanganallur comes alive with the temple organising Carnatic music concerts by leading artistes.

Bhakta Anjaneyar, Alamelumangapuram : In the heart of the city is situated the Bhakta Anjaneyar temple at Alamelumangapuram, Mylapore. The most distinctive feature of this temple is that all distinctions of caste and creed have been overcome, with a constant influx of devotees from all linguistic groups.

The most popular feature here has been the *koti archana*, wherein one crore names of Anjaneya were recited over a period of nearly two years. The temple itself was constructed under the direction of the Kanchi Sankarachaya, Sri Jayendra

Saraswati, who desired that an Anjaneya temple in south Madras should be built with a tall idol. Accordingly, the temple was completed with an 18-foot *vigraham*. The installation was done on March 31, 1985, and the idol consecrated on June 26, 1986.

Hanumath Jayanthi is celebrated grandly here in the Tamil month of Margazhi. The highpoints are the dazzling *alankaram* (decoration) done for the Lord. The decoration with butter, fruits and *vadais* and *tulsi* leaves make the *vigraham* so attractive that one cannot but leave the temple with a full heart.

The *Sri Rama Navami* celebrations are marked by music concerts and discourses. The festival idols of Rama, Sita and Lakshmana with Hanuman are taken on a procession in the area.

As always, the grace of Lord Vinayaka is required for any endeavour and Sri Vijaya Ganapathy has a shrine to himself in this temple. A shrine for Lord Rama has been built and has been consecrated. Rama is seen with Sita, Lakshmana and Anjaneya. New shrines to Hayagreeva, Garuda and Vinayaka have also been constructed and sanctified.

FAST FACTS

How to reach

Air	:	Chennai has two airports – domestic (Kamaraj) and international (Anna) — located adjacent to one another at Meenambakkam, 20 km from the city.
Rail	:	Chennai is well connected by rail on routes towards Mumbai in the West, Jammu in the North, Calcutta in the East and Kanyakumari at the southern tip of India.
Road	:	Chennai is well connected by road to the southern cities like Tiruchirapalli and to the garden city, Bangalore.

...*Temples of Tamilnadu*

Local Transport	:	Tourist taxis, call taxis, auto rickshaws, public buses, private tourist buses and cycle rickshaws are available. The city also has a Mass Rapid Rail Transit system from Madras Beach to Tiruvanmiyur.
Season	:	Throughout the year.
Clothing	:	Tropical, light cottons. A light pullover may be necessary in December - January in the evenings and early morning when there is dew.
Languages spoken	:	English and Tamil.
Accommodation	:	Chennai has a wide range of accommodation from budget to deluxe.

Luxury

	Tariff (INR)	Phone
Chola Sheraton:	5500-6500(+12.5%)	28110101
Moderate		
Nilgiri's Nest	1350-2950 +taxes	28115111
Shelter:	1500-2995(+taxes)	24951919
Budget		
Hotel Karpagam	470-650	24959984
Swagath	394-633	28132971

(Accommodation close to the temples has been selected)

PLACES OF INTEREST NEARBY

Apparswami Temple: This is a shrine for the Saivite saint Apparswami (not to be confused with the saint-poet Appar), nearly 150 years old. A great devotee of Lord Siva, Apparswami lived in Mylapore in the 19th century. He was a consummate *bhaktha*, possessed of extraordinary powers of *siddha* (supernatural powers, especially curative) and believed to be capable of even metempsychosis or transmigration of soul. During his life, devotees thronged the temple in large numbers. When, in 1851, he attained *brahmasamadhi*, his devotee Chidambaraswamy established a *lingam* on top of his tomb. Later it was declared a public temple and came to be known as Apparswami Koil. It is situated on the busy Royapettah High Road opposite Sanskrit College and is a sought after place of worship. A special sight on its premises is the peepul and neem tree, which have fused to present a new botanical entity.

Shirdi Sai Baba Temple: At the Shirdi Sai Baba Temple in Mylapore, it is a silent queue — the young and the old, man and woman, the northerner and the southerner, the Hindu and the Muslim — which moves with a quietude born of intense devotion as they proceed towards the statue of Sai Baba, carved in marble, translucent in its effulgence. The saint, sculpted in a posture of yogic calm and benevolence, is seen seated with a black *tilak* adorning his forehead. Such is the radiance, that one feels that this is not a mere statue. It is also the headquarters of the All India Sai Samaj. How the worship of Saint Sai Baba, a native of Maharashtra, became so popular in Chennai can be known from the life and work of Pujyashri Narasimhaswami.

Narasimhaswami, known in his *purvashram* (prior to renunciation) as Narasimhaier, was a successful advocate of Salem. A tragic event in his personal life, the death of his two young children by drowning in the well of the house, made him lose his attachment to the material. In his quest for peace, he went to Tiruvannamalai and thereafter to Shirdi. This was about 15 years after the *Mahasamadhi* of Sai Baba. When Narasimhaier sat near the tomb of Sai Baba and pleaded for solace, a Chettiar came to him and gave him a bag full of currency notes. To a man who had spurned wealth this seemed ironic. When Narasimhaier told the Chettiar to take away the bag the latter refused, saying that Baba had bade him give the money to a person seated near his tomb! That moment it occurred to Narasimhaier that he had been commanded by Baba to spread his gospel. The money amounted to Rs 11,500 and with that the All India Sai Samaj was founded.

The temple in Alamelumangapuram was established in 1952 and the *Kumbhabhishekam* held in 1953. What began as a tin-roofed shed has now been transformed. The sanctum sanctorum has a massive silver throne with the saint's framed photograph ensconced on it. The priests perform puja in Sanskrit, chanting the Ashtothram and Sai Sahasranamam written by Narasimhaswami. *Abhishekam* is perfomed to the statue. At the *agni kundam* to the left of the main temple, a fire brought from Shirdi burns ceaselessly. The ash from this fire is offered to devotees who assemble at the *Dwarakamayee* (the place of assembly for devotees of Sai Baba without any distinction of race, creed, social position etc) as *vibhuti* and is said to cure any ailment. The Samaj is a philanthropic organisation engaged in charity. It runs a free dispensary, library, school and performs poor feeding twice daily. Thursday is a special day for worship.

Santhome Basilica: With its towering spires, lovely stained glass windows, poignant figure of Christ in the altar, ancient image of Mother Mary and numerous relics of St Thomas, the second apostle of Christ, San

Thome Basilica is a must-see for any visitor to Mylapore. Church literature says that St Thomas himself built the original church here in 52 A D. Tradition has it that the Apostle was buried here after his martyrdom in 68 A D. His remains were later shifted to a Mediterranean island. Even to this day a piece of the lance with which he was mortally pierced, a few bones and some vestments are kept in the crypt below the altar. After some centuries, a bigger church was built here. In 1893, it was decided to build a new cathedral, which was consecrated in April 1896. In 1906, the tercentenary of this great cathedral was celebrated. The Crypt of St Thomas was enlarged and covered with marble and a new altar was erected directly over the sepulchre. In 1956, it was raised to the rank of a Minor Basilica.

Guindy National Park: This is the only national park situated within a metropolis. The vegetation is of the thorny scrub jungle type. There are over 30 tree species including very old banyan trees. The rare Indian antelope, known as the black buck, is found here. Other species of animal and bird life include spotted deer, bonnet monkey, jungle cat and kingfisher, blue jay, koel, dove and robins. Within the limits of Guindy Park lies a children's park with facilities for recreation. Adjacent to this is the Snake Park, which has a remarkable collection of snakes.

Arignar Anna Zoological Park: Located 30 km south of Chennai at Vandalur, this Zoo is special for replication of natural environment. The nocturnal animal house, safari park, aviary, pre-historic animal park and aquarium are some attractions.

Excursions near Nanganallur

Uttara Guruvayurappan Temple: A temple dedicated to Lord Krishna and modelled after the famous Krishna temple in Guruvayur, Kerala.

Raja Rajeswari Temple: This temple is dedicated to Goddess Parvathi, wife of Lord Siva, who represents the force of creation.

Kishkinta: This is a theme park with joy rides and amusement activities.

ASHTALAKSHMI
Temple on the beach

This beautiful temple on the shores of the Bay of Bengal in Chennai enshrines the 8 forms of Lakshmi or Mahalakshmi, the divine consort of Mahavishnu, who are collectively known as *Ashta Lakshmi*. Devotees throng this temple and offer *pujas* to obtain the blessings and bounty of the Goddess.

The 8 Lakshmis according to the *Devi Suktham* are:

Dhana Lakshmi - *"Ya devi sarva bhuteshu pushtirupena samstitha"*....She is the goddess of bounty and wealth.

Vidya Lakshmi - *"Ya devi sarvabhuteshu buddhi rupena samstitha."*....She is the goddess of the intellect.

Dhaanya Lakshmi - *"Ya devi sarvabhuteshu kshudha rupena samstitha"*....She is the Goddess who satisfies hunger.

Veera Lakshmi - *"Ya devi sarvabhuteshu throothirupena samstitha"*....She is the Goddess of courage.

Sowbhagya Lakshmi - *"Ya devi sarvabhuteshu dhushtirupena samstitha"*....She is the Goddess of happiness.

Santhana Lakshmi - *"Ya devi sarvabhuteshu mathrurupena samstitha"*....She is the Mother of all beings.

Karunya Lakshmi - *"Ya devi sarva bhuteshu kaarunya rupena samstitha"*....She is the goddess of compassion.

Mahalakshmi - *"Ya devi sarva bhuteshu Lakshmirupena samstitha"*....She abides as Lakshmi in all beings.

"Namasthasmai Namasthasmai Namasthasmai namo namahah"... "I bow to the Goddess who has all these attributes" goes a prayer.

In Chennai, the main deities in the Besant Nagar Ashta Lakshmi temple are Mahavishnu and his consort Mahalakshmi. In this temple, Goddess Andal is with the Lord. The *utsavar* idols are Lord Srinivasa and Goddess Padmavathy. The main sanctum sanctorum faces the sea.

The temple tank is the sea itself and the *vimanam* is an *ashtanga vimanam* (of 8 parts) similar to those at Tirukkottiyur and Uttiramerur. The temple is an *Omkara Kshetram*, the sound of the sea resembling the *pranava mantram* or the original sound, *Om*.

The temple is built in tiers and as we climb up the winding stairs, each of the 8 Lakshmi idols appears enshrined before our eyes. One has to be careful while navigating the curved steps, especially with the wind buffeting the face. The temple being a contemporary one, it is built with brick and cement and the exterior is painted with multi-colours.

Besides shrines to Dhanyalakshmi, Dhairyalakshmi, Santanalakshmi, Dhanalakshmi and Vidyalakshmi, who are mentioned in the Devi Suktham, the other forms found in this temple are Adhilakshmi (the source or the beginning of everything, She confers *arogyam* or good health), Gajalakshmi (She augurs good beginnings for every new venture) and Vijayalakshmi (She grants devotees victory in all efforts). Blessed are the devotees who get the grace of the Goddess.

The temple was established in the year 1976 mainly from devotees' donations. Poor feeding is carried on regularly. There are also shrines to Lord Ganesha, Lord Ayyappa and Lord Anjaneya.

FAST FACTS

How to reach

Air : Chennai has two airports – domestic (Kamaraj) and international (Anna) — located adjacent to one another at Meenambakkam, 23 km from the city.

Rail : Chennai has direct trains running towards Mumbai in the West, Jammu in the North, Calcutta in the East and Kanyakumari at the southern tip of India.

Road : Chennai is well connected by road to the southern cities like Tiruchirapalli and to the garden city, Bangalore.

Local Transport : Tourist taxis, call taxis, auto rickshaws, public buses, private tourist buses and cycle rickshaws are available. The city also has a Mass Rapid Rail Transit system from Madras Beach to Tiruvanmiyur.

Season : Throughout the year.

Clothing : Tropical, light cottons. A light pullover may be necessary in December - January in the evenings and early morning when there is dew.

Languages spoken : English and Tamil.

Accommodation : Chennai has a wide range of accommodation from budget to deluxe.

	Tariff (INR)	Phone
Luxury		
Park Sheraton	6500-12000+taxes	24994101
Moderate:		
Shelter	1500-2995+taxes	24951919
Budget		
Ramaprasad (Adyar)	130-650	28523251

(Accommodation close to the temple has been selected)

PLACES OF INTEREST NEARBY

Velankanni Church: This important place of worship is close to the Ashtalakshmi temple. Lapped by the incessant waves of the Bay of Bengal, the shrine to Annai Vailankanni is popular not only with Christians but with people of other faiths as well. How this church came to be built is interesting. A parish priest of Chennai, Father P T Arulappa, had a vision in which the Holy Mother directed that a church be built on the shore and called the Annai Vailankanni church. A beginning was made in 1971 in a small hut with a thatched roof. By 1972, an extended structure rose and the Archbishop of Chennai Rev. R Arulappa declared the church open. A bigger church was built and blessed on 15th August 1985 on the feast of Our Lady's Assumption to Heaven. An arresting feature of the church is the commanding 97-ft belfry. The annual church festival in late August and early September is very popular. The whole area comes alive during this period with small vendors crowding the roads leading to the church and families dressed in their best making it a pleasant day out by visiting the church, the temple and the beach nearby.

Marundeeswarar Temple: In the Marundeeswarar temple at Tiruvanmiyur, God is believed to have manifested as a healer of disease and devotees sincerely believe, as do the priests, that the mixture of sacred ash, milk and water offered at the temple and consumed thereafter will cure any ailment. The story goes that Lord Siva is said to have given relief from health problems to sage Agastya, the Sun God and the Moon God here. While Agastya was suffering from a stomach ache after he ingested Vatapi, the Sun and Moon were suffering from a terrible disease because of *Gurupatni Dosham* (planetary ill-effects). It was Agastya, who named the deity Aushadeeswarar, the Tamil translation of which is Marundeeswarar. The Sun and the Moon, it is said, perform *puja* at this temple every evening. The deity faces west, as the Sun does the honours at sunset. Unlike other Siva temples, this temple does not have a shrine to the *navagrahams* because the Sun and Moon are in prayer mode here. The main *lingam* is believed to be Swayambhu, and is also called Palvannanathan because Kamadhenu, the divine cow, used to shower him with milk constantly. The small pit on the 'head' of the deity is supposed to be the mark of Kamadhenu's hoof. The *devi* here is Thiruppurasundari. Apart from shrines to Lord Vinayaka and Lord Subramania, there is a unique shrine here to Valmiki, the sage who authored the Ramayana. Valmiki is said to have performed penance at the spot where the temple stands, and the Lord Thyagarajaswami gave *darshan* in a dancing pose beneath the west tower of the temple. The name Tiruvanmiyur is in fact derived from Valmiki – Thiru Vanmiki-yuur. There is an architectural peculiarity in this temple, since part of it has been built in the Chola style of architecture and part in the Pallava style.

The great temple of
TIRUVANNAMALAI

At Tiruvannamalai is a shrine of great sanctity. The world famous Arunachaleswara temple at Tiruvannamalai, 190 km from Chennai, is one of the *pancha bootha* (5 elements) shrines of Siva. Siva is said to abide here in the form of fire.

When I reached Tiruvannamalai, it was quite late and the town was bustling with life, as the *Karthigai Deepam* festival was the next day. Over 10 lakh people congregate to witness the *Deepam*. This festival involves the lighting of a lamp on the Arunachala hill, believed to be Siva himself, which can be viewed from many miles away. I got lodgings in one of the new hotels with a breathtaking view of the blue-hued hill. The majestic sight of the huge *gopuram* in the morning against the backdrop of the hill was even more striking.

The temple has a well laid out procedure for conduct of worship to the God and Goddess. River Ganga is said to arrive symbolically in a pot carried by an elephant to cleanse the enclosures. After duly waking the Lord and his consort, six *pujas* are performed from dawn to night till the last *puja*, when the couple retire to the bedchamber.

Legend: There is a beautiful story behind how Uma married Siva in Tiruvannamalai.

Once Parvati or Uma closed the eyes of Siva with her hands, in a playful mood, and all the worlds were plunged into darkness. This angered Siva, and Uma had to come down to earth. She went to Kanchipuram, where Siva bade her to go to Tiruvannamalai and perform austerities. He told her that she would then take her place on the left side of his body. (This is the concept of *Ardhanareeswara*, where Siva and Sakthi are found in the same morphology). Accordingly, Uma went to Iruvannamalai (as it was then called) and did penance. She killed the demon Mahishasura and organised a big festival on the day of Karthigai. The Lord appeared as a cosmic flame on the summit of the hill and Uma joined him there as his consort. This is said to be the origin of *Karthigai Deepam*. (It has to be noted that this legend of the separation and subsequent union of Siva and Parvathi is connected with several temples in Tamil Nadu.)

The *lingodhbhava* legend is also associated with this shrine. This is the subject matter of dispute between followers of Siva and Vishnu. According to the Saivites, Siva wanted to prove his supremacy to Vishnu and Brahma, the two other members of the Hindu Trinity. He appeared in the form of fire and challenged both of them to find his head and feet. While Vishnu, in the form of a boar, dug deep into the earth and then told Siva that he could not fathom the depths, Brahma, in the form of a swan, went upwards. He happened upon a piece of floral fibre and learnt that it had been floating down from Siva's head for thousands of years. On this basis, he told Siva that he had reached the top. Siva, angered by the claim — which he knew was false — cursed Brahma that he would not have any temple dedicated to him on earth.

There is another version to this legend, which is oft quoted by Vaishavites. In that, it is Vishnu, who asks Siva and Brahma to find his head and feet and both of them fail. At a metaphysical level, these legends convey that God is infinite and cannot be circumscribed.

It is also said that when Siva appeared as the infinite column of fire, it was so dazzling that Brahma and Vishnu asked him to take a more benevolent and accessible form so that all beings could worship Him. Siva accordingly took the form of the Arunachala Hill, declaring, "As the moon derives its light from the sun, so other holy places will derive their sanctity from Arunachala. This is the only place where I have taken this form for the benefit of those who wish to worship me and obtain illumination. I will appear on the summit of this hill every year at Karthigai in the form of a peace-giving beacon."

Celebrated when the constellation of Karthigai (Pleiades) is in conjunction with the full moon in November-December, a huge bonfire is built on top of the Arunachala Hill on this night each year. From a distance, it looks like a great fiery beacon. It is visible from afar and thousands of devotees gather in Tiruvannamalai to see the flame and walk around the hill along a 12 km trail at its base in a ritual walk called *Girivalam*. (More about *Girivalam* later).

Architecture: The temple is spread out on an expanse of nine hectares at the foot of the hill. Built over centuries with each king adding to existing structures, the temple has an array of *gopurams* (nine in all) and *mandapams*. The oldest, the *kili gopuram* (parrot tower) in the third enclosure, is so called as Saint Arunagirinathar, who was adept at metempsychosis, had entered the soul of a parrot for a brief while. Meanwhile, his enemies interred his physical body. When Arunagiri saw this, he decided to live as a parrot on this *gopuram*, which is ahead of the main shrine.

The tallest is the *rajagopuram* on the eastern side, 41 m tall and 30 m wide, and credited to Krishnadeva Raya, the Vijayanagar king. The eastern gateway has the *Vallala gopuram* named after the Hoysala king Ballala, who made Tiruvannamalai his capital. It is auspicious to view all the 9 *gopurams* at one time. This can be done from a spot in front of the *Maghizham* tree (*sthala vriksham*), which is to the right of the Sambanda Vinayaka shrine, when facing away from the shrine.

The temple has 5 *prakarams*, which originated at various points of time, the first and second are the most ancient. While these have not been dated accurately, the third was built in the 12th century. The fourth and fifth came up in the 16th century. There are residences in the outer *prakarams*, like in the temples of Chidambaram and Srirangam. In the outermost *prakaram* is the 1000-pillared hall with its impressive carvings and the Siva Ganga tank.

The main shrine of Annamalai is in the first *prakaram* and the sight of the massive *lingam* is truly awe-inspiring. On the northern side is Siva's consort in the form of Unnamalai Amman. There is a massive rush of devotees in front of the sanctum sanctorum. In an ambience filled with fervour and devotion and the air thick with incense and myrrh, one can feel the divine presence even in a few seconds!

It is best to visit the temple on a non-festival day to appreciate the many facets of artistic and architectural beauty in the temple. Its carvings and paintings have been attributed to both Hoysala and Vijayanagara periods. Nayak kings also embellished the temple. The poet Sambandar, who lived in the 7th century A D, has sung of this temple.

The temple conforms to the south Indian style of temple architecture. It is interesting to note that even the Hoysalas did not deviate from the Dravidian style of *gopurams*. The *Ballalla gopuram* does not bear any resemblance to the Hoysala structures of Belur, Halebid or Somnathpur. The temple therefore bears the stamp of the Cholas, Hoysalas, Vijayanagaras and Nayáks.

There are 106 stone edicts. One of them narrates how a man hunting deer killed a human being unintentionally. In penitence, he donated cows and oxen to support the expense of lighting a lamp in the temple.

In the second *prakaram* is the famous Sthala Ganapathy installed by the queen of Gandaraditya Chola, under a *Vakula* tree. Sembian Mahadevi was renowned for her numerous benefactions to this temple and others. This temple has 22 idols of Ganapathy. He is present in various forms such as Sarvasiddhi Vinayaka, Anaithiraikonda Vinayaka and Sambanda Vinayaka (one of the largest Vinayaka idols in Tamil Nadu). There is a unique idol here, which people pray to after offering prayers to the God and Goddess (usually, Ganapathy is worshipped before one proceeds to the main shrines). This is a palm-sized Ganapathy, found in a crevice on a pillar near the *Ashtalakshmi mandapam*. In this temple, Ganapathy has a chariot to himself.

There is a shrine of Lord Venugopala (Krishna) in another part of the temple, and many paintings depict scenes from the *Krishna Leela* and the *Ramayana*.

The main temple is actually the second temple to Lord Arunachaleswara in Tiruvannamalai. The original temple is some distance from the town, and it is said the second temple was constructed to make it easier for the Vijayanagara kings to worship. The first, ancient structure is called the Adi Arunachaleswarar shrine. It is near the *Girivalam* circuit. The goddess here is called Abithagujambal.

Outside this temple, to the right, is a Vinayaka idol under a tree. It is believed that he has the powers to restore lost children to their parents. Many a time, when children get lost during the massive crowds at festival time, they are told to go and wait near this Vinayaka, where their parents will come and find them! Another notable Ganesh is the *idukku pillayar*. One has to contort one's body to enter this shrine through one end and exit through the other. This is a recipe for physical fitness, say the locals! From this point, if one looks up at the Arunachala Hill, 5 vantage points on the hill can be seen.

Arunagirinathar - Tiruvannamalai is also the place where the great Tamil poet Arunagirinathar lived and wrote his divine hymns in the 14th century. In his early years, Arunagiri, the son of a courtesan, led a dissolute life squandering all his money on women. He became so diseased that a day came when even women of loose morals shunned him. One day, he approached his sister for money. Whereupon his doting sister, penniless herself, asked him to use her own body to satisfy his lust! Arunagiri was so overcome with shame when she said this that he tried to kill himself by jumping from the *Vallala gopuram* of the Arunachaleswara temple. At that moment, Lord Muruga (Siva's son) appeared in a vision and told him not to despair. He cured him and bade him sing his praise and the debauch was thus transformed into a poet. He wrote the famous *Thiruppugazh*, a collection of 1300 verses on Muruga's glory. As many of these hymns have been set to music they are a popular choice in Carnatic music concerts.

Ramana Maharishi - Tiruvannamalai is also associated with the great sage Ramana Maharishi, who, as a young boy responded to an inner call to go to the Arunachala Hill and meditate. He performed penance in a cave in the hill and later in the temple of Arunachaleswara. The spot where he stayed can be seen near the Pathala Lingeshwara shrine in the temple. You have to go down a steep flight of steps to see the *lingam* where Ramana worshipped. During his time, it was in the midst of a forest. Ramana was guided by Seshadri Swamigal, another great saint who lived in Tiruvannamalai.

Ramana Maharishi attained enlightenment to become a great and powerful preacher and people came from far and wide to listen to him. The Ramanashramam was set up and still serves as a place of retreat for devotees. The Maharishi attained *samadhi* in the year 1940.

In the Ramanashram, there is a shrine to Lord Mathrubhuteswarar and Goddess Yogambika. There is an image of Ramana Maharishi, installed on his *samadhi*, to which *pujas* are done everyday. Poor feeding is carried out at the Ashram everyday. The ambience is pleasant, with a lot of greenery, amidst which peacocks move around freely.

Festivals: *Karthigai Deepam* is what makes Tiruvannamalai so famous. Here, it marks the conclusion of the 10-day *Brahmotsavam* in the month of Karthigai (Scorpio, November 15th to December 15th). *Bharani Deepam* is lit before the *Karthigai Deepam* in the main shrine. Five lamps are lit to symbolize the five elemental forms of Siva.

Preparations begin with a group of men carrying fire inside an earthen container to the summit of the mountain, where a large copper dish filled with ghee and a giant wick made of cloth is placed. Meanwhile at the temple, the various deities are brought out and *pujas* are performed. At an auspicious time in the evening, the lamp atop the hill is lit and the crowd of devotees goes berserk with devotion. People revere the flame of the lamp as none other than Siva himself. As soon as this lamp is lit, the main shrine is closed as it is held that Siva abides there as long as the flame burns till the next morning.

Several other festivals are celebrated through the year. Each *pournami* or full moon devotees congregate in the town, giving a great fillip to commerce for the locals. On this day, devotees perform the *Girivalam* or walk around the Arunachala hill. Devotees walk the 12 km circuit barefoot, because this ritual is said to relieve one from a million rebirths. First, devotees pray at the shrine of *Irattai Pillayar* just to the left of the *rajagopuram*, where you see 2 idols of Ganapathy seated side to side. Then begins the walk. There are 8 *lingams* on the route, where devotees stop to worship. They are the Indra, Agni, Yama, Varuna, Niruda, Vayu, Kubera and Eesana *lingams*. There is also a Surya *lingam*, which faces the main shrine, and is therefore called the '*Thiruner lingam*'. It is not part of the *Girivalam* circuit. There is an Unnamalai

Amman shrine next to the Surya *lingam*. There are shrines to other deities on the route.

Arudra Darsanam in Margazhi (December-January) is special worship performed to Lord Siva. During the *Thiruvoodal* festival, a mock quarrel between Annamalaiyar and Unnamalai Amman is enacted in the presence of the idol of Sundaramoorthy Nayanar in the Tiruvoodal Street (*Voodal* in Tamil means 'lover's tiff').

During this quarrel, the Goddess enters the temple by herself, leaving Siva. The Lord goes around the hill in apparent anger. While doing so, he grants liberation to Rishi Bhringi. Siva's jewels are 'stolen' during the circuit! After recovering them, he enters the temple in the morning. There is also the festival in which the Lord is crowned, as the dauphin, as one of the Hoysala kings, Ballala, did not have an heir.

FAST FACTS

How to reach

Air	:	Chennai is the nearest airport, 190 km away.
Rail	:	There are trains from Tambaram (Chennai) to Tiruvannamalai. Special trains run on *Girivalam* days. If coming from south Tamil Nadu, change at Villupuram.
Road	:	Tiruvannamalai can be reached by road from Chennai and Villupuram (68 km). The route from Chennai has now been shortened from the original 190 km thanks to the construction of a bypass from the Grand Southern Trunk Road just ahead of Tindivanam. Buses to all major towns are there from Tiruvannamalai.
Local transport	:	Tourist taxis, auto rickshaws, cycle rickshaws.
Season	:	Throughout the year.
Clothing	:	Tropical, light cottons.
Languages spoken	:	English and Tamil.

Accommodation (Hotels)

	Tariff Range (INR)	Phone
Ramakrishna	375-550	04175-225004-05
Trishul	350-475	-222219
Ganesh	260	-226701

People who wish to stay in the guest houses run by the Ramanashram, are advised to fax their requests to 91-4175-237491, addressed to

Sri V S Ramanan, Sri Ramanasramam, Tiruvannamalai, India, 606603. People are advised to book three months in advance. For further information, see *www.arunachala.org*

PLACES OF INTEREST NEARBY

Tirukkovilur: This ancient temple is 30 km from Tiruvannamalai on the Tirukkovilur Road that leads to Cuddalore and other southern towns. The 2000-year-old temple has Lord Vishnu in his *Trivikrama* posture as the presiding deity. The idol has the right leg raised to the sky, while the left leg is on the ground. King Mahabali is seen praying to the Lord. The story of how Vishnu put down the egotism of Mahabali is depicted here.

The *shankhu* is held in the right hand and the *chakra* in the left. The festival deity is called Sri Dehalisa Perumal or Gopala. The goddess is Poongovai Nachiyar. The temple is important as it is here that three *mudal* or first Azhwars met and had a vision of God. They were the Poigai, Bhuta and Pey Azhwars. As they composed the first hymns of the *Nalayira Divya Prabhandam* here, this temple is said to be where the great work originated. The huge temple was built was by the Pallava and Vijayanagara rulers over the years, with embellishments being made at different times. It is one of the 108 Vaishnava *Divya Desas*. In a rare occurrence, there is an idol of Vishnu Durga inside the main sanctum sanctorum. She is said to be here to protect the Lord. Built by Pallava and Vijayanagara kings, the temple is said to be over 2000 years old.

Gingee Fort: At a distance of 37 km from the temple town, is an over 700-year-old historic fort dating back to Vijayanagara times. It is famous for its association with Raja De Singh, who revolted against the Nawab of Arcot and became the subject of heroic ballads. He was the son of Sarup Singh, who was appointed chief of Gingee by Aurangzeb, the Moghul Emperor. The fort interconnects 3 hills. It has a number of structures reflecting the Indo-Islamic style of architecture, Vijayanagara and Nayak styles of building. There are some temples inside the complex.

Sattanur Dam: This was built across the river Pennar and is a beautiful picnic spot. It is 35 km from Tiruvannamalai. There is a children's park and a small zoo.

THE NAVA TIRUPATHIS
praised by Nammazhwar

The Vaishnavite saint poets, the Azhwars, traversed over hill and dale to several parts of the country to visit the shrines of Lord Vishnu. They described the beauty and power of these deities in their verses in Tamil, called the *Nalayira Divyaprabhandam* (4000 divine verses).

These shrines are collectively known as the 108 Vaishnava *Divya Desas* (holy sites) or the 108 *Tirupathis*. Actually, 106 of them are on this earth, while two, *Thiruparkadal* (the ocean of milk) and *Paramapadam* (the great feet of the Lord) are said to be attainable after you visit all the others.

Nine of these, the *nava tirupathis*, are of special significance as they have been sung of by perhaps the greatest Azhwar, Nammazhwar. This saint, who composed innumerable divine poems, has sung in praise of these temples in and around Tirunelveli in Tamil Nadu, apart from many others. While one version says he travelled to countless temples on foot, another says God showed them to him in a vision while he was still a child.

Doing a *puja* in all these 9 temples is believed to ensure the blessings of the gods. It is said, God is fonder of those who revere his *bhaktas* (devotees) than those who are fond of him. Honouring a true *bhakta* like Nammazhwar will surely take us closer to His heart. These temples were constructed during the late Pandya and early Chola periods, with

Kulasekara Pandya being responsible for much of the magnificent architecture.

Let us take a tour of these 9 temples, starting with Azhwarthirunagari first, which lies on the Tirunelveli-Tiruchendur road, to the right. It takes about half an hour for the journey from Tirunelveli town to the temple. The beautiful river Tamaraparani flows to the left.

Swami Ramakrishananda, a direct disciple of Sri Ramakrishna, mentions in his book *Life of Sri Ramanuja* that Nammazhwar was the incarnation of Visvaksena, the commander-in-chief of Lord Vishnu's army. He adds that Visvaksena is the alter ego of Vishnu, in other words implying that Nammazhwar was none other than the Lord himself.

The story goes that Udayanangai, a woman devotee of Lord Narayana, married another devotee called Kari. They lived in the town of Thirukkurugur (Azhwarthirunagari). Desirous of a child, they prayed to Lord Adinathar, the presiding deity of the town temple, and observed austerities. Lord Vishnu revealed to them in a vision that he himself would be born as their son.

On Vaikasi Vishakham day in the year 3102 B C, an infant was born who neither cried nor opened his mouth to drink milk. The parents took the baby to the sanctum sanctorum, entreating the Lord to throw light on this strange phenomenon. The child climbed down from his mother's lap, crawled to the base of a *puliyamaram* (tamarind tree) nearby and sat down in a burrow there. He sat in the yogic pose, in *padmasana* (lotus posture), to the wonderment of all, and remained so for many years. Thus did he gain the title *Thiruppuli Azhwar*. The tamarind tree itself is deemed to be none other than Lakshmana or Adi Sesha, the Divine Serpent. The Azhwar apparently did not open his mouth so that he could prevent the noxious vapours of the earth (*sadam* in Tamil), which envelop the human being in the haze of *maya* (illusion). This loss of divinity or fall in mental state makes a child cry. By keeping his orifices closed, he overcame the *sadam*, thereby also gaining the title 'Sadagopan'.

He was so beloved of the Lord that the latter is believed to have once referred to him as *'Nam Azhwar'* (*Nam* in Tamil means 'our'). He is also called 'Sathari' because he is deemed to be Vishnu's feet. In Vaishnava temples after distributing holy water, the priest places a crown, which bears the two feet of the Lord mounted on a crest, on the devotee's head. This signifies total surrender by the devotee. Appillai, a famous Tamil poet, sings of Nammazhwar,

"*Madhavan porpadhugaiyai valarndharulvon vazhiye*"

"Long live the one who is the golden feet of Madhava (Vishnu.)".

Once Madurakavi Azhwar came to Nammazhwar and requested him to expostulate a very complex metaphysical topic. When Nammazhwar gave him a reply, Madhurakavi fell at his feet and became his disciple. Thereupon Nammazhwar gave to posterity the immortal compositions '*Tiruvaimozhi*', '*Periathiruvanthathi*', '*Thiruvasiriyam*' and '*Thiruviruttam*'. These are the quintessence of the four *Vedas* (Ancient Hindu Scripture) – *Sama*, *Atharva*, *Yajur* and *Rig Vedas*, respectively. As Nammazhwar dictated, Madurakavi inscribed the hymns on palm leaves, over a four and a half year period. He also passed on the *Nalayira Divyaprabhandham* to Nathamuni, a great Vaishnavite teacher.

The presiding deity of the temple, Adinathar, in standing posture, is believed to be self-manifested. His consorts, Adhinathavalli and Kurukurvalli have separate shrines. It is said that the head of the celestials, Indra, was rid of the sin of disrespecting his parents after worshipping here.

Another interesting belief is that Lakshmana, the brother of Lord Rama, manifested here as the tamarind tree. The Lord (Vishnu) decided to stay in this place as a *brahmachari* (bachelor). Responding to Goddess Lakshmi's pleas, he wore a garland made of the sweet smelling *Magizham* (*Mimisops elengi*) flower to symbolize Her.

Tiruvaragunamangai: After worshipping at Azhwarthirunagari, we turn back on the road to Tirunelveli and turn across the river to proceed on the right to Varagunamangai.

The Lord here, Vijayasana Perumal, is in seated posture, with the serpent Adi Sesha sheltering him with his hood (Adi Sesha is usually with Vishnu in recumbent posture, serving as the divine bed). The consort is Varagunavalli Thayar, who is by the Lord's side in the sanctum sanctorum.

According to legend, a Brahmin named Vedavith performed penance on Lord Vishnu. The Lord appeared before him in seated posture as his devotee wanted, and so the appellation 'Vijayasana'.

Tiruppulingudi: This temple is just a few minutes away by car from Varagunamangai. It is said that Indra was relieved of a sin by worshipping at this temple.

There is another legend about a Brahmin called Yagnasarma. The sons of Sage Vasishta cursed him to roam as a demon. He was redeemed when the feet of the Lord touched him.

The presiding deity, Kaisinavendan, is in recumbent posture. *Darshan* of his feet can be had from a window outside the sanctum sanctorum. The lotus blooming from the navel of the Lord conjoins with the lotus of Brahma, sculpted on the wall as a frieze. The goddess is Malarmagal Nachiar. The *utsava murthy* of the consort is Pulingudivalli.

Tirutholaivillimangalam (**Irattai Tirupathi**): If temples can be called pretty, the two temples in the town named Tirutholaivillimangalam fit the bill. They can also be approached from Azhwarthirunagari by crossing the Tamaraparani, a distance of around 3 km.

Together, they constitute one of the 108 *Divya Desas*. The first temple is virtually on the banks of the river, with Lord

Srinivasa in standing position as the presiding deity. The second temple, near an adjacent canal, has as the presiding deity, Senthamaraikannan, also called Aravindalochana. In seated posture, He takes your breath away by the beauty of his mien.

A legend tells us how this place got its name. A sage built a *yagasala* (hermitage) here. Once he came upon a beautiful balance and a bow, which on being picked up, turned into a girl and a youth. They had been relieved of a curse. As *thulai* (balance) and *villu* (bow) got salvation, the spot became Thulaivillimangalam.

These temples being in the interior, and away from the main road, it is advisable to visit them during the day.

Thirukkulanthai: Taking the same road for about 10 km, we reached Thirukkulanthai.

We worshipped the main deity Lord Srinivasa, happy to see him so far away from his main abode, Tirupathi. There are two consorts, Alamelumangathayar and Kulandaivalli. Garuda, the vehicle of Vishnu, as an *utsavar*, is by the side of the Lord.

The *utsavar* idol of the Lord is called Mayakoothan, or 'Divine Dancer'. As per lore, a demon called Achmasaran was troubling the *Devas* (celestials), who prayed to the Lord for help. In response, the Lord fought the demon at this place, earlier called Palikavanam. Taking hold of the demon's foot he smashed it to the ground, even as he performed a dance. So, the name Mayakoothan.

There is another interesting story. Kamalavathi, the daughter of a Brahmin, Vedarajan, performed severe penance to attain Lord Vishnu as her husband. Vishnu is said to have appeared before her and married her in this place. The name Palikavanam could also have been derived from this episode, as a *palika* (maiden) did penance here.

Thirupperai (Then Thirupperai): The main deity here is Makara Nedunkuzhai Kadhan or Mukhil Vannan. He is in seated posture, facing the east. His consorts Kuzhaikathuvalli Nachiyar and Thirupperai Nachiyar, have separate shrines.

As per lore, Lakshmi asked Sage Durvasa to make Bhoodevi look like her. Bhoodevi, reciting the *Ashtaksharam* (the divine mantra *Om Namo Narayanaya*), taught to her by Durvasa, did penance. The place therefore got the name Sriperai (Thirupperai), meaning the corporeal form of Lakshmi. During her penance, Bhoodevi went for a bath in the river Tamaraparani. She found two fish-shaped earrings, which she presented to the Lord. He thus came to be known as *Makara Nedunkuzhai Kadhan*.

Varuna, the God of Rain, is said to have been relieved of the sin of insulting Guru here. The King of Vidharbha is said to have conducted *pujas* here to pray for rain when drought affected his kingdom.

This temple is five km from Azhwarthirunagari. It can also be approached from Tholaivillimangalam

Thirukolur: From Then Thirupperai, on the route to Azhwarthirunagari, at a distance of about 2½ km, a small road turns to the right to lead to this temple, about 1 km ahead.

There is a beautiful legend associated with this temple. Kubera, the God of Wealth, was cursed by Goddess Parvathi because he was disrespectful, and became impoverished. Therefore, Parvathi in turn lost all her *navanidhis* (nine forms of wealth) that were the *mahapadma* (sacred lotus), *padma* (lotus), *shankhu* (conch), *makara* (crocodile), *kachyapa* (tortoise), *mukund* (quicksilver), *kund* (jasmine), *neelam* (sapphire) and *kharva* (dwarf). These *navanidhis* did penance in this place and prayed to Vishnu to marry them. He responded and appeared as *'Vaithamanidhi'* (one who kept the wealth safe), the protector of the *nidhis*. Kuberan was freed of his curse here.

In *bhujangasayana*, the recumbent Lord is also called Nikshepavithan. His consorts, Kumudavalli and Kolurvalli, have separate shrines.

The war between *Dharma* (righteousness) and *Adharma* (wickedness) took place at this spot. *Dharma* stayed here, praying to the Lord. One day, *Adharma* attacked him and was sent fleeing by *Dharma*. Therefore this area got the title *Adharmapisunam*.

Thirukolur is also the birthplace of Madurakavi Azhwar.

Srivaikuntam: We had to double back on the Tiruchendur-Tirunelveli road and take the same turn across the river that we had taken much earlier in the evening to reach Varagunamangai. But after crossing the river, we turned to the left to reach Srivaikuntam.

We witnessed the temple priests and volunteers carrying the idol, placed on a pedestal, on their shoulders and performing an intricate dance. Was it a snake dance, we wondered as the Lord jumped forward, sideways and back with insouciance? A temple priest standing nearby clarified. "The Lord is playing *Pandi*" (the game hopscotch played by children). The natural smile on the Lord's face made us feel he was enjoying it as much as we were!

The presiding deity is Sri Vaikuntanathar, also called Kannabhiran, in standing posture, with Adi Sesha holding an umbrella as shelter. His consorts, Vaikuntavilli and Bhoodevi, have separate shrines.

The legend goes like this. A thief called Kalathushakan vowed that he would give half his ill-gotten wealth to Sri Vaikuntanathar. He was caught while robbing the palace. He prayed to God for help. The Lord assumed the garb of the thief, and taught philosophical truths to the King. The king, thinking that Kalathushakan was no thief but a *yogi*, became his friend. As per the king's prayers, the Lord assumed the name Kallabiran.

According to another legend, a demon named Somakan stole the creative knowledge of Brahma. Brahma did penance here. Lord Vishnu appeared, retrieved the creative expertise from the demon and restored it to Brahma.

Visiting and praying at the *nava tirupathis* is indeed a unique experience.

FAST FACTS

How to reach

Air	:	All these shrines can be accessed from Tirunelveli. The nearest airport to Tirunelveli is Madurai, 151 km away.
Rail	:	Tirunelveli is an important rail junction connected to major cities.
Road	:	There is good road connectivity to major towns in the south.
Local Transport	:	A tourist taxi is the best way to visit, if you do not have your transport. Public buses are also available.
Season	:	Throughout the year.
Clothing	:	Tropical, light cottons.
Languages spoken	:	English and Tamil.

Accommodation

Tirunelveli

	Tariff (INR)	Phone
Hotel Aryaas	400-1800	0462-2339001
Hotel Barani	330-1200	0462-2333234
Hotel Janakiram	350-1200	0462-2331522
Hotel Blue Star	330-650	0462-2334495
Hotel Nainar	240-590	0462-2331618
Hotel Nellai	100-150	0462-2331618

Courtallam

Anantha Classic	350-650	04633-223303

Tiruchendur

Rathna Lodge	150-400	04639-242383
Hotel Thilagam	195-600	04639-245185

PLACES OF INTEREST NEARBY (DISTANCES FROM TIRUNELVELI)

Thirukkurungudi about (40 km) This magnificent temple has remarkable architecture in stone. Cameos from epics and legends are chiselled so intricately that it looks like carving on wood. Actually a complex of temples, there are three principal deities - Ninra Nambi, Iruntha Nambi and Kidantha Nambi - inside the main compound and two outside. The goddess is Kurungudivalli Nachiyar. There is a shrine for Siva inside the main compound.

There are two other temples outside, at a distance. One is beside a rivulet, and has a shrine to Tirupparkadal Nambi. The other is on a hillock about 10 km away. The Lord here is Malaimel Nambi. Praying at all five constitutes visiting one of the 108 Vaishnava *Divya Desas*. The temple on the hill closes early in the afternoon. Among the Azhwars, Tirumangai Azhwar has sung many hymns of the glory of this temple. The Thirukurungudi *Jeeyar* (pontiff) administers these temples.

Nanguneri (Thirucheerivaramangai): This impressive temple is on the way from Tirunelveli to Tirukkurungudi. Lord Thothadrinathar is the main idol and Lord Deivanayaka is the *utsava murthy*. The former is said to be self-manifested. The goddesses are Upanachiyar and Seerivaraimangai Thayar. There is an oil well here, believed to be around 1000 years old. All the oil used in the temple for oblation is poured into this well. Devotees who visit this temple climb up a flight of steps to the well and dip their hands in the holy well briefly. This temple is the seat of the Vanamamalai Mutt. Bhoomidevi, who became tainted when the Lord slew some demons on earth (*Bhoomi*), did penance here and regained her pristine purity. The Lord here is seen in joyous aspect with Sreedevi and Bhoodevi on the *vimanam*.

Tirunelveli: A bustling town with a 2000-year-old history, it was the capital of the Pandya kingdom for a while. The ancient name of Tirunelveli was Salippathiyoor. It is famous for its temples and centres of education. The Kanthimathi Nellaiyappar temple is dedicated to Parvati and Siva. The great Tamil poet Subramania Bharathi studied in this town.

Tiruchendur (48 km): This temple, situated on the shores of the Bay of Bengal, is one of the six abodes of Lord Muruga. It is renowned for its Skanda Sashti festival in praise of Lord Muruga.

Kalakkadu Wildlife Sanctuary (47 km): It is situated on an area of 223 sq.km. The sanctuary has tigers, lion tailed macaque, panther, gaur and many other fauna. Trekking can be undertaken with permission from the Forest Department. The best season is September-March. Accommodation is available at the forest rest house at Sengaltheri, with catering facilities.

Courtallam (59 km): Known as the spa of the south, it is situated 167 m high on the Western Ghats. The falls are best visited during the July – September season.

THIRUNANGUR
Town of temples

Who would not like to visit a temple town that has in its vicinity 12 of the 108 Vaishnava *Divya Desas*, amongst them the birthplace of Thirumangai Azhwar, and also the temple that is known as the southern Badrinath? In addition, once a year, the *utsava murthys* of all these temples congregate in the latter temple for a grand *Garudotsavam* (temple festival). The town is none other than Thirunangur, 15 km from Sirgazhi, near the famous temple town of Chidambaram.

Though it is the fervent wish of every devout Hindu to visit Badrinath in the Himalayas in his or her lifetime and have *darshan* of Lord Badrinarayana (believed to ensure *moksham*), not everyone from the south of India can undertake a pilgrimage to Badrinath even today. Therefore, it was wonderful to learn that Lord Badrinarayanana is very much resident in Tamil Nadu, in similar majesty as in his snowy abode.

The southern abode of Sri Narayana Perumal, where Lord Vishnu is in the same *roopa* (form) as in Badrinath, is the little hamlet of Thirunangur. The main deity is in seated posture along with Sreedevi and Bhoodevi. The goddess is Pundarikavalli.

During his lifetime, the Vaishnavite saint Thirumangai Azhwar accompanied by his wife Kumudavalli Thayar walked through the paddy fields to the 11 *Divya Desas* in and around Thirunangur and finally reached the temple of Narayana Perumal to celebrate the *Garudotsavam*. The Azhwar sang verses in praise of all the gods and performed *aradhanai* (adulatory worship) for each of them. It is believed that as he walked on the paddy fields, the harvest would always be plentiful.

In the Sri Narayana Perumal temple, on the day following new moon day in the Tamil month of Thai (Jan-Feb), eleven forms of Vishnu and Thiruvali Thirunagari Thirumangai Azhwar assemble for the *Garudotsavam* festival. Garuda, the golden eagle, is the vehicle of Lord Vishnu.

The gods who assemble at the Thirunangur Sri Narayana Perumal temple for the festival are Kudamadukoothar with Amuthakadavalli, Semponnarangar with Allimamalaral, Lakshmiranganathar with Senkamalavalli, Sreenivasaperumal with Alarmelmangai, Venpurushothaman with Purushothamanayaki, Varadarajaperumal with Sreedevi and Bhoodevi, Vaikuntanathar with Vaikuntavalli, Madhavaperumal with Madhavanayaki, Parthasarathy with Senkamalavalli and Rajagopalan with Rukmini and Sathyabhama.

But why do the 11 forms of Vishnu assemble in one place? The legend goes that Lord Siva had to get rid of the *Brahmahatti Dosham* – the sin of having decapitated Lord Brahma. He conducted a *yaga* (oblation) for this purpose. At the conclusion of the austerities, Lord Vishnu appeared before Siva along with the celestials. Siva then requested Vishnu to show him his 11 forms of himself. Vishnu obliged and revealed himself in 11 different and beautiful forms. So, the 11 *Divya Desas* in Thirunangur, it is believed, came about to please Lord Siva.

The twelfth *Divya Desa* nearby is Thiruvaliyum Thirunagariyum, the birthplace of Thirumangai Azhwar. These temples were built by the Cholas. Stone plaques say this was the only town in the Chola kingdom to have so many temples. In Chola times, 4,000 Vedic Brahmins lived here and it was called Chathurvedhi Mangalam or 'Village of the Chathurvedis'.

On the night of the *Garudotsavam,* all the world and its friend head for Thirunangur, by car, motobike, tourist van, tractor, bullock-cart, bicycle, on foot! The mass of humanity proceeds in convoy stopping *en route* to buy souvenirs from the numerous small shops lining the roads. They sell anything from laughing Buddha to hair clips.

After *darshan* of the main deity, we come out and see that the curtains covering the deities on *Garuda Vahanas* have been removed. It is god's plenty. The sight of the various manifestations of Lord Vishnu all seen together is breath taking. We move slowly from alcove to alcove, getting a bunch of *tulsi* (basil) leaves here and *sathari* there. The flame of camphor lights up the faces of the idols. The milling crowds, bright illumination and the air of piety invest the place with a transcendental quality. A location difficult to leave.

FAST FACTS

How to reach

Air	:	The nearest airport is Tiruchirapalli, 148 km away.
Rail	:	The nearest railhead is Sirgazhi, 15 km away.
Road	:	One can access both from Sirgazhi (15 km) and Chidambaram (35 km)
Local Transport	:	Tourist Taxis, Auto rickshaws and Bullock Carts.
Season	:	Throughout the year.
Clothing	:	Tropical, light cottons.
Languages spoken	:	English and Tamil.

Accommodation

As the facilities in Sirgazhi are not up to the mark, it is best to stay in Chidambaram:

	Tariff (INR)	Phone
Hotel Saradaram	375-645	04144-221338
Hotel Akshaya	200-545	04144-220192
Everest Lodge	90-375	04144-222543

Paces of Interest Nearby

Thirunangur temples: These temples are all part of the 108 Vaishava Divya Desas.

1. ***Thiruarimeya Vinnagaram:*** The presiding deity here is Kudamadukoothan, in seated posture and facing east. The *utsava murthy* is Gopala, with four arms. The goddess is Amruthakadavalli.

2. ***Thiruvanpurudothamam:*** The main deity is Purushottaman, in standing posture and facing east. The goddess is Purushottama Nayaki. The temple is 8 km from Sirgazhi.

3. ***Thirumanimadakkoil:*** This is the temple of Sri Narayana Perumal described earlier, where all 11 deities of Tirunangur assemble for the *Garudotsavam*.

4. ***Thiruthettriyambalam:*** Popularly known as Pallikonda Perumal temple, the Lord here, in *bhujanga sayana* (recumbent posture), with four arms, is variously called Senganmal, Ranganatha and Sreelakshmirangar. The goddess is Sengamalavalli. The four temples listed above are 8 km from Sirgazhi, in close proximity to each other in Thirunangur.

5. ***Thirukkavalambadi:*** The Lord here appears as Gopalakrishna with his consorts Rukmini and Satyabhama. He is in standing posture and facing east. The local names for the goddesses are Madavaral Mangai and Sengamala Nachiyar. The temple is 10 km to the east of Sirgazhi.

6. ***Thiruchemponchei Koil:*** The deity is Perarulalan, in standing posture and facing east. The *utsava murthy* is Hemarangar or Chemponnarangar. The goddess is Allimamalar Thayar. This temple too is 8 km from Sirgazhi. According to legend, Lord Rama, after vanquishing the demon Ravana, stayed here at the *ashram* (hermitage) of Sage Thridanethrar. As per the sage's advice, Rama made a cow of gold and donated it to a Brahmin. This temple was built by the Brahmin with the help of the gold and the temple thus got its name.

7. ***Thiruvaikuntha Vinnagaram:*** The Lord is Vaikuntanathan or Thamaraikannudaiyabiran (One with the lotus eyes). The Lord is in seated posture, as are the goddesses and the *utsava murthys*. The goddess is Vaikuntavalli. The temple is 8 km from Sirgazhi.

8. ***Thirupparthanpalli:*** The Lord is Thamaraiyal Kelvan and the goddess Thamarai Nayaki. The *utsavar* is Parthasarathy. Both the presiding deity and the *utsava murthy* have four goddesses – Sreedevi, Bhoodevi, Neeladevi, and Jambavathy. There is another *utsava murthy* called Kolavalli Rama, who manifests with the conch, discus and mace. A

bow and arrow have been placed on this beautiful idol. It is said that the *moolavar* (presiding deity) of this idol can be seen in a temple within a garden nearby.

9. **Thirumanikkudam:** The presiding deity is Varadaraja Perumal, also called Manikkooda Nayakan, in standing posture, facing east. The goddesses are Sreedevi (Thirumamagal Nachiyar) and Bhoodevi. The temple is 9 km from Sirgazhi, and 1 km east from the outskirts of Thirunangur.

10. **Thiruvellakkulam:** This is part of the 11 *Divya Desas* of Thirunangur, though it is located 10 km from Sirgazhi on the way towards Nagapattinam. The presiding deity is Lord Srinivasa, and the goddess is Alarmelmangai. He is also called Kannan, Narayanan and Annan Perumal, indicating He is the elder brother of Srinivasa. The festival idols of the goddesses are Padmavathi and Poovar Thirumagal. This temple is called *Then Tirupathi* (Southern Tirupathi). Vows to Lord Venkateswara of Tirupathi can be fulfilled here.

11. **Thiruthevanar Thogai:** This temple is in a place called Kizhachalai, 6 km southeast of Sirgazhi in the direction towards Tiruvenkadu. The Lord is Deivanayakan, in standing posture and facing East. The *utsavar* is Madhava Perumal. The goddesses are Kadalmagal Nachiyar and Madhavanayaki. This temple is one among the 11 *Divya Desas* of Thirunangur. It is said that the celestials had an assembly here.

Thiruvaliyum Thirunagariyum: These are twin temples. Tiruvali is on the Sirgazhi-Thiruvenkadu bus route, about 8 km away. The presiding deity is Lord Lakshmi Narasimha, also called Vayalalimanavalan. He is in seated posture, facing east. While the festival idol is Thiruvali Nagaralan, the goddess is Amruthakadavalli. As the idol of Vayalali Manavalan, who has been sung of in the Nalayira Divya Prabhandham is now in the Thirunagari temple and not in Thiruvali, the two are considered one *Divya Desa* in combination.

Thirunagari: This temple is located 5 km from Thiruvali via Neppathur. The *moolavar* (presiding deity) is Vedarajan or Vayalalimanavalan, in seated posture and facing east. The *utsavar* is Kalyana Ranganatha and the goddess is Amruthavalli. This is the *avathara sthala* of Thirumangai Azhwar. Of the 5 Narasimha idols he worshipped, 2 are still here. There is a separate shrine for Tirumangai Azhwar in the temple, in the garb of a hunter. Beside him, there is a small idol called *Chindanaikkiniyan*, which the Azhwar worshipped in his lifetime. As he is said to have performed many miracles, this place is locally known as Azhwar Koil. It was at a place called Vedarajapuram, 1 km from here, that

Tirumangai Azhwar was blessed with the *Tirumandiram* (sacred mantra) after intense prayer to the Lord. It was here too that Lord Ranganatha gave *darshan* to the Azhwar with his consort, in the form of a young couple. That is why he got the name Kalyana Ranganatha. It is believed that obstacles to marriage will be removed if one prays here.

Sirgazhi Vishnu Temple: The Lord here is Trivikraman, also called Tadalan. He is in the *Ulagalanda Perumal* posture, with his left leg lifted and measuring the sky. This story refers to the Vamana incarnation of Lord Vishnu, where he appeared as a dwarf before King Mahabali of Kerala to put down his arrogance. When the king said he would give anything to the dwarf, Vamana asked for just 3 ft of land he would measure out himself. Vishnu then assumed his original huge form and with one foot measured the whole of the earth, with the other the whole of the heavens and then asked Mahabali where to put the third foot. Whereupon the penitent king asked that he put it on his own head. It is rare to find a temple to this form of Vishnu. The temple, one of the 108 *Divya Desas*, is called Thirukkazhicheerama Vinnagaram. It is 1 km from Sirgazhi railway station. It is also the place where Tirumangai Azhwar defeated the Saivite saint Thirugnanasambandar, in an argument, and obtained his *Vel* (spear) as the prize.

Sirgazhi Siva Temple: The temple has 3 shrines to Lord Siva called Sri Brahmapureeswarar, Sattanathar and Thoniappar. There is a separate shrine to the goddess Thirunilai Nayaki. There is also a shrine to the Saivite saint Thirugnanasambandar.

Union of art and spirituality in
THANJAVUR BIG TEMPLE

Some temples become famous for their art and architecture, their sculptural excellence and their marvellous construction. Some temples gain renown for the spiritual power of their deities, and for their powerful religious associations. It is in the Thanjavur Brahadeeswarar temple that there is an astonishing union between the two. The effulgence of the *lingam* matches the beauty of the stone structure.

Only one other temple in Tamil Nadu displays this synchrony — the Nataraja temple at Chidambaram. And the common thread that links these temples is that both are products of the magnificent munificence of the Chola dynasty, whose rulers possessed an infinite imagination coupled with the ability to translate it into tangible achievement. While at Chidambaram, the Cholas' contribution was complemented by the input of various other dynasties, at Thanjavur, Raja Raja Chola must be given sole credit!

Raja Raja Chola was a ruler who revelled in his regality. Ascending the throne at a time when the Rashtrakutas had humiliated the Cholas, he conquered much of south India in just 20 years. And what better tribute to the Gods who graced him than to build a magnificent temple for them?

Sometimes temple history is clouded in confusion and doubt. Not so in the case of the Thanjavur Big Temple. Thanks to extant inscriptions carved on the walls, we know the temple was completed exactly 25 years and 275 days after Raja Raja's ascension in 985 A D. The inscription, on the walls of the *vimanam* (roof over the sanctum sanctorum) records for posterity the gifts made by the king and his family for the 'sacred stone temple called Sri Rajarajeswaram which we have caused to be built in Thanjavur', an inscription over a 100 paragraphs long! The completion was marked by Raja Raja gifting the golden *kalasam* (finial) for the temple *vimanam*.

The *vimanam* marks out this temple as unique from the architectural point of view. In most temples in south India, for that matter in India, the temple *gopuram* (pyramidal tower at the entrance to the temple) is bigger than the *vimanam*. At the Srirangam Ranganatha temple and the Srivilliputhur Vatapatrasayee temples, for instance, the *gopuram* is magnificent, while at Thanjavur and in three other temples built by Chola kings, the *vimanam* dominates.

The dimensions of the *vimanam* in Thanjavur clearly indicate the ingenuity and skill of Chola architects. Its 13 tiers are totally 58 m tall. The square base of 29 m supports the octagon-shaped *shikara* (cupolic dome). This dome that weighs 81 tonnes rests on a single block of granite, which is a square of 7.8 m. How it was transported and installed without the aid of modern machinery and gadgets is a wonder! It is said the stone was carried up an inclined plane from a spot 6 km north east of Thanjavur, called *sarapallam*, or 'scaffold hollow'. The four corners of the *shikara* are ornamented by two *Nandis* (bulls) each, while the pinnacle is the finial or *kalasam*. A unique architectural feature of the *vimanam* is that its shadow never falls on the ground.

As with all temples, legends surround the Thanjavur temple too. In particular, there are legends associating the huge *shikara* with a devotee of the Lord, a dairymaid. The *shikara*, it is said, was lying in the woman's house, about 30 km from Thanjavur. She heard of the temple being constructed at Thanjavur and yearned to give it for this purpose. The Lord appeared in a dream to the king and told him of this, upon which the king obliged.

Numerous stucco figures can be seen on the thirteen storeyed *vimanam*, which is often referred to as *Dakshina Meru* (Meru of the South). Mount Kailash is *Uttara Meru* (Meru of the North).

The *vimanam* shelters the huge *lingam*, which is 8.7 m high. The deity, Lord Siva, is called variously, 'Dakshina Meru Vitankan', 'Adavallan' or 'Rajarajeswaran'. The most famous among the names, of course, is 'Brihadeeswara'.

The sanctum sanctorum, which houses the *lingam* is itself very large by the usual standards, as a square of over 25 m. There are two storeys, each with a huge overhanging cornice. The sanctum sanctorum stands on an *upapitham* (platform) and *adhistanam* (base). There are two surrounding walls, the inner and the outer. Between the walls is a corridor, also of two storeys, with astounding murals and sculptures.

There is such plenty that the visitor needs some guidance on what to look out for. For those interested in iconography, there are three large Siva sculptures, which depict the Lord holding a spear, wielding a sword and a trident and in dancing posture. For the aficionado of sculpture, there are bas-reliefs depicting 51 of the 108 dance poses mentioned in the *Natyashastra* (Science of Dance) of Bharata. Art buffs can drink in the sight of magnificent murals typical of the Chola style. The fact that some of the Chola murals have been painted over with Nayak murals makes the whole experience more interesting!

Some of the remarkable murals are those of Siva in his manifestations as Nataraja, Dakshinamurthi and Tripurantaka. The last mentioned is an eye-catcher, occupying an entire wall. It is a fearsome sight to see Siva conquering the demons with his might. King Raja Raja Chola figures in many of these murals, often with his queens and attendants.

Lord Siva is again the repeated theme in the sculptures that adorn the outer surface of the walls that surround the sanctum sanctorum.

There are three *mandapams* (halls) in front of the sanctum sanctorum. They are called the *ardha* (half), *mukha* (facing) and the *maha* (main) *mandapams*. The fourth *mandapam* in the temple, the *Nandi mandapam,* is a little distance away. The huge *Nandi* is 3.7 m high, 6 m long and 2.5 m broad. The monolith is said to have been carved out of stone brought from a distant quarry. In fact, not only this, but much of the stone used in the temple had to come from long distances as there is no stone available in the immediate vicinity of Thanjavur.

The story goes that the *Nandi* is said to have been growing continuously, much to the alarm of the people. They finally drove a nail into its back and it stopped growing. Another version says that there was a live toad inside the *Nandi* and this made the stone bull grow and grow. The toad was finally discovered and removed, and the *Nandi* stopped growing!

There are more *Nandis* to be seen near the walls of the massive *Prakara* (courtyard) of the temple. One Krishnaraman, who was a minister and general of King Raja Raja, built the walls at the same time as the temple. There is a vast pillared-cloister running all around the wall. Here, one can see many *lingams*.

The temple had many other shrines, but only some are extant today. Notable are the shrines to Indra, Chandeswara and Varahi.

Experts have dated the shrine of the goddess as belonging to a later period than the main temple. The Pandyas built it in the 13th century. There are paintings from the *Devi Mahatmayam* (a text on the glory of the Goddess) on the ceilings of the *mandapam*. There is a small shrine to Subramanya, which is dated to the 15th century A D. There is another shrine to Lord Ganesh. The temple has to be entered after passing through two *gopurams*.

FAST FACTS

How to reach

Air	:	Tiruchirapalli, 55 km away, is the nearest airport.
Rail	:	There is a direct train on the Broad Gauge to Thanjavur from Chennai.
Road	:	Thanjavur is an hour's drive from Tiruchirapalli. There is a good national highway connecting the two places.
Local Transport	:	Tourist taxis and auto rickshaws.
Season	:	Throughout the year.
Clothing	:	Tropical. Light cottons.
Languages spoken	:	English and Tamil.

Accommodation

Thanjavur

	Tariff (INR)	Phone
Hotel Sangam, Trichy Road,	1300-1650	04362-239451
Hotel Oriental Towers, 2889 Srinivasa Pillai Road.	800- 2200	04362-230742
Hotel Tamil Nadu, Gandhiji Road.	275-700	04362-239451
Hotel Parisutham, GA Canal Road.	1250-1600	04362-231601
Ganesh	170-610	04362-231113

There are Retiring Rooms at Thanjavur Railway station.

PLACES OF INTEREST NEARBY

Darasuram: If Raja Raja Chola excelled in temple building, his son Rajendra Chola was not far behind. Like Gangaikondacholapuram, the Airateswara Temple in Darasuram (34 km from Thanjavur) is a fine example of Rajendra Chola's contribution. Built in the 12th century, it is in good condition. Look out for the miniature sculptures in the temple's frontal columns.

Thirukkadaiyur: Thirukkadaiyur is a temple famous for many reasons. First, Lord Siva defeated the God of Death, Yama, here, to save the life of Markandeya. It therefore forms part of 8 temples where Lord Siva performed such heroic deeds, called *Atta Veerathanam*. Second, this is the place where Goddess Parvathy, in the form of Abhirami Amman, graced the devotee Abhirami Pattar, who went on to write the famous poem *Abhirami Anthathi*. The Lord is called Mruthyunjayeswara or Kala Samharamoorthi here, while the goddess is Abhirami. It is said that praying here can alleviate any malefic effects owing to Saturn. The temple also has a famous shrine to *Kalla Pillayar* – Ganesha who stole the divine ambrosia to keep it away from the *asuras* (demons). The architecture is striking. This temple is the place of choice for celebrating *Sashtiabthapoorthi*(where the 60th birthday of an individual is celebrated in a grand manner akin to a marriage ceremony) The temple is close to Mayiladuthurai.

Thanjavur Palace: The magnificent palace, surrounded by impressive fort walls, was built partly by the Nayaks and partly by the Marathas. Located just 1 km from the Big Temple, the Maratha royal family continue to stay in the palace. The tall towers, roomy halls, ornate rooms, long corridors, frescoed walls and ceilings and artistic stuccowork make the palace a visitor's delight. Ask for details about the underground tunnel!

Sangeetha Mahal: In the palace precincts, is the Sangeetha Mahal. This acoustically perfect music hall is an excellent illustration of the skill of ancient builders.

Royal Museum and Serfoji Memorial Hall: This too is located in the palace complex. It plays host to the royal families' antique collection. Whether weapons, regal robes or handicrafts made of lacquer, glass, jade, ivory and wood, the display is an antique lover's paradise. The Marattah Durbar Hall is striking for its pillars and paintings – frescoes and stuccoes. The Sharajah Madi, on the other hand, is famous for its ornamental balconies. Raja Serfoji built this six-storeyed building in the eastern part of the palace in the Saracenic style. A bird's eye view of Thanjavur can be had from this *Madi*. There is a nominal entrance fee for these attractions.

Rajagopala Beerangi: Go to the eastern gate of the Fort and you will see this impressive *beerangi* (cannon). One of the largest in the country, the cannon is good proof of the mastery over metallurgy achieved in India many centuries ago.

Art Gallery: The whole Thanjavur area is famous for its bronzes. Some of the best pieces are showcased in the Thanjavur Art Gallery. Bronze icons are complemented by the stone sculptures. The pieces are antique and have fascinating historical associations. Many of them represent gods and goddesses from the Hindu pantheon. The best of Chola art can be found here. There is a nominal entrance fee.

Saraswathi Mahal Library: No lover of books should miss this library. It is one of the few libraries in the world, which specialises in the medieval period. The Maratha and the Nayak rulers took great care to collect rare manuscripts, books, maps and paintings for this library. Described by the Encyclopaedia Brittanica as 'the most remarkable library in India,' this is definitely a must-see.

Schwartz Church: Rev. C V Schwartz was a Danish missionary who was much loved by the local people. He was the tutor of Rajah Serfoji. The king built this church in 1779 A D as a memorial for his teacher.

Tamil University: This University was established in 1981 with the aim of fostering the study and growth of the Tamil language. Some of the interesting courses it offers are Literature, Grammar, Linguistics, Religion and Philosophy, Manuscriptology, Epigraphy, Folklore, Engineering, Computer Science and Medicine.

Rajarajan Mani Mandapam and Tholkappiya Sadukkam: Both these were built during the World Tamil Conference held in Thanjavur in 1995. The former is a memorial to Raja Raja Chola. The latter is a square with a tower, named after the Tamil classic, *Tholkappiam.*

Thiruvaiyar: A short drive from Thanjavur (13 km) is Thiruvaiyar on the banks of the Cauvery. This is where the saint poet Thyagaraja, who wrote more than 2,000 songs on Lord Rama, attained *samadhi.* Thiruvaiyar is also the place where the other two members of the Trinity of Carnatic music, Muthuswamy Dikshitar and Shyama Sastri, passed away. Every year the Thyagaraja Samadhi day in January is commemorated with a big gathering of musicians – vocalists, instrumentalists and percussionists – who sing the *pancharatna kritis* (five gems among Thyagaraja's compositions) in concert.

Poondi Matha Basilica: Fr. Constantine Beschi, who was called Veeramamunivar in Tamil, built this shrine in the 18th century. The statue of Mother Mary in this church was made in Paris. Praying to 'Our Lady of Immaculate Conception' is believed to confer a cure from ailments. Many miracles are spoken of in connection with this church, which is 35 km from Thanjavur. The annual festival is in May.

Papanasam: In this town steeped in history, the granary constructed by the Nayak rulers in the 17th century has been declared a monument by the Tamil Nadu State Archaeological Department. Of interest here are the Pallaivanatha Temple and the 108 Sivalayan Temple (with 108 Siva Lingams). Papanasam is 30 km from Thanjavur.

The God who eats no salt
OPPILIAPPAN

Kumbakonam, 300 km from Chennai, is second to Kanchipuram as another famous temple town of Tamil Nadu. Every street and corner of this town has a temple. Of course, some of these temples are better known than the others, for reasons of antiquity, architecture, or simply the power that the presiding deity exudes.

One such is the ancient temple of Lord Oppiliappan or Uppiliappan, lying 4 km from Kumbakonam. Often called the southern Kasi and *Bhoologa Vaikuntam* (Heaven on earth), the Lord here is with a benign and smiling countenance. Described as 'without equal' by the Vaishnavite saint poet, Nammazhwar, he has the name Oppiliappan *(Oppilla-Appan)*.

His other name is Uppiliappan or 'One who has eschewed salt'. The legend behind this is fascinating. Sage Markandeya, after performing rigorous penance was graced with a beautiful girl child who emerged from the Earth, whom he named Sree Bhoomi Devi. The child was so devoted to the Lord that He wanted to marry her. Markandeya submitted before the Lord that as his daughter was so young, she did not know even how to cook, and that the Lord might well have to eat food without salt! So gracious was the Lord that he assured Bhoomi Devi's father that henceforth he would eschew salt and eat food prepared without *uppu* (salt). Therefore the name 'Uppiliappan'.

This is also the reason why this temple does not use salt in any of its culinary preparations or *prasadam*.

Though normally, food without salt is inedible, here, it tastes divine!

The temple, which has an imposing façade, has one of the most majestic and kind forms of Lord Mahavishnu in a standing pose, with the conch and the discus, like in Tirumala. The Lord here is seen with the *abhaya hastam* on which is the inscription in diamonds, *Mam ekam charanam vraja*, ('I am the only one, surrender to me'). On either side of the lord are Bhoomidevi and sage Markandeya. There is no separate shrine for the consort in this temple. She is on his right, kneeling in the marriage posture. The *utsava murthy* of the beautiful goddess is in standing posture, bedecked with jewels.

In the past, it used to be said that Lord Oppiliappan is the elder brother of Lord Srinivasa of Tirumala. Nowadays, the temple priests describe Him as Srinivasa himself. Other names of the Lord here are Thiruvinnakarappan, Sree Venkatachala-pathi and Sreenivasan. He is also known as Ennappan, Ponnappan, Maniappan and Muthappan. The Vaishnavite saints Poigai Azhwar, Peyazhwar, Thirumangai Azhwar and Nammazhwar have composed 47 divine verses called *pasurams* on this temple and its presiding deity.

On Saturdays and on Sravana Nakshatra day, (Sravana is the birth star of Lord Srinivasa) the main deity and the festival idol wear a crown of rubies. On Thursdays one can see the Lord wearing a big *thirumann* (caste mark) on the forehead.

Devotees are not allowed to take salt beyond the shrine of Garuda in this temple. The custom is to buy salt outside the temple and dispose of it at a receptacle kept for the purpose. Many devotees offer a number of items such as coconut, jaggery, crystal sugar, rope, butter, rice and coins on a scale against their weight in fulfillment of vows. This practice is called *thulabaram* and is particularly famous in temples like Guruvayur in Kerala. This is also a popular shrine for people to conduct weddings in the family.

FAST FACTS

How to reach

Air	:	The nearest airport is Tiruchirapalli, 94 km away.
Rail	:	Kumbakonam lies on the Chennai-Kumbakonam Broad Gauge Line via Thanjavur.
Road	:	Kumbakonam is easily accessed by road from Thanjavur (39 km) and Tiruchirapalli (94 km).
Local Transport	:	Tourist taxis and auto rickshaws.
Season	:	Throughout the year.
Clothing	:	Tropical, light cottons.
Languages spoken	:	English and Tamil.

Accommodation

	Tariff (INR)	Phone
Hotel Rayas	250-1575+ 10%	0435-2423172, 2422545
Hotel Aditya	440-660	0435-2421794
Siva International	300-700	0435-2424014

NEARBY ATTRACTIONS

Sarangapani Temple: This 2000-year-old temple is a masterpiece of Pallava architecture, built by the Cholas. The sanctum sanctorum is in the form of a chariot. The exquisite wooden temple chariot was dedicated by Thirumangai Azhwar to the Lord in 7th century A D. Sarangapani, also called Aravamudha, is in the rare *Uttanasayi* posture—half rising and half lying down—on Adi Sesha, with his right hand under his head, facing east. The festival idol has the conch, discus and mace, apart from the bow, Saranga. There is an idol of Lord Krishna, by holding which couples will be blessed with progeny. The goddess is Komalavalli. This temple has been sung of by 7 of the 11 Azhwars and is one of the 108 Vaishnava *Divya Desas.* There is an intricate, carved 12-pillared hall and a lofty temple tower.

The Lord, it is said, was originally in recumbent posture. Thirumazhisai Azhwar asked the Lord in one of his compositions why he was lying down – was he tired after defeating Ravana in his incarnation as Rama, or was he weary after rescuing Bhoomi Devi from the netherworld? Upon which the Lord began to get up, but stopped when the latter began praising him! The monumental devotional work *Nalayira Divyaprabhandam* would not have been available to us but for Saint Nadamuni's (9th century A D) efforts. One day he heard a devotee uttering some beautiful poems in praise of the Lord. On learning that the full text was not available, he expended much effort, travel and prayer to recover the Azhwars' work *Tiruvaimozhi* and *Nalayira Divyaprabhandam*. The temple is 2 km from Kumbakonam bus stand and railway station.

Chakrapani Temple: In this unique temple the Lord is present in the form of the divine discus, Sudarshana. He is fully armed, with all his weapons. As we approached the temple, Sangita Kalanidhi M S Subbulakshmi's rendition of the *Vishnu Sahasranama* (1000 names of Lord Vishnu) rang out, chanting the words which list Lord Vishnu's weapons.

*"Vanamali Gathi Sharangi, Shankhi Chakri Cha Nandaki
Shriman Narayano Vishnur Vasudevo Abhirakshathu"*

In the sanctum sanctorum, is a *chakra* (discus), with eight arms each holding a weapon, exuding an indescribable power.

Ramaswamy Temple: A king of the Nayak dynasty, which ruled Thanjavur, built this temple in the early 17th century. The idols of Lord Rama and Sita were installed after King Raghunatha found them while digging for a tank. The Lord gives *darshan* in the *Pattabhisekham* (coronation) posture. The temple is replete with carvings and murals from the Ramayana.

Mahamaham Tank: The name of the town, Kumbakonam, is linked to this sacred tank (*Kumbha-* pot, *Kona* –corner). In ancient times Lord Brahma put divine nectar (ambrosia), the Vedas and the seeds of creation in a pot, sealed it and placed it on top of Mount Meru. During the *pralayam* or deluge, which signals the end of every *yuga* or cycle of creation, the pot was washed away to rest in a place in south India. In response to the celestials' request, Lord Siva used an arrow and pierced the pot. The nectar flowed out into two spots—Mahamaham Tank and Potramarai Tank. (The latter is the temple tank of Sarangapani Temple). The *Mahamaham* festival is celebrated every 12 years, when devotees take a holy dip in the tank to wash off all sins. Idols from all the temples in Kumbakonam are brought to the tank for the festival. The last festival was held in March 2004.

Sri Adi Kumbeswara Temple: It is the most ancient among the Saivite temples in this town. When Siva pierced the sacred pot and the nectar spilt out, some of it flowed on to the temples in Kumbakonam, one of which is the Adi Kumbeshwara temple. It is said the idol in the temple is made of a mixture of nectar and sand. It has a large entrance *gopuram* and two other *gopurams*.

Thirunageswaram: Of the 9 *navagrahams*, Rahu and Kethu are said to be the most fierce. This temple is dedicated to Rahu and praying here is believed to remove any malefic effects that may befall a person on account of Rahu.

Swamimalai: This Muruga temple is ever popular for its beauty. It is about 15 km from Kumbakonam and is one of the *Aru Padai Veedus* (six houses) of Lord Muruga. One has to climb up a flight of steps to have *darshan* of Lord Subramanya. Swamimalai is famous for its metal work and one can pick up beautiful artifacts such as idols of various Gods and Goddesses, bells, lamps and other devotional items.

Tiruvalanchuzhi: There is a beautiful shrine of Lord Ganapathy in Thiruvalanchuzhi, 20 km from Kumbakonam. There are three reasons why this place got this name, which means 'curved to the right'. One is that the name represents the *Pranava Mantra, Om*. The second is that the trunk of the Vinayaka idol here is curved to the right, signifying spirituality. The third is that when the river Cauvery, nearby, was in floods, she skirted the temple in an arc curving to the right.

The idol here is known as *Vellai Vinayakar* or white Vinayakar as it is believed to have originated from the foam of the sea. According to legend, the *asuras* and *devas* were churning the ocean to get *amritham* or ambrosia, which confers immortality. Many stories are associated with this episode, but this little known one says that before they began the churning, they forgot to pray to Lord Vigneswara, the Remover of Obstacles. This resulted in the ocean spilling out poison. The *devas* and *asuras*, realizing their error, made a small *vigraham* of Vinayaka using foam. They prayed to him and started the churning again. As for how the idol came to earth, the *Puranas* say that Indra brought it with him when he came to earth. The foot high idol is never given the customary ablutions, because it is believed to be made of foam. The only offering is *pachai kalpooram* or edible camphor. It now looks to be made of white stone.

The ancient temple also houses the shrines of Kapardeesar (Siva) and Periyanayagi Ambal. There is a shrine to Erandamunivar, who sacrificed his life to save the temple from floods. The best time for a visit is early morning or evening. It is better known as the Vellai Vinayakar Koil.

The powerful deity of
PALANI

Lord Muruga is very dear to the people of Tamil Nadu and a pilgrimage to Palani is like looking at a mirror reflecting the culture of the people of this south Indian state. Muruga is the leader of Siva's armies, and he is usually found in hill shrines. Palani is the third of the six *Arupadai veedus*. Most beatific is the smile of Lord Dandayuthapani, as Muruga is called here.

There is a legend behind how he got this name. Idumban, a demon, carried the hills of Sivagiri and Sakthigiri by dangling them on either side of a rod. When he was near the area that is Palani, he placed the hills down to rest. At that time, Muruga ascended the hill and made it his abode. When Idumban tried to dislodge the young god, a fierce battle ensued and the demon was slain with the Lord's baton (*Dandayutha*). Just before his death, Idumban prayed that those who bear a *kavadi* and come to Palani should be blessed and that he himself should be allowed to be the sentinel at Palani. God granted both wishes and that is how one can see the Idumban shrine at Palani. Even today, we can see groups of men performing the folk dance called the *kavadi* in Palani, where the dancer balances a hemisphere-shaped structure on his shoulders and dances in a trance-like state.

There are many other rituals associated with Lord Muruga, though not all of them practised in Palani. There are devotees who walk all the way to the hill shrine, barefoot and clad only in a loincloth, from their homes hundreds of miles away. There are those who engage in the ritual of 'fire walking' with devotees walking with bare feet over hot coals arranged on the ground. Some even pierce their tongues with the Lord's weapon, the *vel* (spear.)

The other important legend relates how Palani got its name and why Muruga came here. The story goes that Sage Narada brought a mango, which was the fruit of knowledge, to Mount Kailash, Siva's abode. The mango would be efficacious only if eaten whole. Narada offered it to Siva, who gave it to Parvathi. She however wanted to give it to her children. Narada maintained that the fruit had to be eaten whole and suggested a competition. The task given to Ganapathy and his younger brother Muruga was, that they should go around the world three times. Whoever finished first, would get the fruit!

Muruga set off immediately on his peacock. Ganapathy, on the other hand, went around his parents thrice, saying that, to him they were the entire world! He was awarded the prized fruit. When Muruga came back after his travels and was told the outcome, he became furious at what he felt was unfair treatment and left home in the garb of a mendicant to Palani.

The enchanting story bears repetition if only to convey how Palani got its name. Siva and Parvati, it is believed, rushed to this hill to pacify their disconsolate child. Siva is believed to have told Balamuruga, "*Pazham Nee*". In Tamil this means "You are the fruit (of knowledge)". This in due course got syncopated to 'Palani'.

The smiling Muruga is a surprise! What was the expectation? A snarling and sulking God? The very idea is preposterous! How often do human feelings and angst get imposed on divine beings? How often is it forgotten that legends and myths about Gods and Goddesses are parables, not to be taken literally? Scholars aver that Muruga's forsaking the world when a mere child and deciding to do penance in Palani should not be mixed up with a human beings' wish to eschew the material. Rather it is an action of great philosophical import.

The *moolavar vigraham,* 3.5 ft tall, is said to have been made by the renowned *Siddhar,* Bhogar (father of the Siddha system of medicine) who lived 3000 years ago, from 9 rare herbs called *Navabhasanam.* There is a shrine to him. Recently a new *panchaloha* idol has been installed to serve as the *utsava murthy.*

You can reach the hill temple either by walking up the 679 steps or by using the cable cars that are pulled by a winch, which go up and down in quick succession, carrying small batches of pilgrims. As the car climbs, the first part of the temple to come into view is a sculpture of Lord Muruga's elder brother Lord Ganesha, set high into the walls. An auspicious beginning—having *darshan* of the 'Remover of Obstacles.'

Enter the large temple *prakaram* and you will see many rows of shops selling idols, pictures, puja materials and the famed *Palani Panchamrutham* (a concoction of fruit, jaggery and rare herbs with medicinal quality). Everywhere, people of all ages, attired in bright clothes, are sitting or standing, the festive spirit high. Along the courtyard, and into a large open space, is a point from which there is a breathtaking view of the Western Ghats from an eminence of 1500 feet above sea level. Palani is a lone hill amid the surrounding plains.

Palani is also known as Thiruavinankudi. Cheeman Perumal, a Kerala king, is believed to have constructed the temple in the 7th century AD. This probably accounts for the large numbers of devotees from Kerala who throng this temple. Later, the Nayaks and Pandya Kings built additions such as the *Navaranga Mandapam.* The style is of the south Indian temple architecture with pillared bays, *gopurams* and *vimanams.*

After partaking of the heavenly *Palani Panchamrutham*, we descended to the base of the hill. The temple cautions devotees against buying the *panchamrutham* from sources other than the temple counters, as spurious versions abound.

The important festivals celebrated here are: *Panguniuttiram, Thai Poosam, Kandha Sashti, Agni Nakshatram, Vaikasi Visakam* and *Thai Kartikai.* An event looked forward to is the taking out of the golden chariot or *Thanga Ther.*

This temple has the distinction of being the richest shrine in Tamil Nadu and the second richest in India after Tirupati. It has grown from receiving a handful of devotees in the past to five lakh devotees during festival days lately. The Government of Tamil Nadu's Hindu Religious and Charitable Endowments Department administers the temple.

FAST FACTS

How to reach

Air	:	The nearest airport, Madurai, is 140 km away.
Rail	:	Palani is on the Dindigul-Pollachi metre-gauge rail route. There are plenty of trains from Chennai to Dindigul. Dindigul is 60 km from Palani.
Road	:	Palani is 130 km drive from Madurai and 60 km drive from Dindigul. Driving down the hills from Kodaikanal is a distance of 64 km.
Local Transport	:	Tourist taxis, auto rickshaws and cycle rickshaws.
Season	:	Throughout the year.
Clothing	:	Tropical, light cottons.
Languages spoken	:	English and Tamil.

Accommodation

The Arulmigu Dandayuthapani Devasthanam, which is under the government, has created adequate infrastructure for the stay of pilgrims. They can be contacted through e-mail at lordmuruga@eth.net or on Phone 91-4545-241417.

	Tariff (INR)	Phone
Hotel Tamil Nadu (TTDC hotel)	AC - Rs.495, Non AC Rs.250	04545-241156
Hotel Subham	AC - Rs.1350, 700 Non AC Rs.460	04545-242672
Hotel Tiruppur	AC - Rs.1000, 700 Non AC Rs.420, 260	04545-242303

NEARBY ATTRACTIONS

Palani Town: Palani Town has a number of temples. The most important is the Thiruvavinkudi temple, which is the original shrine at Palani. It is situated at the foothills. It is this shrine, which the famous Tamil poet Nakkeeran sang of, as the third martial abode of Muruga. It was later that Lord Muruga is believed to have moved up to his hilly home after slaying the demon Idumban.

Kodaikanal: The famous hill station is only 3 hours away from Palani. The drive from Palani to Kodaikanal is uphill. The salubrious hill station is located at an elevation of 2100 m. Some of the scenic spots in Kodaikanal are Dolphin's Nose, Pillar Rocks, Silver Cascade, Coker's Walk and Botanical Gardens. There is an excellent golf course.

The Kurinji Andavar Temple dedicated to Lord Muruga is 3.2 km from the centre of the town. Named after the Kurinji flower, which blooms once in 12 years, the temple is under the administration of the Dandayudhapani Devasthanam.

Bestowing all good
KARPAGA VINAYAKA

*"Suklam bharadharam vishnum shashivarnam chathurbhujam
Prasanna vadanam dhyayeth sarva vignoba shanthaye"*

This invocation to Lord Vinayaka, son of Siva and Parvathi and the remover of obstacles, is the first verse of the *Vishnu Sahasranama,* (the thousand names of Lord Vishnu) which Bhishma uttered while lying on his bed of arrows, at the request of Lord Krishna himself. Vinayaka or Ganapathi is the god every devout Hindu, whether Saivite or Vaishnavite, prays to before beginning any auspicious venture.

The easiest of deities to please, He wants no costly offerings or rich vestments and asks for sincere prayer alone. Of all the gods, He alone can be worshipped in any form, whether as a lump of clay or a cone of turmeric paste. You find shrines to him, both big and small, throughout the Indian subcontinent. In Vaishnavism, he is called *Thumbikkai Azhwar,* with reference to the *thumbikkai* (trunk) on his elephant visage.

So important is the Karpaga Vinayaka Temple in Pillayarpatti that the very town is named after the presiding deity. This temple, which is on the Thirupattur-Karaikudi Highway, is special in many ways. The presiding deity in the form of an exquisite bas-relief sculpture is Karpaga Vinayakar or Desi Vinayaka, whose very presence is said to be the fount of wealth and prosperity. Like the *Karpaga Vriksham* (Tree of Prosperity), which bestows all prosperity, praying to this idol will shower all good. Little wonder then that people are drawn to this shrine in large numbers. He faces north, the direction of Kubera, the demi-god of wealth, and is a *valampuri vinayaka*, with his trunk turned to the right.

The deity, 6 ft tall and 5 ft wide, has two arms and does not have any weapons. The hands are in *gaddi* (hand on the hip) and *varada* (granting boons) *hastam* posture, indicating his peaceful and benign aspect. While the left arm is placed on the waist, the right holds a *modaka*, his favourite dish (made of steamed rice stuffed with coconut and jaggery). Always clad in white, He is seated in *ardha padmasana* (half lotus posture). In place of the sacred thread or the snake waist belt, He wears the *udharabanda*, whose three bands are similar to the cummerbund used by gentlemen to keep their midriffs trim!

The temple is said to be of the Pandya period (5th century A D) and is situated in a cave. As a rock cut cave temple, it calls for comparisons with structures in Mamallapuram. However, this temple conforms to the Pandya style of rock cut temple architecture and not the Pallava. History bears this out, as the Pallavas did not advance beyond Tiruchirapalli.

The *garba graham* (sanctum sanctorum) is in apsidal shape, like an inverted lotus. It is also described as the *gajaprastha* shape, (resembling the back of a seated elephant) and carved out of one single rock form. In the sanctum sanctorum, there is a rare panel of Harihara (as conceded by archaeologists after much debate), as a standing figure with headgear and a crown and the combined features of Siva and Vishnu. On one side is Garuda in a supplicant posture and on the other is Chandikeswara, a devotee of Siva. On the side wall of the inner shrine, is a panel depicting Lingodhbhavamurthy. The head of Siva, unlike other such depictions, has a crown of matted hair. There is also a *lingam* in the sanctum sanctorum, which has been scooped out of rock.

The temple has two *rajagopurams* and grand *vimanams*. You enter the temple through a small *gopuram* to immediately see the main deity. The *gopuram* has been painted in *vannakalabam* (multi-colours). There have been several *Mahakumbabhisekhams*. There are shrines to Siva and his consorts. Siva is called Thiruvengaikudimahadevar or Thiruvisar. The consorts are Meenakshiamman and Vadamalarmangai.

Inscriptions mention Vikrama Pandya Thevar, Kulothunga Chola III, Sundara Pandya Thevar and Kulasekhara Thevar as benefactors of the temple. The Nattukottai Chettiars in the 13th century endowed the temple with lands and jewels and made a number of structural additions.

Having *darshan* here is equal to worshipping in all the six houses of Vinayaka. (All deities, whether Muruga, Parvathy or Siva, have some shrines which are more special than others, called *veedus* or houses. Another commonly used word is *sthalams*). The campus is dotted with a number of Vinayaka idols. A priest belonging to the Sivacharya lineage performs *pujas* five times a day.

The festival of *Vinayaka Chaturthi* is celebrated over 10 days. The festival idol is taken around atop vehicles shaped like the bandicoot, lion, demon, ox, lotus, elephant, peacock and horse. On the 9th day he rides on the temple chariot and on the 10th and final day, women carry silver idols in pots of water, in a ritual that is believed to fulfil all desires. That day, a huge *modhakam* made of 25 kg of rice is prepared over three days and brought to the sanctum sanctorum by ten people, to be offered to devotees after offering to the Lord.

The ambience is pleasant, with a number of trees and a pond. A quaint little town filled with the serenity of divinity, Pillayarpatti is a place you should take time to visit, for an atmosphere which is both vibrant and quiet.

FAST FACTS

How to reach

Air	:	The nearest airport is Madurai, 82 km away. Tiruchirapalli is 100 km away.
Rail	:	The nearest railhead is Karaikudi, 8 km away.
Road	:	Karaikudi is 8 km away. One can also drive or take a bus from Tiruchirapalli, 100 km away.
Local Transport	:	No local transport is available.
Season	:	Throughout the year.
Clothing	:	Tropical, light cottons.
Languages spoken	:	English and Tamil.

Accommodation

Karaikudi

	Tariff (INR)	Phone
Hotel Subhalakshmi Palace	365-1800	04565-235200
Hotel Malar	300-900	04565-239601

NEARBY ATTRACTIONS

Karaikudi: This is an interesting town full of old buildings with fine woodwork and carvings. Ornate Chettiar houses, many of which have been dismantled, have led to a good antique market in Karaikudi.

Pudukottai: Pudukottai Museum is worth a visit for the glimpse it gives into the life of its royal family and its people, when Pudukkottai was the centre of power.

Thirumayam: This temple lies between Karaikudi and Pudukkottai. The presiding deity is Meyyappan. The *utsavar* is Satyagirinathan. The goddess is Uyyavantha Nachiyar. It is believed that this shrine is under the protection of Adi Sesha. Carved out of a rock, the temple is among the 108 *Divya Desas.*

Thirukottiyur: This famous temple can be approached from Karaikudi via Tirupattur. It was from here that the Vaishnavite saint Ramanuja, gave the *Ashtakshara mantra, 'Om Namo Narayana',* to the people. The temple is fascinating for its fort-like construction, in 4 levels. Getting from one level to another involves bending double and climbing up steep steps! The presiding deity is Uragamellaiyan, in *bhujanga sayana,* while the *utsava murthy* is Sowmya Narayana. The goddess is Thirumagal Nachiyar. There are other idols of Narayana in various postures. This temple too is one of the 108 *Divya Desas*.

Pilgrimage to
RAMESWARAM

Few pilgrimages evoke the kind of fervour and enthusiasm as a visit to the holy island of Rameswaram does. The life of a Hindu is considered incomplete without a visit to the holy city of Varanasi in north India and the island of Rameswaram in the south.

The journey to Rameswaram is in itself very different as it involves the crossing of the sea across the Gulf of Mannar by rail or road. While the road bridge is sufficiently elevated to allow free passage of ships, the rail bridge folds up at the centre with the help of a complex mechanism of gears and chains as ships approach. Gales are so common that trains are signalled to stop during high winds. It is a wonder how, in ancient days, pilgrims used to cross these choppy waters. It is even more amazing how such a massive temple was built in the conch-shaped Rameswaram Island, transporting huge blocks of rock and timber across the sea (since the island is largely sandy, resources could not have been obtained locally).

Legend: The origins are traceable to the time of Lord Rama. Ravana, a Siva *bhakta*, was a good being and a good king, till his desire for Sita blinded him. When Rama, on his return from Lanka, had to expiate the sin of killing Ravana, he decided to worship Siva as soon as he reached the shores of India, at Rameswaram. He bade his devotee Hanuman get a *lingam* from Kashi, while he prepared for worship. But when the auspicious time for the *puja* approached, there was no sign of Hanuman. Upon which Sita fashioned a *lingam* from the beach sands for Rama to offer worship. Hanuman arrived soon after and was crestfallen to see that worship had been completed. Rama noticed Hanuman's sorrow and directed that the *lingam* brought by him should also be installed and that all those who visited Rameswaram should pay obeisance to that *lingam* first. Both *lingams* are worshipped in the temple. The one made by Sita is known as Ramalinga, Ramanatha or Rameswara, meaning the Lord of Rama, while the one brought by Hanuman is called the Visvalinga as it came from Kashi (Varanasi).

There is also another legend. Rama and his army of monkeys and bears sought to build a ford across the sea. During the day, they would toil hard and build the bridge but Ravana, who had imprisoned Sita on his island, would destroy their work at night. When Rama was losing hope, the wise bear, Jambavan, advised him to place a Siva *lingam* on the bridge, since Ravana being a Siva *bhaktha*, would not destroy anything, which had a *lingam* on it. This came true and Rama could cross over this bridge called Sethu to Lanka. It is said that as a symbol of thanksgiving, Rama built this temple fashioning the *lingam* himself for worship.

The magnificent temple grew bigger as monarchs of dynasties like the Rashtrakutas and Hoysalas erected columns of victory, commemorating their pilgrimages. It covers an area of half a square kilometre and is the heart of the island.

Architecture: A nine-storeyed *gopuram* adorns the eastern entrance. The temple has 3 enclosures or *prakarams*. The outermost that measures 196 m in length and 120 m in width has over 4000 pillars erected on a base that is over a metre in height. The carved pillars are 3.7 m high. Poised on the pedestal along the long corridor, they are an amazing sight. The visual impact of a row of pillars progressively appearing thicker and shorter and finally dissolving into the distant darkness is marvellous. Some scholars say this is the longest temple corridor in the world.

There is a massive *Nandi,* over 15 ft tall and equally long beyond the second *prakaram.* On either side are portraits of Visvantha Nayak and Krishnappa Nayak, kings of Madurai and benefactors of the temple.

In the main sanctum sanctorum is the Ramalinga made by Sita. It has a three-storeyed *vimanam* over it. The *lingam* brought by Hanuman is enshrined in another *garba griham* on the northern side. One should worship here first. There are shrines to Visalakshi, the consort of Visvanatha and Parvathavardini, consort of Ramanatha.

There is a separate shrine for Lord Vishnu, located behind that of Ramanatha. Here Lord Vishnu is called Sethumadhava, or God of the Sethupathis, who ruled here. He is also the guardian of the *sethu* (bridge). Some say His name is *Shweta Madhava,* meaning the White Lord, since the idol is made of marble (*shweta* in Sanskrit, means white).

There is a story in connection with this shrine. Punyanadhi, an ardent devotee of Vishnu, performed a big *puja* in Rameswaram to propitiate Vishnu. To test his devotion, Vishnu sent Lakshmi, his consort, as an orphan girl to him. The man adopted the child and brought her up with care. One day Vishnu entered her chambers as an ascetic and learning of this, Punyanadhi had him chained. That night, the Lord appeared to him in a vision as Vishnu with his divine consort, in full effulgence. The man ran to his daughter's chambers and saw the same sight. He then ran to the temple and found the Lord in shackles. Aghast at his action, he fell at the feet of the Lord, who consoled him, saying that he would forever remain in Rameswaram in shackles with Lakshmi, as if bound by the love of his devotee.

It is believed that whoever bathes in the nearby tank and worships gets all the benefit of bathing in the Sethu and those who offer worship here with the sand from Dhanushkodi get all the benefits of a pilgrimage to Varanasi.

There is a 24 m tall *gopuram* on the western side, much smaller than the eastern *gopuram*, which is 38.4 m high Unfinished towers are seen in the northern and southern directions. The temple, spread over an area of 15 acres, has massive walls. The ancient shrine was housed in a thatched hut until the 12th century. Parakrama Bahu, a king of Sri Lanka, built the first masonry structure. The Sethupathy rulers of Ramanathapuram completed the rest of the temple. Much of the additions were carried out between the 12th and the 16th centuries. The long corridor (third *prakaram*) is as recent as the 18th century.

Another important facet of a pilgrimage to Rameswaram is bathing in the sacred baths or *theerthams* that number 22, some of them situated outside the temple. You can see hordes of pilgrims having their first dip in the *agnitheertham*, which is the sea itself, and rushing to the temple in wet clothes bringing in their wake a trail of sand and water. The final dip is taken in the *kodi thirtham* that is inside the temple. Some ingenious pilgrims collect a little of the water from all 22 *theerthams* and have one 'compact' bath! None other than Lord Krishna is said to have bathed in all these 22 bathing places in the prescribed order.

About 2.5 km from the temple is Gandamadhana Parvatha, where one can see Rama's footprints. This hillock affords a breathtaking view of the sea and the littoral scenery. The multicoloured hues of the Indian Ocean are a photographer's delight. On the way to Dhanushkodi is the Kodandaramaswamy temple. It has an image of Lord Rama with the *Kothandam*, his bow. It is said that Vibhishana, brother of Ravana, was crowned here.

Rameswaram is famous not only among the Tamils but pilgrims from all over India. They come in large numbers, as it is believed that a visit propitiates one's ancestors.

This is also one among the 12 *jyotirlingams* (self-manifested *lingams* that can be seen as columns of fire by the enlightened). Ramalingeswara is the southernmost while Kedarnath is the northernmost. Worshipping them is believed to free one from rebirths.

The important festivals here are the two annual *Brahmotsavams*. They are in the Tamil months of Masi (Feb15th – March 15th) and Adi (July 15th – August 15th). There is a festival dedicated to Lord Rama in Ani (June 15th – July 15th).

FAST FACTS

How to reach

Air	:	Madurai, 170 km away, is the nearest airport.
Rail	:	Rameswaram has direct trains to Chennai. It is linked by rail to Madurai too.
Road	:	It is well connected by road to major South Indian towns through Madurai.
Season	:	Through the year.
Local Transport	:	Tourist taxis, auto rickshaws, public buses, tourist buses.
Clothing	:	Tropical, light cottons.

Accommodation

	Tariff (INR)	Phone
Hotel Tamil Nadu	425-650	04573-221277
Hotel Maharaja	280-825	04573-221721

PLACES OF INTEREST NEARBY

Thirupullani: This temple is located near Ramanathapuram, which is 60 km from Rameswaram. The main deity is Kalyana Jagannatha. There is another important shrine to Lord Chakravarthi Raghavan (Rama). While the first idol is in standing posture, the second is in *darba sayana* (lying on a bed of grass). Lakshmana in the form of Adi Sesha is serving his brother in this shrine. There is also a shrine to Rama in his *Pattabhisekha* posture. The consorts are Kalyanavalli and Padmasani. A sage called Pullar recited the *Ashtakshara Mantram* here innumerable times, upon which the Lord appeared before him under an *Aswatha* tree. Hence, this place got the name Pullaranyam. This is one of the 108 *Divya Desas* of Vaishnavites.

Sethu: Rama is believed to have built the bridge to Ceylon at this spot, which is 5 km from Tirupullani and 11 km from Ramanathapuram. It is also called Adhi Sethu. Pilgrims bathe in the sea here. In the temple, the presiding deity is Srinivasa and the goddess Alarmelumanga. There is a shrine to Hanuman. Notable is a statue of sage Agastya made of white marble. Close by, at a place called Devipattinam, there is a spot called Navapashanam, just submerged by the sea., where there are nine stones here symbolising the 9 planets or *navagrahams*. It is believed that prayer at Thirupullani and Devipattinam will bless the childless with progeny.

Dhanushkodi: Dhanushkodi was at the tip of the Rameswaram Island where the Bay of Bengal joins the Indian Ocean, before it was destroyed in a cyclone. In Tamil, Dhanushkodi means 'end of the bow'. This is derived from the belief that Lord Rama destroyed the bridge to Sri Lanka with his bow, responding to Vibhishana's pleas. This is also the spot where Vibhishana surrendered to Rama. The idols of Rama and Sita, which used to be here, are now in the Rameswaram temple.

Kurusudai Islands: These islands are a paradise for nature lovers. There are coral reefs here and a variety of marine flora and fauna. The islands are 20 km from Rameswaram via Mandapam. Entry needs permission from the State Fisheries Department.

Twin temples at
MAMALLAPURAM AND KADALMALLAI

To have *darshan* of Lord Vishnu without his weapons, the *Shankhu* and the *Chakra*, and without his customary 'bed' that is Adi Sesha, is somehow a humbling experience. Lying on the ground with one hand supporting his head and the other raised up in the traditional gesture of invitation, the Lord somehow seems defenceless, though the rational mind says this is not true. Of course, the Lord has assumed this posture without the customary conch and discus, to convey how accessible He is to true devotees. In this particular case, it was Sage Pundarika, a great devotee of Lord Vishnu, who was the recipient of His grace.

The temple being referred to is the Sthalasayana Perumal temple in Mamallapuram, which has been described by the Azhwars as Kadalmallai. Considering that it was built 600 years ago, it is in good condition and has a quiet charm about it.

The story goes that when Sage Pundarika came to Mamallapuram, he saw a tank with a lovely lotus flower having 1000 petals. Desiring to offer it at the feet of the Lord, he plucked the flower from the tank (that is now called *Pundarika Pushkarani*) to offer it to *'Par kadalil pallikollum paraman'*, or 'the Lord who lies on the sea'.

He began to bale out the water from the sea with his own hands. The Lord, Anaatharakshaka (Protector of the helpless) came to his rescue in the form of an old and weakened man.

The old man asked for food, and immediately Pundarika went in search of it. Meanwhile, the aged man started bailing out the water. When the sage returned with food, he saw that the sea had dried up. In the place where the water had been, a beautiful figure was lying in recumbent posture. The sage realized that the old man was none but the Lord himself. He placed the lotus at the feet of the Lord. Because the Lord touched the sea for bailing water, it is now called *Artha Sethu*.

The idol being referred to is none other than the idol of Lord Vishnu in the shore temple at Mamallapuram. This is dated to the 9th century A D. Around 500 years later, in the 14th century A D, the Lord is said to have appeared in a vision to the rulers of Vijayanagar and commanded them to build a temple for Him at a spot well away from the eroding waves of the sea.

The ruler Parangusan, built the present Sthalasayana temple, which lies in the heart of Mamallapuram town, with an idol that is a replica of the one in the Shore Temple. The Lord's feet are on a lotus, and *darshan* of the *padam* (feet) confers great good. The goddess here is *Nilamangai*, the goddess of the earth. There are also shrines to Andal, Lord Lakshmi Narasimha and to Boothathazhwar, who incarnated here. Once this temple was consecrated, *pujas* were stopped at the shore temple.

Thirukadalmallai is one of the 108 Vaishnava *Divya Desas* sung of by the Azhwars. Set in the middle of a crowded town and yet away from it, the temple should be part of any visit to Mamallapuram.

FAST FACTS

How to reach

Air	:	The nearest airport is Chennai, 55 km away.
Rail	:	The nearest railhead is Chengalpattu, 30 km away. Trains from Chennai further south halt at Chengalpattu.

Road	:	Mamallapuram is 55 km from Chennai on the East Coast Road. The Tamil Nadu state transport corporations operate buses to Mamallapuram. Tours run by the TTDC touch Mamallapuram.
Local Transport	:	Tourist taxis, auto rickshaws, public buses and bicycles for hire.
Season	:	Throughout the year.
Clothing	:	Tropical, light cottons.
Languages spoken	:	English and Tamil.
Accommodation	:	One can stay in Mamallapuram or Chengalpattu.

Mamallapuram

	Tariff Range (INR)	Phone
Ideal Beach Resorts	1500-2400	954114-242240
Hotel Tamil Nadu	500-1000	954114-242361
GRT Temple Bay	3500-9000	954114-242251
Fisherman's Cove	4500-8000	954114-272304
Mamalla Bhavan	825-950	04114-242060

Chengalpattu

Hotel Ganesh	380-660	954114-22637
Hotel Kanchi	*160-420*	*954114-231019, 226819.*

PLACES OF INTEREST NEARBY

Excursions: There is a lot to see in Mamallapuram itself, apart from which there are beautiful picnic spots a short drive away. Mamallapuram has bas-reliefs, pagodas, rock cut caves and single-stone crafted chariots, all belonging to Pallava times (600 A D to 750 A D).

Arjuna's Penance: This is the world's largest bas-relief measuring 27 m x 9 m. This huge whale-backed shape rock contains figures of gods, demi-gods, men, animals and birds and serves as a picturesque backdrop for the dance festival that takes place in Mamallapuram every year in December-January.

Five Rathas (chariots): These are 5 monolithic temples, each in a different style. They are also known as the *Pancha Pandava Rathas,* named after the heroes of the epic Mahabharatha. Four of the *Rathas* are said to have been scooped out of a single formation. They are richly carved with artistic motifs and have wall panels depicting Hindu gods and royal personages. The Shore Temple stands right at the edge of the sea, and is one of the oldest temples in south India. Said to have been built by the Pallava King Rajasimha in the latter half of the 7th century A D, it is enclosed by a row of bulls carved out of rock. It has two shrines, one dedicated to Lord Vishnu and the other to Lord Siva. The monuments are floodlit at night. The Cave Temples are noted for their simple plan and decoration. King Mahendravarman I initiated the rock cut cave tradition, represented by over a dozen caves here. Some of the cave temples of note are Mahishasuramardhini Cave, Varaha Cave and Krishna Mandapa. Krishna's Butterball is a huge boulder that rests on a narrow rock base near the Ganesha Ratha. The legend goes that several Pallava Kings tried to move it, using men and elephants, but it would not budge an inch! Tiger's Cave is 4 km north of the main monument complex. It was an open-air theatre where cultural shows used to take place in Pallava times.

Thirukkazhukunram: This small Siva temple, 17 km from Mamallapuram, is situated atop Vedagiri hill. There is also a larger Siva temple in the town below. At the town's southeast end there is a large tank whose waters are said to be curative. Once every 12 years, a conch is discovered in the tank and thousands of devotees throng for a bath. A legend attached to the hill temple says that two kites come to feed here every day. They are believed to be sages in the form of birds.

Thirupporur: 16 km from Mamallapuram, Thirupporur lies on the Old Mahabalipuram Road. There is a fascinating legend about the building of the temple. Over 450 years ago, one Chidambaraswamy, an ardent worshipper of Madurai Meenakshi, was on a fast desiring a vision of the goddess. Many days passed and he was almost in a coma. Suddenly he heard the sound of anklets and when he opened his eyes, he glimpsed the divine feet. The goddess then raised him, and as her hands touched him, his skin turned golden. She told him that six earlier attempts to establish a temple at a place called Thirupporur had failed and bade him build a temple there. Chidambaraswamy reached Thirupporur to find a dense forest of palm trees. He could not make out where earlier attempts had been made. Lord Muruga appeared as a small boy and gave him the vision of the sanctum sanctorum. He unearthed the *Swayambhu Moortis* of Muruga with his consorts and established the temple.

Lord Muruga, son of Lord Siva, is said to have waged three battles — in Tiruchendur, Tiruparankundram and Thirupporur, to symbolise the defeat of evil. On a metaphysical plane, the battle at Tiruchendur, fought on sea against the demons Soora and Padma, can be viewed as the battle against *Maya* (illusion); the battle in Tiruparankundram, against Kadaipatta Asura, who symbolised *karma* (past deeds and their effect) was fought on ground; and the battle of Thirupporur was fought against Thalayaya Asuran in ether or air to connote the defeat of arrogance or pride.

Sadras: This was once a Dutch settlement. Called Chathurangapattinam in Tamil, there is a fort built by the Dutch and a cemetery with old, carved tombstones. There are some temples, besides a pretty beach. The river Palar joins the sea here. 16 km south of Mamallapuram, it is well worth a visit.

Vedanthangal: 55 km away, it is a national sanctuary visited annually by thousands of migratory birds. They come during winter to breed, some from as far as Siberia. The large marshy area harbours nearly 100 species of birds. Some years, bird watchers have reported seeing up to 100,000 birds here. Carry a pair of binoculars!

Alamparai Beach: The sand dunes at Alamparai, 50 km from Mamallapuram, are a pretty sight. There is a damaged fort built by the Nawabs. You can go for a boat ride with the help of local fishermen. The landmark for Alamparai is Kadapakkam village.

Lord Venkateshwara at
GUNASEELAM

The experience of having *darshan* of Sri Venkateshwara at Tirumala is unparalleled. While ordinary mortals feast their eyes on the beauty of the Lord in his sacred abode, and leave the shrine with a full heart hoping to return soon, ancient India had saints who had the faith to ask the Lord to leave Tirumala and go with them to their *ashram*. Amazing, but true!

The story of Gunaseelar, an ancient sage, is an engrossing illustration. Gunaseelam, a small hamlet, about 16 km away from Tiruchirapalli, on the Salem-Tiruchirapalli Road, is the site where the *rishi* performed penance that brought none other than Lord Venkatachalapathy himself to reside on the banks of river Cauvery. The place soon came to be known after the saint.

Gunaseelar, the disciple of Saint Sreethalpya, served his *guru* (teacher) with such sincerity that he was bestowed with the superior knowledge of his guru. One day, Gunaseelar went on a pilgrimage to the Seven Hills and had *darshan* of Lord Venkateshwara. So stirred was he that he pleaded with the Lord to go with him to his *ashram* because he felt he could not be separated from Him anymore. The Lord, ever moved by the true love of his devotees spoke to Gunaseelar and told him that as he was in a state of debt (the story of Kubera – see chapter on Lord Srinivasa of Tirumala), he could not leave Tirumala. He directed Gunaseelar to return to his retreat on the banks of the Cauvery and perform penance. The Lord told the saint that none other than Vaikuntavasa Sri Narayana would appear before him.

Gunaseelar did as the Lord directed. Many years later, in the *Kritha Yugam* (according to the Hindu calendar, time is divided into *yugams*, which run into many thousands of years), on a Saturday in the month of Purattasi, on *Sravana Nakshatram* (the star of Sravana), Venkatachalapathy appeared in the *ashram* of Gunaseelar as a *swayambhu*. Gunaseelar was overjoyed and spent his days performing *puja* to the Lord. At the time, his guru Sreethalpya wanted to go to Badrinath and perform penance. He however did not want to part from his disciple. Gunaseela could sense the desire of his *guru* and his quandary. He too was in the horns of a dilemma – whether to go with his guru and in the process forsake his dear Lord, or forsake his guru and stay with his Lord?

The ever-compassionate Narayana was so moved at seeing the predicament of his devotee that when Gunaseelar prayed to Him to clear his mind and make him do the right thing, the Lord blessed him and bade him serve his guru. Since Venkatachalapathy cleared his mind, Gunaseelar prayed that all those who prayed to the Lord at Gunaseelam should be rid of illusions and delusions and be blessed with clarity of mind. This is why there is a belief that praying at this temple will cure insanity.

Gunaseelar left the Lord after appointing a small boy to take care of the *vigraham* and do the daily *pujas*. Unfortunately, the boy grew fearful of the wild animals and the swirling waters of the Cauvery in spate. He ran away. In the efflux of time, an anthill grew over the *vigraham* of Venkatachalapathy and serpents lived in it.

Many years later, a local king Gnana Varman, who had his capital at Uraiyur, established his cowshed near present day Gunaseelam. One day the cowherds noticed that the level of milk in the milk jugs had gone down mysteriously. The puzzled cowherds reported this to the king and he came to see the mysterious disappearance of the milk. At that point, an old Brahmin appeared and told the king that if the anthill was dissolved with milk, the king could see the Lord himself. The anthill was dissolved with milk and the idol of Venkatachalapathy with a conch, discus, whip and sceptre was revealed. The Lord blessed the king who immediately took upon himself the job of constructing a temple.

The Lord here is known as Prasanna Venkatesa Perumal and it is believed that those who are not able to visit Tirumala can obtain the grace of Venkatachalapathy here. The most important feature in this temple is the belief that the lord bestows special grace on the mentally challenged.

The Lord holds the conch and the discus in two hands. One hand points towards his feet, while another rests on his leg. Interestingly, there is a stick resting on him. The temple priests explain that this is the Lord's way of telling the devotee that he is striking at the demons afflicting the devotee's mind. Goddess Lakshmi abides on the chest of the Lord. There is no separate shrine for her for She is ever with Him.

The *pujas* are done here as per the *Vaikanasa* (a form of worship named after Maharishi Vaikanasa) tradition. The temple is administered by hereditary priests, who become trustees in turn in a system of rotation. The temple has three *choultries,* besides one for the mentally challenged. It is believed that staying for 48 days and taking the *theertham* (holy water) twice a day will cure insanity. Whether one subscribes to this belief or not, the beauty and benevolence of the deity beckons devotees to this temple.

FAST FACTS

How to reach

Air : The nearest airport is Tiruchirapalli, 16 km away.

Rail	:	The nearest railhead is also Tiruchirapalli.
Road	:	Gunaseelam is on the Salem-Tiruchirapalli road. There are buses from Tiruchirapalli to Gunaseelam. Private tourist taxis can also be hired.
Local Transport	:	Walking is recommended.
Season	:	Throughout the year.
Clothing	:	Tropical, light cottons.
Languages spoken	:	English and Tamil.

Accommodation

Tiruchirapalli	*Tariff (INR)*	*Phone*
Hotel Femina	350-1950	0431-2414501
Hotel Abbirami	270-720	0431-2415128
Hotel Guru	240-840	0431-2415881
Hotel Anand	215-825	0431-2415545

Temple choultries are available. There is room for 13 patients suffering from mental problems. One needs a nativity certificate and a psychiatrist's reference to approach the temple authorities for treatment that lasts 48 days and costs Rs.1650. The temple has its own panel of psychiatrists who examine the patient before admission. An escort for the patient is necessary. One can contact the Manager on phone 04326-275310.

PLACES OF INTEREST NEARBY (ALL IN TIRUCHIRAPALLI OR NEARBY)

Rock Fort: Rock Fort, atop which Uchi Pillayar Temple is situated, is an attraction in itself. Experts deem this rock to be 3,800 million years old, making it older than the Himalayas and as old as the ancient rocks of Greenland. The rocky outcrop is 83 m high. There are 420 steps leading to the summit, where there are inscriptions dating to the 3rd century B C. Not much remains of the fort ramparts, but the Main Guard Gate is intact. The fort played a crucial role in the Carnatic Wars.

Tiruvanaikkaval: This temple is famed for its architecture. It is a *panchalingam* (one of the shrines of Siva representing the 5 elements) shrine of Lord Siva. He is present in the form of Water here. The *lingam* installed under an ancient *Jambu* tree is partially submerged by water. The temple is also called Jambukeswara temple, after an elephant which worshipped Lord Siva here.

Samayapuram: 20 km from Tiruchirapalli, Samayapuram is a famous temple dedicated to Goddess Parvathy, called Mari Amman here. It is believed that those who are mentally ill will be cured if they visit this temple. The kind and beautiful mien of the goddess is unique.

Grand Anaicut: An engineering marvel, accomplished in the 2nd century A D. The Grand Anaicut, also called *Kallanai*, is a stone dam built by King Karikala Chola to harness the waters of River Cauvery. It is close to Srirangam Island. The dam is 329 m long and 20 m wide. There is now a road bridge on top of the dam, from where there is a good vista of pleasant greenery.

Upper Anaicut: This 685 m-long dam lies at the head of Srirangam Island, 18 km from Tiruchirapalli. It was built across river Kollidam in the 19th century. It is also called Mukkombu, because the dam forks into three.

The grand temple of
MYLAPORE

Mylapore, or Thirumayilai, one of the oldest areas of Chennai in Tamil Nadu, has a unique ambience. In ancient days, Mylai is supposed to have been a forest where peacocks danced joyously (*Mayil* in Tamil means peacock). Its most striking feature is the commanding tower of the Kapaleeswarar Temple that is dedicated to Lord Siva. There is a saying that goes '*Kayilaye Mailai, Mailaiye Kailai*' that means 'Mylapore is Kailash, the abode of Siva in the Himalayas, and Kailash is Mylapore'. The grand temple, built on an expanse of 33 grounds, has a spiritual and devotional fervour that is at once inspirational and calming. Once inside, we can hardly imagine that just outside the quiet and peaceful precincts, there is a welter of humanity rushing about the business of life.

Leave the busy *mada veedhis* (streets around a temple) and the milling shops of Mylapore. Forget the metro rail station, which looms on the horizon and enter the Kapaleeswarar temple to experience stillness, for it is a stillness that will persist even when the temple is filled with devotees on festival days and other important religious occasions.

There are some fascinating legends about how Mylapore got its name and how the temple got its name. Brahma, the Creator and one among the Hindu trinity, was being told of the creation of the *lokas* (different worlds) by Lord Siva. Siva's consort Parvathi too was with him. A lapse on Brahma's part made the Lord pluck off one of Brahma's five heads with his hand. Brahma begged forgiveness and was advised to do penance at Mayilai (Mylapore). Brahma did as directed and Siva appeared before him. Brahma requested Siva to permit him to carry out the mammoth job of creation. He also gave him the title Kapaleeswara (*Kapala* – skull).

For his hasty act, Siva too was punished as the skull got stuck to his hand and he could not shake it off. A short distance away from the Kapaleeswarar temple is the Adi Kesavaperumal temple, where Siva prayed to Lord Vishnu and atoned for the sin he had committed! The skull then fell off.

The other story relates how Parvati, in the form of a peacock, prayed to a Siva *lingam* at this spot. How did this come about? Legends say that once Lord Siva was elucidating the significance of the letters in the word 'Kailash' to Parvati. At that time a beautiful peacock came by and began dancing, displaying its resplendent plumes. Parvati was captivated and her attention was diverted. She missed a little of what her husband was saying and asked him to repeat it. Enraged, Lord Siva cursed her to become a peacock. Parvati pleaded for forgiveness and Siva told her to perform penance at Mayilai to regain her divine form.

Parvati performed *puja* as a bird to the *Sivalingam*. The Lord gave her *darshan* and she regained her original form. She then desired that the place she had lived in as a peacock and worshipped her Lord should be known as Mayilai.

The main shrines in the temple are that of Kapaleeswarar and his consort Karpagavalli. The Lord here is in *lingam* form, facing the west. As he gave *Saba Vimochana* (redemption from curse) to both Brahma and Parvati here, he is believed to be in benign frame of mind here. The Siva idol that is used for festivals is in anthropomorphic form.

Goddess Parvati here is Karpagavalli, the goddess of unlimited plenty. She is like the divine cow *Kamadhenu* and the tree *karpaga vriksha*, both of which confer bounty. She has inspired numerous poets who have sung of her as 'Karpagavalli of Mylapore'.

Most people with Tamil as their mother tongue have learnt the song,

'Karpagavallinin Porpadangal Pidithen
Nargathi Arulvai Amma
Parpalarum Potrum Padimayilapuriyil
Sirpam Migunda Uyar Singara Kovil Kondu'.

This verse translates to 'I seek refuge in the golden feet of Karpagavalli, who is resident in a resplendent temple replete with finest sculpture and praised by one and all........Oh goddess grant me a good standing....'

The main shrines of the Lord and Goddess here form two points of an angle so that it is possible to worship both of them from one spot. The goddess faces south. There are also shrines to a number of gods and demigods of the Saivite tradition.

The temple has two entrances. The one on the eastern side appears as the main entrance with the 40 m high *rajagopuram*, drawing the attention of all those who pass by. This lies on a narrow bylane, which is difficult to access. The normally used entrance is on the western side, opposite the temple tank, which leads you to the main deity, Kapaleeswarar.

On either side of this entrance, we can see shrines of Lord Vinayaka and Lord Muruga, the sons of Siva and Parvathi. There is a small shrine to Angam Poompavai, who was brought to life by the great saint Thirugnanasambandar. On the eastern precincts, we can see a sculpture depicting the *puja* performed by the peacock (Parvathi) to the *lingam* under the *Punnai* (Alexandrian Laurel) tree, which is the *sthalavruksham* (tree special to this temple). It has white blossoms and seeds that are poisonous.

Further east one can see the shrine of Lord Sundareswarar in *linga roopam*. Close by is the shrine of Saneeswara, one of the *navagrahams* or 9 planets. To the south of the Sundareswarar shrine are the *navagrahams* together. Devotees go around the planetary gods and light lamps with gingelly oil to propitiate them, following a common custom in south India. Jagadeeswara, another form of Siva in *lingam* form, can be seen to the south of the *navagrahams*.

Facing the *rajagopuram* is the pleasing Narthana Ganapathy known in this temple as *Koothadum Pillayar* (one who dances merrily) Close by are shrines to Annamalaiyar and Unnamalaiamman. (Siva and Parvati as found in the temple of Tiruvannamalai).

On the southern precincts, one can find the shrine of Singaravelar, none other than Lord Muruga, accompanied by Valli and Deivanai, his consorts. There is a beautiful hall with majestic pillars on the face of the shrine. The festival idol of Muruga is seated on a peacock *vahanam* and his consorts are on elephants. Facing north is another form of Muruga, Palani Andavar. The fierce forms of Idumban and Kadamban, demons who were killed by the gods, can also be seen.

On the west of the Palani Andavar shrine is Vailar Nainar, a devotee who attained salvation in Mayilai. It is said this shrine was built in the early 20th century. There is also a shrine to Arunagirinathar, who composed numerous devotional verses on Muruga, and a *Nandi*, which faces Lord Kapaleeswarar.

To the left of the Kapaleeswarar shrine is the sanctum sanctorum of his consort Karpagambal. To her right are the shrines to the *Arupattumoovars* — the 63 *Nayanmars* or Saivite saints, and Dakshinamurthy, who is Lord Siva in meditation. One can see a huge congregation of devotees on Thursdays, *Guruvaram*, in front of the Dakshinamurthy shrine, where it is customary to light lamps. Dakshinamurthy is said to confer knowledge on those who pray sincerely to him. He also mitigates ill effects caused by other planetary positions in an individual's horoscope.

Four *pujas* are conducted daily. They are the early morning *puja*, the day *puja*, the *pradosha kaala puja* and the night *puja*. The auspicious *pradosha puja* marks the time when Lord Siva swallowed the *halahala* (poison) that rose from the ocean when it was churned by the celestials in quest of *amrta*. The poison, which threatened to exterminate the gods and the demons, was swallowed by Siva to save the others. Parvathy, who clamped her hands round his neck and prevented the poison from going into his system, saved Siva. Because of the poison Siva's throat turned blue and he got the name Neelakantan or 'One whose throat is blue' (*neela* –blue, *kanta* –throat).

There are differing views among scholars about the antiquity of the temple. A publication brought out by the temple authorities states that the original temple was on the seashore of the Bay of Bengal, and was destroyed by the Portuguese in the 15th century. One Muthiappa Mudaliar of Mylapore constructed the present temple in the 16th century.

The temple architecture is of the Dravida style with a pyramidal multi-tiered *gopuram* at the entrance and a curved covering over the sanctum sanctorum called *vimanam*. The temple is full of large courtyards and paved spaces abutting dais-like structures, indicating the temple's role as a place of congregation for appreciation of the fine arts. The temple has been recently renovated at a cost of Rs. 1.6 crore. The *mahakumbabhishekam* was performed on Aug 30, 2004. A unique feature of the renovation was the use of herbal treatment on the ceilings of the sanctum sanctorum. A combination of sandalwood, *pachai kalpooram* (camphor), *manjal* (turmeric) and other herbs has been used to keep pests away. The treatment will be repeated at frequent intervals.

In addition, the sancta sanctora of all deities have been repaired. Security has been improved with the provision of brass grills for all shrines and reinforced doors for the strong room.

The shrines of Lord Kapaleeswarar and Goddess Karpagambal have been air-conditioned. The *kalasams* of the *raja gopuram* and 21 *vimanams* have been gold plated. A gold plated flagstaff for the Singaveralan shrine has been installed, replacing the old one. The seven-tiered *rajagopuram* has been painted colourfully. The stone pillars have been sand blasted and cleaned and special varnish applied, to prevent accumulation of grime.

The temple often organises grand festivals during which the various deities are carried around the streets of Mylapore on *vahanams* (vehicles) like the bull, elephant, bandicoot, peacock, goat and parrot. Recently a golden chariot was commissioned.

In the Tamil month of Panguni, corresponding to March-April, the *Arupatthumoovar* festival takes place, when the 63 Saivite saints, the *Nayanmars* are taken out in procession. The entire neighbourhood of the temple comes alive with a fair-like atmosphere. Mylapore takes on a rustic hue, more village-like with no buses and automobiles for 10 days in the area. Time travels backwards and we can see the past flashing in our eyes in images of lights burning in oil soaked cloth, young girls with plaited hair and bright ribbons, mounds of sticky dates and hawkers who sell all kinds of goods.

FAST FACTS

How to reach

Air : Chennai has two airports — domestic and international — located adjacent to one another at Meenambakkam.

Rail	:	Chennai has trains running towards Mumbai in the West, Delhi in the North, Calcutta in the East and Kanyakumari at the southern tip of India.
Road	:	Chennai is well connected by road to the southern cities like Tiruchirapalli and to the garden city, Bangalore.
Local Transport	:	Tourist taxis, call taxis, auto rickshaws, public buses, private tourist buses and cycle rickshaws are available.
Season	:	Throughout the year.
Clothing	:	Tropical, light cottons.
Languages spoken	:	English and Tamil. There is a sizeable population from other parts of India too, living in Chennai.
Accommodation	:	Chennai has a wide range of accommodation from budget to deluxe.

Luxury

	Tariff (INR)	Phone
Chola Sheraton	5500-6500 (+12.5%)	28110101
Moderate		
Nilgiri's Nest	1350-2950 +taxes	28115111
Shelter	1500-2995(+taxes)	24951919
Budget		
Hotel Karpagam	470-650	24959984

Places of interest nearby

Though Mylapore is famous for the Kapaleeswara Temple, few know that there are six more Siva temples in a radius of 2 km in the same locality. The 7 Siva *sthalams* (temples) are Kapaleecharam (Kapaleeswarar), Velleecharam (Velleeswarar), Karaneecharam (Karaneeswarar), Vaaleecharam (Vaaleeswarar), Virubatcheecharam (Virubatcheeswarar), Valleecharam (Malleeswarar) and Theerthabaleecharam (Theerthabaleeswarar).

Karaneeswarar Temple: The 12th century Karaneeswarar temple is situated on busy Bazaar road that runs perpendicular to Kutcheri Road, to the north. The *Karunaimigu* (merciful) Karaneeswarar attracts a stream of devotees. The *sthala puranam* talks about a young Brahmin who renounced his family and after many years of wandering, settled down in Mylapore. He performed pujas to Lord Siva in *linga roopam*. He realized through his penance that Lord Siva was the Cause of Creation, Maintenance and Destruction of the World. The Lord was said to be so pleased that one day he manifested within the *lingam* and said, "I am here. Let this *lingam* henceforth be known as Karaneeswara ('One who is the Cause', from the Tamil *karanam* or 'cause'). At the portal there is an idol of Sarvamangala Vinayaka who is the Pradhana Vinayaka (most important Vinayaka idol in the temple). On the other side are Dandapani and Durga, Lakshmi and Saraswathi. To the right of the main deity is Porkodi Ambal, also known as *Pon Alandhidum Ambal* as prayers to her are said to bestow gold. The Vishnu Durga is worshipped during *Rahu Kalam* (the time when the demon Rahu attains powers of a demi-god) by childless couples.

Velleshwara Temple: Lord Velleeswarar is believed to cure devotees of eye ailments. Legends say that during the Vamana incarnation of Lord Vishnu, Sukrachariar who was the preceptor of the *asuras* tried to prevent the gifting of land to Vamana by King Mahabali. Angered, Vamana poked the eye of Sukra with the *darba* grass, blinding him. When Sukra prayed to Lord Siva in the form of Velleeswarar in Thirumayilai, his sight was restored.

The temple, on South Mada Street, is easily approached and despite the busy vegetable market just outside, it is very peaceful and quiet. A *rajagopuram* was recently built and consecrated. The Lord is in *linga roopa* here and his consort Kamakshi has a separate shrine. The Sengunthars established the temple and are traditional trustees. An annual celebration is held in honour of the Sengunthar poet, Ottakkoothar, in the Tamil month Avani. Here, Kamakshi is said to possess attributes of both Saraswati and Lakshmi. The Lord and goddess here rest in a 'mirror palace' called the *'ardhajama palliarai'*. Vinayaka, accompanied by consorts Siddhi and Buddhi, can be seen at the forecourt. Vinayaka, as the *brahmachari* (bachelor) also gives *darshan*. Muruga is here as Muthukumaraswamy. In the outer precincts are the *navagrahams*. Just opposite is Sukra worshipping Lord Siva under a tree.

Adhikesava Perumal Temple: The Adhikesava Perumal Peyalwar temple in Mylapore is located near Chitrakulam, a well-known landmark. Periakulam is now called Mylapore tank. The 1000-year-old temple with intricate carvings was built by a royal clan of the Raojis, according to an edict in the main shrine. The family maintains links with the temple though they are no longer in Tamil Nadu. The insignia of the Cholas, the tiger, is also found at the entrance to the sanctum sanctorum. The Raojis installed the main deity Adhikesava. The stone idol holds the conch in one hand

and the *chakra* in the other. The third hand is in the *abhaya hastam* posture while the fourth rests on the hip in *gaddi* posture. The consort is Sree Mayuravalli Thayar, after whom, Vaishnavites say, the name Mylapore is derived. She was the daughter of Brighu Maharishi. Vaishnavite legend goes on to say that Lord Vishnu incarnated here to rid Lord Siva of the *Kapalam* (skull) that got stuck to His hand when he decapitated Lord Brahma. Siva had to be relieved of the *Brahmahatti dosham* by taking alms from Vishnu. Adhikesava means the first and the originator. He holds within himself all other deities of the earliest times, even before the Vedas got divided into four for learning convenience. The form of worship here precedes Vaishnavism and is called *Vaikanasam,* named after Maharishi Vaikanasa. Sharing the name of the temple is Pey Azhwar, who incarnated here. He is said to have emerged from a *Sevvalli* (red lily) flower. He was so devoted to the Lord that he never thought of anything else. One day a person called Siva Vakkiar, a great scholar in search of God, came to Mylapore. He found the Vishnu *bhakta*, who later became his *guru*, planting a *tulsi* sapling upside down, drawing water using a broken rope and pouring it into a container with a hole. Siva Vakkiar asked "Why are you behaving like a *Pey* (spirit) and doing totally foolish things?" The *bhakta* replied "If there is faith anything is possible. The *tulsi* plant will grow anyway. And it did!

Siva Vakkiar experienced the glory of Narayana and got the name Thirumazhisai Azhwar. He has sung about this temple in conjunction with Parthasarathy temple of Triplicane. The waters of the temple tank, though now sullied, had medicinal properties once. The moon was cured after he bathed in the *chandra pushkarani* here and had *darshan* of the Lord. Apart from the Pey Azhwar shrine to the right of the main deity, there are shrines to other Azhwars, Veera Anjaneya and Garuda. Rama's shrine in this temple is unique, since apart from the idols of Lord Rama, Sita, Lakshmana and Anjaneya, those of Bharatha and Shatrughna are also present. The legend associated with Bharata's and Shatrughna's presence is that the shrine depicts Rama's coronation. The other legend says that this is where Rama stayed before going to the forest.

Vedanta Desikar Devasthanam: Some temples attract devotees by their grace and simplicity and the mercy of the presiding deities. One such is the Srinivasa temple near the Chitra Kulam in Mylapore, which is administered by the Sri Vedantha Desikar Devasthanam. It has an over 350-year-old history. An idol of Vedanta Desika was brought from the adjacent Adikesava Perumal temple and installed here. Since elders felt the *acharya* (teacher) should not preside alone, a *vigraham* of Lakshmi Hayagriva was installed. The shrine of the great teacher faces north. Vedanta

Desika lived over 730 years ago in south India. He wrote erudite commentaries on Ramanuja's *Sribhashyam* and was a great exponent of *Visishtadvaita*. Hayagriva was the *upasana deivam* (the deity who is the object of worship) of Vedanta Desika and worshipping him here is doubly beneficial. He is said to have performed penance in Sivasamudram on the banks of the Cauvery river for 10 years. He left behind 5 noted disciples *(Jeeyars)*. Apart from the sancta sanctorum of Srinivasa and Alamelumanga Thayar, there are shrines to Lord Rama, Lord Narasimha and the Azhwars. Recently, a golden *Garudavahanam* was commissioned with devotees' contributions.

Universal Temple: The Universal Temple of Sri Ramakrishna Paramahamsa was consecrated in Chennai in February 2000, by Swami Ranganathananda, President of the Ramakrishna Math and Mission. A Kapaleeswar temple priest performed the *mahakumbabhishekam*. The imposing white temple, presenting a synthesis of various temple idioms of India and other parts of the world, is testimony to the universality of Saint Ramakrishna's spiritual message. Situated inside the Mission premises on Ramakrishna Mutt Road (R K Mutt road) in Mylapore, the striking edifice has an attractive interior. It is called the Universal Temple because Saint Ramakrishna ' does not belong to any religion or sect', say his devotees. He cannot be tied down to any *agama shastra* (system of worship). His creed was unity and universality of religion. He believed in attaining spiritualism as a tool for emancipation of self, not just for one's own good, but for the good of the universe. What catches the eye is the cathedral-like dome that towers 104 ft, made of Dolpur white sandstone. The red sandstone of Agra can be seen in the lower levels. The façade, which presents a three-tower front, has the swan motif of the Ramakrishna Math. Ganapati, Krishna and Kartikeya, are also represented. The extremes are occupied by Garuda and Hanuman. A grand staircase leads to the main prayer hall, which can accommodate a 1000 people. A 7 ft high, life-like marble figure of Saint Ramakrishna Paramahansa housed in a marble *garbhamandira* (sanctum sanctorum) adorns the hall. On either side are pictures of Swami Vivekananda and Mother Sarada Devi in smaller shrines. The big prayer hall with its vaulted roof of 40 ft is inspired by the concept of Buddhist Chaityas where devotees engage in congregational meditative worship. Below the prayer hall is the basement with an auditorium.

Kumariamman at
KANYAKUMARI

One of the most captivating aspects of Hindu religion is the depiction of the divine love between Lord Siva and his consort Parvati. It has not only been the staple of many a poetic effort but also the inspiration for many glorious shrines. One of the finest examples of this is the Bhagavathiamman temple at Kanyakumari.

Kanyakumari is itself a fascinating place — land's end and the cradle of the waters of the Indian Ocean, Arabian Sea and the Bay of Bengal. The venue of this unique fusion is lifted to a higher plane by the presence of the temple of Bhagavathiamman, who is said to be meditating on her Lord. In this mood of intense contemplation and devotion, She is mercy personified bestowing unequalled blessings on the devotee.

The temple, which always draws droves of eager devotees, is virtually on the sea with the eastern portal (that is always kept closed) opening on to the Bay of Bengal.

The surpassingly beautiful idol of the goddess, who faces east, is decorated in vermilion. The goddess is adorned with a brilliant gold necklace and is in a standing pose of penance. At Her foot is a lotus in full bloom. Her nose stud is so bright that legend has it that in olden days, sailors used to take it for a beacon and come to grief on the rocky shores of Kanyakumari! This, some say, is the reason why the eastern portal is kept closed. In all probability, it might be just to ensure that nobody falls into the sea, which is right at the doorstep.

The name Kanyakumari originates from Bhagavathiamman being a *kanni* (virgin), waiting for Her Lord. The story goes that the marriage of Bhagavathi and Sthanumalayan (Lord Siva) was arranged at Kanyakumari. The ceremony had been scheduled for before sunrise. Sage Narada, known for his *kalagam* (mischief), made a cock crow the night before the wedding. The Lord, hearing the rooster, thought it was already day and that the time of the *muhurtham* (appointed auspicious hour) had passed. So, he returned to Suchindram. Bhagavathiamman waited for him and when it turned out to be in vain, she decided to perform penance at that spot and remain unwed.

Another fascinating legend about the *mookkuthi* (nose stud) of the goddess, says that the gem in the nose stud is said to be a *naga mani* (the jewel dropped by a serpent). The king of Kanyakumari is said to have offered a reward to any one who brought him the *naga mani*. Many people who tried to retrieve the jewel became victims of the serpent, which used to guard the *mani* relentlessly. However, one clever man observed the habits of the serpent and noted that it was on a full moon day that the serpent would drop the *naga mani* from its mouth at the foot of a palm tree. The man climbed the tree with a handful of cow dung and no sooner had the serpent dropped the jewel, than he dropped the dung on it. The snake soon went away puzzled and the man handed over the *naga mani* to the king, who was so dazzled by the brilliance of the *mani* that he decided that such a jewel would befit only the Goddess.

This temple is over 1000 years old, having been built in 984 A D. It has several *mandapams* and a number of figurines. A number of sculptures of dance poses dating back to the 11th century A D are also found here. *Chitra Pournami*, *Vaikasi Vishakam* and *Navarathri* are important festivals.

Kanyakumari has a number of other attractions. But it is the sight of the Kumariamman with the seas at her foot and the different coloured sands — believed to be the sugar cane, paddy and gold brought for her wedding — that leave a mark on the devotee's mind.

FAST FACTS

How to reach

Air	:	The nearest airport is Thiruvananthapuram, 90 km away.
Rail	:	Kanyakumari is a terminal with direct trains to important cities all over India.
Road	:	Kanyakumari is 19 km from Nagercoil, a big town.
Local Transport	:	Tourist taxis and auto rickshaws are available.
Season	:	Through the year.
Clothing	:	Tropical. Light cottons.
Languages spoken	:	English and Tamil.

Accommodation

	Tariff (INR)	Phone
Hotel Tamil Nadu	550-900	04652- 2346257
Cape Hotel	250-900	04652-2346259
Cape Residency	250-900	04562-2346239
Singar International	750-1495	04652-2347992

PLACES OF INTEREST NEARBY

Guganathaswamy Temple: This is a 1000-year-old temple believed to have been built by Raja Raja Chola. The architectural style of the Cholas is evident.

Suchindram: 13 km from Kanyakumari, is the famous Sthanumalayan Temple dedicated to Siva, Vishnu and Brahma. This 9th century temple is testimony to the skill of sculptors. Musical pillars, a huge 18 ft Hanuman statue and a unique bas-relief of Vainayaki are of note.

Nagercoil: The Nagaraja Temple, 19 km from Kanyakumari, is notable for images of Jain Theerthankaras. The entrance reminds one of Chinese architecture. The idol of Nagaraja was installed where it was originally found. Soil is the *prasad* (offering).

Kanyakumari Beach: This is the confluence of the Indian Ocean, the Bay of Bengal and the Arabian Sea. The waters of the sea at Kanyakumari are unique. The sands themselves are a mixture of colours – red, black and white. The best time to visit the beach is at dawn, to watch the sunrise, or in the evening, to watch the sunset and the moonrise. Full moon days are spectacular.

Vivekananda Rock Memorial: About 200 m offshore are two rocks, which jut out from the sea. One is a memorial for the great spiritual leader, Swami Vivekanda. On an adjacent rock is a memorial to the Tamil saint poet, Thiruvalluvar. The 133 ft statue corresponds to the 133 chapters of Thiruvalluvar's *Thirukkural*. There are ferry services to the memorials.

Gandhi Memorial: The ashes of the Father of the Nation, Mahatma Gandhi, were immersed in the confluence of the three seas. A memorial has been built at the spot where the ashes were kept in an urn for public homage. Close by is Kamaraj Memorial, a tribute to the great freedom fighter.

Udayagiri Fort: This fort, at a distance of 34 km, was built during the reign of King Marthanda Varma (1729–1758 A D) It had a foundry for casting guns. The fort has the tomb of De Lennoy, a Dutchman. He was captured when King Marthanda Varma defeated the Dutch at Colachel. He soon earned the king's trust and trained his soldiers in European warfare. There is another 18th century fort 6 km away. Called *Vattakottai* (circular fort), this Dutch fort overlooks the sea.

Padmanabhapuram Palace: In the ancient capital of the Travancore rulers, this palace has wonderfully intricate woodwork. There are a number of antiques worth seeing, including armoury. The adjoining Ramaswamy Temple has scenes from the Ramayana carved in panels. Padmanabhapuram is 37 km from Kanyakumari.

Meenakshi Amman at
MADURAI

Madurai, the second largest city in Tamil Nadu today, has a teeming population. Visitors from north India often remark that Chennai, the state capital is less representative of the culture of the state than Madurai, which is in the heartland. While centres of commerce and industry flourish and fade in this great town, one symbol of permanence is the Meenakshi temple, which is the life breath of the city.

On a physical plane too, the towering *gopurams* of the Meenakshi temple dominate the landscape like looming colossi. They seem to keep a caring eye on the land and its people, who throng to the temple every day to offer worship to the supreme embodiments of Shakti and Sivam in the form of Meenakshi and Sundareswara.

The entry to the temple is through a massive gate that opens out immediately from the road. Just opposite the portals are stalls selling large flower garlands, yards and yards of the closely strung *Madura Malli* (jasmine flower) and bright chrysanthemum. The festive effect does not diminish as you step into the outer temple premises that are filled with the ubiquitous sellers of flowers, fruits, neatly piled up mounds of *kumkum* (vermilion) and sandal paste. Unlike most Siva temples, which have an air of solemnity and sobriety, the Meenakshi temple is always imbued with a spirit of *joie de vivre*. Men and women dressed in sparkling white *dhothis* (Indian dress for men) and bright *saris* can be seen relaxing at various places in the temple precincts either after they have had *darshan* or during a wait for the crowds to clear.

This joyous serenity is particularly evident in the long queue that seems ever present outside the shrine of the Mother or *Amman* as she is lovingly referred to here. The queue is so long that the person who is at the far end cannot possibly catch a glimpse of the beautiful deity. Still the worshipper's eyes are riveted towards the sanctum sanctorum.

Legend: There are numerous legends connected with the origin of this temple. The foremost is that of Indira, the king of the celestials, who wandered from place to place in search of expiation after performing a sinful deed. He stopped at a spot (present day Madurai) in a *Kadamba* forest because he suddenly felt at peace after the torment he was undergoing. Members of his retinue, who found a small *Sivalingam* in the midst of the forest beside a lake, told Indra that this must have been the source of his newfound relief. Convinced of this, he built a small temple at the spot where the *lingam* stood. It is believed that this is the very *lingam* that is worshipped in the Meenakshi temple today.

The origins of the city and the temple are also traceable to Dhananjaya, a merchant of Manavur, who stopped to rest overnight at the shrine built by Indra. The next morning he was amazed to see that the *lingam* had been worshipped with flowers. He informed the Pandya king, Kulashekhara, of this miracle. The king immediately ordered the building of a temple and a city at the spot.

His successor Malayadhvaja Pandya performed a sacrifice to Lord Siva along with his wife Kanchanamala, seeking offspring. A beautiful girl with eyes like fish and three breasts sprang out from the ritual fire. The Lord told the king in a vision that the third breast of the child would vanish the moment she met her future husband. The child was brought up more as a boy than a girl and was trained in military skills.

She was called Thadhathagai and on her father's death, she ascended the throne. After many a local victory she marched to Kailash to take on Siva. When she came face to face with Kailasanatha (Siva), her third breast vanished. She knew that she had met her Lord.

Another version of the legend has it that it was Indra, whom she decided to conquer. Indra ran to Mount Kailash, Siva's abode, to escape from her. When Thadathagai reached there, she encountered Siva, and her third breast vanished. She was told by Siva to return to Madurai and await his arrival. He arrived in eight days and the celestial wedding took place.

Lord Vishnu, the brother of Meenakshi (Parvathi), was to give her away to Siva in marriage. He was delayed on the way and could not arrive in time. The wedding went on without him. Vishnu, in his form as Kallazhagar, stopped at the banks of the river Vaigai when he heard that the festivities were over. Even to this day, this event is commemorated. The golden *utsavar* of Azhagar is brought from the Kallazhagar temple to the banks of the Vaigai after the *Meenakshi Kalyanam* (wedding of Meenakshi) is celebrated.

As always, legends are innumerable and vary from one to the other. In another, Lord Vishnu gives away the bride in marriage to the groom. This is depicted in several sculptures in the temple complex. Following the wedding, Siva ruled Madurai in the name of Sundara Pandya. After a lapse of some years, the divine couple left for heaven after leaving the city in the custody of their son, Ugra Pandya, who is said to be none other than Lord Subramanya. This is related in the *Thiruvilayadal Puranam*, written by Sage Paranjyothi in the 16th century. This work is deemed the *sthala puranam* (lore) of the temple. The story of Meenakshi is related through sculpted pillars in the *Ashta shakti mandapam* inside the temple.

History: While the antiquity of the temple cannot be specified exactly, experts say that the structures, which can be seen today, were built over the period from the 12th to the 18th century. Apart from the two main shrines, there are 12 *gopurams* and any number of *mandapams*. A hymn of the Saivite saint Sambandar (7th century) refers to the *Kapali Madhil*, referring to the present inner walls of the Lord's shrine. This is the earliest recorded reference to the existence of the temple. When the Muslim invasion took place in the 14th century, the temple was closed for nearly 50 years.

The temple in its present form was constructed primarily by the Nayak kings, who were originally governors of the Vijayanagara dynasty. With the fall of Vijayanagar in 1565, the Nayaks became independent rulers of Madurai. Foremost among the Nayak rulers who added to the glory of the temple was Tirumalai Nayak, who ruled from 1623 to 1659.

Among the many *gopurams*, the four tallest are located at the outer periphery in each principal direction. The southern tower is the tallest of these at 48 m. These *gopurams* are remarkable for their symmetry and artwork. The west *gopuram* bears the famous Pandya crest of two carps indicating that this was the work of the Pandya kings. Notwithstanding the fact that the 4 *gopurams* were built during various periods are separated by centuries, they bear a striking similarity to each other as though the construction was simultaneously undertaken. This is an indication of the continuity in temple architecture traditions and of the high degree of culture and civilisation where the past is respected and not ignored.

However, as the tradition here is to worship at the Meenakshi shrine first, devotees do not use these entrances. Instead, they enter through a *mandapam* which has no tower, that leads directly to the Meenakshi shrine. This grand *mandapam* has a hemispherical ceiling. One of the bas-reliefs depicts the divine marriage. The *mandapam* is called *Ashta*

Shakti as it contains the sculptures of the eight *shaktis* (powers), constructed by the consorts of Tirumalai Nayak. This leads to a series of *mandapams* culminating in the *Samagam Meenakshi Nayakar mandapam*, a huge hall with 110 stone columns and a beautiful brass stand holding 1008 lamps. The entrance from this *mandapam* to the shrine complex of the goddess has over it the *chitra gopuram*, which is replete with sculpture. The seven-tiered *gopuram* is the tallest among those over the Meenakshi shrine.

After several *mandapams* you can see a beautiful tank — the *Potramaraikulam* or 'Tank of the Golden Lotus'. It is said that during the period when Tamil Sangam literature flourished, many works used to be composed and offered to the tank. While works of true merit floated, those of spurious value sank to the bottom! The corridors around the tank are called the *chitra mandapam,* acknowledging the many paintings adorning the walls. The northern corridor leads to the shrine of the goddess. Close by are two *mandapams,* the *oonjal* and *kilikootu mandapams,* where the swing (*oonjal*) for the divine couple and parrots (*kili*) of the temple are found respectively. The latter is the most ornate of the temples *mandapams*.

The main shrine is entered from the *kilikootu mandapam* through a three-tiered *gopuram*. This is one of the most ancient parts of the temple as it was built in 1227. The shrine of the goddess is located in a square *garba griham*. Images of *Icha Shakti*, *Kriya Shakti* and *Gnana Shakti* symbolising Desire, Action and Wisdom respectively, are found.

There is a lovely story relating to the Goddess. Close to the flagstaff is a six-pillared structure. At Tirumalai Nayak's request, a noted poet Kumaragurubarar, composed verses in praise of Her. He recited the poems in this part of the temple. in the king's presence. As he was reciting, a small girl went up to the Nayak, took a pearl necklace from him, gave it to the poet and vanished. Who could she have been but Meenakshi?

While on the subject of miracles wrought by the goddess, let us tell the story of Rous Peter, a Collector in the early decades of the 19th century. The people of Madurai loved him so much that he was called Peter Pandya. He would go around the temple every night on horseback. On a rainy night Peter was asleep in his house when a little girl woke him up and asked him to rush out. No sooner did he do that when lightning struck his house. The girl then disappeared. The collector felt sure that his saviour was none other than goddess Meenakshi. He gifted precious jewellery to the temple.

Going back to our journey in the temple, the approach to the Lord's shrine is through two *gopurams*. The *nadu kattu gopuram* stands over a doorway leading from the *kilikootu mandapam* and the *gopura nayaka mandapam* towers above the actual entrance to the shrine. Each is of five storeys. Beyond the former, facing south is the huge image of Lord Ganesh. He is called the Muḳkuruni Vinayaka. Every Vinayaka Chaturthi day a huge *kozhukkattai* (rice dumpling) made from 34 kg of rice is offered to him.

The flagstaff of the Lord's shrine is found in the *Kambathadi mandapam*, which also has some outstanding examples of Baroque sculpture. This *mandapam* also has a number of huge sculptures of Siva in various forms and the 10 incarnations of Vishnu.

A three-storeyed *gopuram* stands over the entrance to the shrine. The base of the shrine is a wonder of sculpture. It is supported by 8 elephants, 32 lions and 62 *ganas* (the soldiers of Vinayaka). Above the sanctum is a three-storeyed *vimanam* with a gold-plated *shikara*.

Among the many famous spots, here is the *Velliambalam* where Lord Nataraja (Siva) performed the cosmic dance. There are numerous Nataraja idols in this temple. Look out for the one, which has the right leg lifted as against the usual *idathu padham* or left leg.

Among the numerous *mandapams*, those of note are the *Kalyana Mandapam*, (marriage hall), which has exquisite woodwork. It is here that the marriage of the god and goddess is celebrated every year. Next is the *Pudhu Mandapam* built by Tirumalai Nayak, which has the figures of all the 10 Nayak rulers commencing from Viswanatha to Tirumalai. Adjacent is the *Vasantha Mandapam*, which is used during festivals.

There are fascinating stories connected with the building of these *mandapams*. One relates how the king personally made a *pan* (betel nut freshener) for an artisan who was engrossed in work, another relates how the king gave the child of an artisan a golden mango as the child was pestering his father for a mango when it was not the season for the fruit. The most poignant is the story of how the image of a consort of the king kept developing a flaw in the thigh. The minister advised the artist to leave the flaw as such. When the king came to know of this he grew angry, wondering how his minister knew of the scar. When the king summoned the minister, he found to his shock that the minister had already blinded himself. He then composed a verse beseeching the goddess to restore the minister's vision if he was innocent. And the minister's sight was miraculously restored!

The munificence of Goddess Meenakshi is truly wonderful.

FAST FACTS

How to reach

Air : Madurai has an airport with flight connections to important cities.

Rail : Madurai is a major rail terminal of Southern railway.

Road : Madurai is 461 km from Chennai.

Local Transport :	Tourist Taxis, Auto rickshaws, Cycle rickshaws and buses.
Season :	Throughout the year.
Clothing :	Tropical light cotton.
Languages Spoken :	Tamil, English.

Accommodation

	Tariff (INR)	Phone
Pandyan Hotels	2200-2700+	0452-2537090
Park Inn	1800-2600+	0452-2371155
Sangam	1800-2500+	0452-2537531
Tamil Nadu (TTDC)	370-520	0452-2537461
Taj Garden Retreat	2500-4000 +	0452-2371601
Vijay	500-150	0452-2336322
Saratha Rajans	390-1190+	0452-2537501

PLACES OF INTEREST NEARBY

Koodal Azhagar temple: Vishnu is depicted in sitting, standing and reclining postures. This is a temple where the *vimanam* towers over the *gopuram*.

Azhagarkoil: This is the temple dedicated to the brother of Meenakshi. The presiding deity is Vishnu or Kallazhagar. It is 20 km from Madurai.

Pazhamudhircholai: One of the six martial abodes of Lord Muruga, it is very close to Azhagarkoil.

Tiruparankundram: Another martial abode of Lord Muruga, it is 8 km from Madurai towards the south. The hillock is an arresting sight.

Thirumalai Nayak Mahal: Situated 1 km from the Meenakshi temple this was the palace of the king and is an imposing edifice with high roofs, imposing pillars and sprawling spaces. It is a fine example of Indo-Saracenic style of architecture. A Sound and Light Show on the life of Thirumalai Nayak is held every day in the courtyard of the *mahal*.

Vaigai Dam: Located 69 km from Madurai, it is a picnic spot of choice for the people of Madurai. It is illuminated on Sunday nights.

The Dance of Nataraja
CHIDAMBARAM

To appreciate the concept of Siva as both the Creator and the Destroyer, and the complexity of His role in the Hindu trinity in the customary *lingam* form, requires much effort. And it is definitely easier to relate to an anthropomorphic entity where divinity is defined in human contours. The finest illustration of this is the Nataraja of Thillai or Chidambaram, where one can behold Siva performing the cosmic dance. No wonder it is said that when a Saivite speaks of going to the temple, he refers to the Chidambaram Nataraja temple, just as a Vaishnavite means the Srirangam Ranganatha temple.

Welcome to Chidambaram. An ancient town and a centre of learning too, thanks to the Annamalai University. Just over 250 km from Chennai, its main attraction — for locals and foreigners alike — is the awe-inspiring temple that extends over 51 acres. Tradition has it that the temple was built by Simhavarman (also called Hiranyavarman), in the 5th century A D. While some scholars believe that Simhavarman was a Chola, others state that he was a king of the Gauda country (Bengal) who came to Thillai (the ancient name for Chidambaram), seeking relief from an ailment.

A fine example of the Chola style with *gopurams* and *vimanams*, most of the temple structure is ascribed to various Chola emperors, who also made gifts of gold, jewels and precious stones and added new structures. They patronized literary works, particularly the *Peria Puranam,* which relates the story of the Nayanmars. Over time, the temple was enlarged, in different periods, by the Pandyas, Vijayanagara rulers and Nattukkottai Chettiars.

The temple of Thillaikoothan, as Lord Siva is called here, has four imposing towers in the east, west, south and the north, which enhance its splendour. Each of these towers rise 135 ft above the ground in 7 storeys and finish in 13 copper finials. The thresholds of the four towers are impressive, each 40 ft high, and they can be seen collectively when one travels towards Killai village on the Chidambaram-Pichavaram route. It is believed in Hinduism, '*Gopura darsanam papa vinasanam'* which means 'The sight of a *gopuram* destroys the ill effects of sins'. On each side of the *rajagopuram* (eastern tower) are sculptures of Bharatanatyam poses. As Lord Nataraja dances facing the south, his banner is flown over the south tower.

The Lord has his abode in two places - Tirumulattanam and Thiruchitrambalam. In the first shrine, believed to be the oldest part of the temple, He is known as Tirumulanathar and Mulattaneswarar, because the energy of Siva in all other Saivite shrines is believed to withdraw into this *lingam* after midnight worship. The goddess is Umai Ammayar.

In Thiruchitrambalam, Nataraja performs the eternal dance of joy. Literature describes him as Koothaperuman, Nataraja, Vidangar, Meruvidangar, Dakshina Meruvidangar et al.

The Lord here abides in the inner *prakaram* under a golden *vimanam* performing the *Ananda Thandava* (Dance of joy), and is accompanied by Goddess Sivakamasundari. Here two – the *Chit sabha* and *Kanaka sabha* – of the five *sabhas* (halls) are linked together and are known as *chitrambalam* and *ponnambalam* respectively.

The *ponnambalam* rests on 64 wooden rafters representing the 64 arts. There are 21,600 tiles on the roof, indicating the number of breaths taken by man everyday. The 72,000 nails binding the roof signify the *nadis* or pulse, the very essence of life. The five steps leading to the shrine represent the *panchakshara mantra (mantra* with five syllables) – *na-ma-si-va-ya*.

Devotees can worship the Lord in all his glory when the camphor is lit. To the right of the Nataraja is a curtain, with just a golden garland of *bilva* leaves indicating that God is present there as Space. Chidambaram is the *Akasa sthala* (Siva is worshipped as Earth in Kanchipuram (Ekambareswara), Water in Thiruvanaikaval (Jambukeswara), Fire in Thiruvannamalai (Arunachaleswara), Air in Srikalahasthi (Srikalahasthiswara) and Space or *Akasa* in Chidambaram). This is an excellent example of the permeating omnipresence of God, who is formless and abides everywhere, and is referred to as the *Chidambara Rahasiyam* (Secret of Chidambaram). To the left of Nataraja is Goddess Sivakamasundari, who, as the name denotes, is the very embodiment of beauty.

A unique aspect of this temple is that it houses a very important *Vaishnava sthala*, which is one of the 108 *Divya Desas* sung of by the saint-poets, the Azhwars. Here Lord Govindaraja in *Bhoga sayana* (restful recumbence) is believed to be judging the dance competition between Siva and Durga, which took place in Chidambaram. Even rarer is the fact that both Siva and Govindaraja (Mahavishnu) can be seen from one point at the same time. This, savants say, was to impress on feuding groups that Saivism and Vaishnavism were one and the same.

There is a separate shrine for Goddess Sivakamasundari next to the temple tank, which is called the Sivaganga. Among the innumerable shrines in the temple are those dedicated to Sarabeswara, Vinayaka and Subrahmanya. Notable also is the 8 ft high Mukkuruni Vinayaka.

The *kanaka sabha, chit sabha, deva sabha, raja sabha* and *nritya sabha* are the famous *sabhas* in this temple that continue to be the venues of major literary recitations, dance recitals and sacred rituals as in the past.

There are a number of legends behind the Dance of Siva at Thillai, now known as Chidambaram. One says that as Mahavishnu, the Protector among the Trinity, was lying on his snake mattress on the *Ksheerasagara* (the ocean of milk), when He suddenly smiled. The 33,000 crore *devas* (celestial beings), who were worshipping him by his feet, were delighted at the sight, and wished to know why. Whereupon the Lord answered that He was watching Nataraja dance.

Naturally, the sages wanted to have a vision of this awesome spectacle. The *rishis* Patanjali and Vyagrapada, came to Thillai and did stringent penance. Vyagrapada even prayed for and acquired tiger's paws so that he could climb trees with ease and gather flowers for the Lord before the honeybees took away the nectar. Patanjali, none other than Adi Sesha himself, taught his disciples the *yoga sutras* (key to yoga) hiding behind a veil to protect his disciples from the poisonous vapours that emanated from his mouth. When Lord Nataraja gave them *darshan* on *Thai Poosam* day, the sages were overjoyed and appealed to him to stay in Thillai for the benefit of humanity. The Lord obliged. This place was called 'Thillai' because the Thillai (mangrove) tree grew in profusion here.

Another story is that a dance competition between Siva and Kali took place in Chidambaram, with Lord Vishnu as adjudicator. During the competition, Nataraja's earring fell down and was replaced it by picking it up with one foot. As it would not be decorous for a woman to imitate this movement in front of a man, Kali withdrew from the contest and went away angrily to the border of the town where she still abides as Thillai Kaliamman. The adjudicator chose to stay on in Chidambaram as Govindarajaswamy, to continuously enjoy the dance of Thillaikoothan. In one of the sculptures at the temple, one can see the impossible feat of replacing an earring with one foot, frozen in the Oordhvathandavamurthy idol that is plated in silver. It is in front of this image that famous dancers of today perform. The horse-drawn chariot-shaped *Nritya Sabha* (Dance Hall) also has 56 exquisitely carved pillars.

The Puranic account of the origin of the cosmic dance is more metaphysical. The *rishis* of Dharuka Vanam questioned the relevance of God, arguing that since *karma* was everything, only action mattered. To remove their *agnyana* (ignorance), Siva took the form of a most beautiful man, Sundaramoorthy and came to Dharuka Vanam. Enchanted, all the women followed him. Lord Vishnu enticed the *rishis* in his female form, Mohini. Enraged that they had been fooled, the *rishis* conducted an *Atharva Vedic homa* (ritual) to destroy Lord Siva whose idea it was to deceive them.

From the *homa* fire emerged Muyalagan, the demon (*Apasmarapurusha* in Sanskrit). The cosmic dance began. Muyalagan was trampled underfoot by Lord Siva. The snakes from the fire became Siva's garlands after the venom was removed. A deer with huge antlers is held in one hand. The menacing tiger became his waistcloth, the raging fire was captured in another hand and the sound of evil incantations his anklets. Thus transformed, all the evil aspects became beneficial.

Each aspect of Nataraja is significant. The circular frame is the aura, while His hair flies in all the 8 directions. The whole universe is His body and the swirling *swastika* the life force. Without His vibration, the world cannot be sustained. All sound is music to His dance. His ornaments are all the celestial bodies while the demon underfoot signifies the suppression of pride. The sound of His steps and the *damaru* (drum) in one hand are the sounds of creation. The deer indicates purity and the fire, alchemy and transmutation. The hand pointing downwards shows the way to salvation, while the lifted foot is salvation itself. The whole signifies the *omkaram* (the original sound).

Sivam itself means auspicious. The Lord here is guiding Man to become like Him. The whole world is His dance and people, his dancers. What is the cosmic significance of Nataraja? There are five *khoshas* or aspects — *annamaya* (physical), *pranamaya* (energy), *manomaya* (emotions and mind), *vignanamaya* (unification and expansion of consciousness) and *anandamaya* (atomic consciousness), the life giving force. This is the *amsa* (element) of Parameswara. Nataraja activates each of them and the *jeevatma* (living spirit) evolves, gathering experience and capacity in each birth.

FAST FACTS

How to reach

Air	:	The nearest airport is Tiruchirapalli, 168 km away.
Rail	:	Chidambaram lies on the metre-guage rail route from Chennai (Tambaram) to Kumbakonam.
Road	:	Chidambaram is 230 km, eight hours drive, Chennai. It can also be reached from Thanjavur and Tiruchirapalli.
Local Transport	:	Tourist taxis, auto rickshaws and cycle rickshaws are available.
Season	:	Throughout the year.
Clothing	:	Tropical, light cottons.
Languages spoken	:	English and Tamil.

Accommodation

	Tariff (INR)	*Phone*
VandayarGateway Inn	200-650	04144-238056, 238060
Hotel Ritz	455-834	04144-223312

Lodge Abhi Plaza (old name Sri Nataraja Lodge)	120-450	04144-222968
Hotel Saradaram	375-645	04144-221338
Hotel Akshaya	200-545	04144-220192
Everest Lodge	90-375	04144-222543

PLACES OF INTEREST NEARBY

Thillai Kali Amman Temple: All those who come to the Nataraja temple visit this temple, on the northern outskirts of Chidambaram town, where Kali is said to have come in anger and sorrow after losing the celestial dance competition to Siva. The idol is smeared with *kumkum* to propitiate the deity. It is customary to buy *kumkum* at the entrance and offer it to the goddess. Kopperunjingan, who ruled between 1229 A D and 1278 A D, built the temple.

Vaitheeswaran Koil: This temple is famous for its curative powers. Located 24 km from Chidambaram, Lord Siva is said to have come down here to cure 4,448 types of diseases, which were afflicting human beings on earth. This Chola temple has *rajagopurams* on the east and west. The main deity is Lord Vaidyanathaswamy. (*Vaidyan* – doctor). The goddess is Thayalnayaki. The waters of the temple tank or *Siddhamirthatheertham* are said to have medicinal properties. It is customary to throw jaggery into the tank after making three circular motions with it around the head. Another custom is to deposit rock salt and pepper in the receptacles kept to the side of the tank. Apart from the main shrines, the others of note are the *Jatayu Kundam* – said to be the place where the Eagle King, Jatayu, who fell fighting Ravana, was cremated by Lord Rama – and the *Sevvai Graham,* known as Angarahan (Mars), prayers to whom will bestow health.

Pichavaram: This is a beautiful scenic spot just 16 km from Chidambaram. The mangrove forests with their dense foliage and bird life present a unique biodiversity. Don't miss taking a rowboat ride on the backwaters (for a fee of between Rs. 75 and Rs. 100). The Tamil Nadu Tourism Development Corporation has a few rooms for lodging besides a restaurant that serves both vegetarian and non-vegetarian cuisine. To get to Pichavaram from Chidambaram take an auto rickshaw if you do not have private transport.

Poompuhar: 40 km from Chidambaram lies Poompuhar, which has an ancient history dating back to the 2nd century A D. Once the biggest port on the East Coast, Poompuhar, also called Kaveripumpattinam, has been extolled in Sangam literature and in the Tamil epics *Silappathikaram* and *Manimekalai*. Apart from a nice beach, there is a period art gallery here, which recreates the glory of the past. TTDC has built some conch shaped and shell shaped cottages here for stay. Archaeological excavations have uncovered several interesting remains like buildings, brickware, a water reservoir, a Buddhist *vihara* and copper coins.

Gangaikondacholapuram: Of archaeological significance, it has the Brihadeeswara temple, which exemplifies the best of Chola architecture. King Rajendra Chola, who built it in the early years of the 11th century A D, wanted to emulate the achievement of his father, Raja Raja Chola (who built the Brihadeeswara Temple at Thanjavur). He acquired the title of 'Gangaikondan' after he brought water from the river Ganges in north India in a golden pot and sanctified the water sources near the temple. Hence the place name, Gangaikondacholapuram.

You will be amazed by the tall *vimanam*, rising to a height of 55 m, with its intricate carvings. It also has beautiful sculptures, noteworthy among them being Nataraja, a dancing Ganesha and the coronation of Rajendra Chola. The sanctum sanctorum has a 4 m tall *lingam*. This temple is said to have some Chalukyan influence too, in its construction. There is a huge fortress wall, and different rulers used this place as a fort.

Nityakalyana Perumal in
TIRUVIDANTHAI

Have you ever heard of a beautiful boar, who was so attractive that countless maidens queued up to marry him? There were so many of them that there had to be a wedding celebration everyday! This is none other than Varaha Perumal of Tiruvidanthai, also called 'Nityakalyana Perumal' because of his predilection for connubial bliss – he married the 360 daughters of Kalava Maharishi on 360 days! And this was in response to a boon the Lord granted to the sage.

The lovely Tiruvidanthai temple, over 1000 years old, is situated on the East Coast Road just a few kilometres short of Mamallapuram or Mahabalipuram. It is one among the 108 *Tirupathis* sung of by the Vaishnavite saints, the Azhwars. The temple can be accessed through a mud road branching off from the main road from the temple pond. There is a bus stop on the main road called Tiruvidanthai.

Varaha is the third incarnation of Lord Vishnu, who defeated the demon Hiranyakshan, the elder brother of Hiranyakashapu, father of Prahlada. The beneficent idol of Varaha here is a *swayambhu*. With him is his consort Komalavalli. She embodies all the maidens Varaha Perumal married (in Tamil, '*Ella Manaviyarum adakki oru thayaraga amaithar*').

Lord Varaha's foot is on Adi Sesha, the divine serpent. Before the main shrine is a small *sannidhi* to Garuda. There are separate shrines to the goddesses Komalavalli and Andal.

This temple has a steady stream of aspiring grooms and brides from all parts of India. Those who find it difficult to get a good 'match' come to this temple to solve their problem. As per tradition, the devotee buys a garland of flowers, offers it to the Lord, and then dons it, after which he/she then goes round the sanctum sanctorum 9 times. There are many devotees who speak of the success of this exercise in faith.

As you complete the circumambulation, you come across a shrine to Lord Ranganatha. He is in relaxed recumbence with right hand under his head, both Sridevi and Bhoodevi seated by his side. Ranganayaki too is there as a standing *Panchaloha* idol. Worshipping the feet of the Lord is said to be a sure way of obtaining his benediction. There is a specialty in this temple. The *Thamarai Thiruvadi* (feet resting on a lotus) of Lord Ranganatha should not be missed when the priest is lighting the camphor.

Yes, there is a reason why Ranganatha is gracing this temple. While attending with his consorts the wedding of Varaha Perumal, he found that there was a wedding day after day, and so decided to stay on in Tiruvidanthai!

FAST FACTS

How to reach

Air	:	Madras, 55 km away, is the nearest airport.
Rail	:	The nearest railhead is Chengalpattu. Chennai will be more convenient.
Road	:	Thiruvidanthai is 15 km from Mamallapuram, towards Chennai.
Local Transport	:	Auto rickshaws and Public buses.
Season	:	Throughout the year.
Clothing	:	Tropical, Light cottons.
Languages Spoken	:	English and Tamil.
Accommodation	:	One can stay in Mamallapuram.

Mamallapuram

	Tariff Range (INR)	Phone
Ideal Beach Resorts	1250-1700	954114-242240
Hotel Tamil Nadu	600-1000	954114-242361
GRT Temple Bay	2500-2995	954114-242251
Fisherman's Cove	4100-5600	954114-272304
Mamalla Bhavan	825-950	04114-242060

PLACES OF INTEREST NEARBY

Mamallapuram: Around 55 km from Chennai and a short distance from the Nityakalyana Perumal Temple, Mamallapuram is famed for its sculptures on rock. The monuments date to the Pallava period. See under 'Kadalmallai' for details

Dakshina Chitra and Cholamandalam: Both are artiste's villages, with a difference. Dakshina Chitra is a 'living museum' which showcases the life styles of different groups like weavers, potters, agriculturists, from the four southern states, Cholamandalam is an artist's colony where many well known artists live and work. Driving along the East Coast Road (ECR) from Chennai, Cholamandalam comes first on the left, while Dakshina Chitra is further down, to the left after MGM Dizzee World.

Crocodile Bank: Among the many attractions on the East Coast road linking Chennai and Pondicherry is the Crocodile Bank. At a distance of 44 km from Chennai, this is a crocodile breeding and research centre. The numerous crocodiles lying lazily in pools of water is quite a sight.

Muttukadu: 36 km from Chennai, the backwaters are ideal for a picnic. There are boating facilities provided by the Tamil Nadu Tourism Development Corporation.

Amusement Parks: The ECR plays host to a number of amusement parks like VGP Golden Beach, MGM Dizzee World, Little Folks and Maya Jaal. There is also a popular go-karting track off the East Coast Road.

The famed Parthasarathy temple of
CHENNAI

The *Mahabharatha* tells the story of how Lord Krishna, unarmed, took on the role of charioteer to Partha or Arjuna. And how it was His presence that made the difference between triumph and defeat, in the battle of Kurukshetra. Thus was added one more name to address the Lord, 'Parthasarathy' (*Sarathy* – charioteer, in Sanskrit). On a metaphysical plane, He is the charioteer who guides life itself.

It is in the famous and ancient Sri Parthasarathy temple in Chennai that one can get *darshan* of Lord Krishna in this form. The main deity here is seen with a luxuriant moustache marking him out as a charioteer. The Lord is also found only with the conch and without his discus in accordance with his vow to be unarmed during the battle. The festival idol is seen bearing the scars of wounds and pit marks, inflicted by myriad arrows shot at him by the rival group during the battle.

The story goes that when the battle of Kurukshetra became unavoidable, Lord Krishna declared that since both the Pandavas and Kauravas were his nephews, he would not fight the war with weapons. He decided that the two warring factions could choose between his massive army and himself, alone and unarmed.

How would the opposing factions make the choice? Duryodhana representing the Kauravas and Arjuna, for the Pandavas, went to Lord Krishna's abode. Duryodhana, who reached first found him asleep and decided to sit by the Lord's head.

Arjuna who came later stood by his foot. When Krishna woke, he set eyes on Arjuna first. He then turned to greet Duryodana and asked them what had brought them to Dwaraka.

Duryodana, speaking first, asked for Krishna's support in the impending war. He pointed out that he had arrived first and therefore should receive preference as per *dharma* (righteousness). Krishna replied that though Duryodana had come first, he had seen Arjuna at his feet, first. So, both of them were of equal merit. Further, it was traditional, while distributing favours, to begin with the juniormost, who in this case, was Arjuna.

Krishna said, "The Narayanas, my tribesmen, are my equals in battle, and constitute a host, large and almost invincible. In my distribution of assistance I place them on one side and me individually on the other, but I shall wield no weapon and take no part in actual fighting".

Turning to Arjuna, he asked, "Partha, think it over well. Would you want me, alone and weaponless or would you prefer the prowess of the Narayanas?" Without hesitation, Arjuna replied that he would be content if Krishna was with the Pandavas. An overjoyed Duryodhana, thinking Arjuna's choice injudicious, gladly settled for Krishna's army.

And Krishna's grace went on to make the difference between triumph and defeat, in the battle of Kurukshetra.

To quote the inimitable C Rajagopalachari's Mahabharatha – 'The Gods came down to watch the combat between Bhishma and Arjuna. These were two of the greatest warriors on Earth. From either side, flew arrows in countless number. Shaft met shaft in the air and sometimes the grandsire's missile hit Arjuna's breast and that of Madhava. The blood flowing made Krishna more beautiful than ever, as he stood like a green *palasa* tree in full bloom with crimson flowers'.

The idol of Parthasarathy in Chennai embodies this beauty. Full of stately majesty, the Lord is unarmed, yet exudes a more potent power – the ultimate omnipotence of God. In the sanctum sanctorum of this ancient temple, one can see Him in the company of his divine consort Rukmini, brother Balarama, younger brother Satyaki, son Pradyumna and grandson Anirudda.

It is believed that the Chola king Sumati Raja Chola, who was a great devotee of Sri Venkatesa of Tirumala, wanted to see Venkateswara as Krishna. The Lord, who ever delights in fulfilling the desires of his devotees, appeared as Parthasarathy in Tiruvellikeni in Chennai. Appropriately, the name of the *moolavar* in this temple is Sri Venkatakrishnan. There is an edict in the temple dated 808 A D., signifying a grant by Pallava king Nandi Varman that is proof of the antiquity of this temple. There are also edicts of the Vijayanagara Empire.

Apart from Parthasarathy, you can find separate shrines to Sreemath Nadhan, Narasimha, Rama, Gajendra Varada, Vedavalli Nachiyar and Andal. The sculpture of Anjaneya to the right of the main *prakaram* is a favourite point with all worshippers in this temple.

Throughout the year, there are festivals. The most important is *Vaikunta Ekadesi* when the *Paramapada Vaasal* or 'entrance to the heavens' is opened in the early hours. Thousands of devotees brave the chill in the month of Margazhi (December-January) to have *darshan* of the Lord in his 'permanent abode'.

During this festival, the *Nalayira Divyaprabhandam* is recited by *acharyas* (scholars) for 21 days. The Lord wears *kabai* winter wear, for 10 days after *Vaikunta Ekadesi*. On the eastern side of the temple is the temple tank that is the site of the float festival in the Tamil month of Masi. The *sampradayam* (tradition) followed in this temple is *Tenkalai* (southern) Vaishnavism while the *pujas* are done as per the *Vaikanasa Agamas*.

The temple is surrounded by four *veedhis* (streets), which exude an old-world charm. Subramanya Bharati, who used to live close by, used to visit the temple daily. Swami Vivekananda and Saint Thyagaraja also worshipped in this temple.

The *Mahabharatha* is replete with instances of how Krishna saved the life of Arjuna during battle. He not only stuck fear into the hearts of adversaries but also shored up the confidence of Arjuna, who at various points in the battle was overcome by despair. For us too, worshipping Parthasarathy at Triplicane is a sure way to seek protection from all ills.

FAST FACTS

How to reach

Air	:	Chennai has two airports — domestic and international — located adjacent to one another at Meenambakkam.
Rail	:	It is south India's biggest rail terminal. Chennai has trains running towards Mumbai in the West, Delhi in the North, Calcutta in the East and Kanyakumari at the southern tip of India.
Road	:	Chennai is well connected by road to the southern cities like Tiruchirapalli and to the garden city, Bangalore and to the north towards Vijayawada.
Local Transport	:	Tourist taxis, call taxis, auto rickshaws, public buses, private tourist buses and cycle rickshaws are available.
Season	:	Throughout the year.
Clothing	:	Tropical, light cottons.
Languages spoken	:	English and Tamil. There is a sizeable population from other parts of India too, living in Chennai.
Accommodation	:	Chennai has a wide range of accommodation from budget to deluxe.

Luxury	Tariff (INR)	Phone
Chola Sheraton	5500-6500(+12.5%)	28110101
Moderate		
Shelter	1500-2995(+taxes)	24951919
Budget		
Hotel Karpagam	470-650	24959984
Swagath	394-633	28132971

(Accommodation has been selected for proximity to the temple)

Places of interest nearby

Madhava Perumal Temple: In the 800-year-old Madhava Perumal temple at Mylapore, the Lord is indeed in a state of bliss. Along with *Tirumagal* and *Manamagal*, he is seated on the *Anandanilaya Vimanam*. 'Vangakkadal Kadainda Madhavane Kesavane,' sang Andal in her immortal verses, the *Tiruppavai*. In another verse, she talks of Mayan, Madhavan, Vaikuntan. In the first *pasuram*, the divine daughter of Periazhwar describes Madhava as the embodiment of love.

There are two *utsava murthys* —the *Peria Madhavar* and the *Siria Madhavar*. Monthly festivals are dedicated to the latter while yearly celebrations are in honour of the former. This area to the south of the Parthasarathy Temple used to be called Sri Madhavapuram according to the text *Mahatmiyam*. Of Puranic fame, this beautiful temple is mentioned in the *Mayurapuri Mahatmiyam* in the *Brahmanda Puranam*. In reply to Veda Vyasa's query of Lord Narayana as to which place in *Kali Yuga* was free of the *doshas* (ills) associated with this *yugam*, and therefore fit for penance, the Lord answered, 'Madhavapura'.

Sage Brighu had his ashram here. The third of the Mudal Azhwars, Peyazhwar, was born close by and worshipped Madhava everyday. The temple has a shrine for him. In 1956 the Kanchi Sankaracharya Chandrasekarendra Swami, who was sojourning at the Sanskrit college nearby, had his daily ablutions at the *Santana Pushkarini* (tank) of the temple and worshipped the Lord. On *Masi Maham* and *Pournami*, sacred waters from various spots are believed to flow into the large temple tank. Bathing here that day and praying is said to confer the devotee with *putra bhagyam* (children) There is a shrine to Mahalakshmi in the form of Amrithavalli, who is said to have manifested here as a beautiful baby in response to the prayers of Sage Brighu, who was childless. Lord Narayana appeared as Madhava and sought her hand. The sage celebrated the wedding grandly during *Panguni Uttaram*.

There is also a *sannidhi* (shrine) for Varaha, one of the 10 *avataras* (incarnations) of Lord Vishnu, beside the temple tank. Other deities present are Rama with Sita, Lakshmana and Anjaneya, Veera Anjaneya in another shrine, Viswaksena, Sampathkumar, Andal and the other Azhwars. Lord Madhava being analogous to Lord Krishna, the *sthalavriksham,* the *Punnai* tree (Alexandrian Laurel), is found behind the sanctum sanctorum. The architecture is simple, and the once faded stone has been painted in myriad colours.

Mundaga Kanni Amman Temple: Almost every street and gully in Chennai has a temple dedicated to the many forms of the Divine Mother. One such is the Mundaga Kanniamman temple on the street known by the same name, which links Royapettah High Road near Sanskrit college to Kutchery Road near Luz. As the Goddess appeared as a *swayambhu* (self formed) with *trisoolam* (trident), in a tank full of lotuses, she came to be known as Mundagakanniamman. The Goddess's eyes resemble a lotus, therefore she is called *mundagakanni*, or 'lotus-eyed' *mundagam* – lotus.

The main deity resides in a thatched sanctum sanctorum, identifying with the poor. Devotees worship Amman here in a number ways. The sacred waters offered here are considered a panacea. To the right of the main deity are the *sapta kannigas* (7 virgins). Behind is an ancient banyan tree with a large anthill. It is believed that the cobras, which dwell here, visit the shrine at midnight to worship the Amman.

Thiruvalluvar Temple: A few metres away from the Mundagakanniamman Temple is this temple, built at the spot where Thiruvalluvar, the famous Tamil saint poet, was born, and brought up by a childless couple. The street too is named after him. His biological parents are said to have left the newborn child under the shade of an *Iluppai* (south Indian Mahua, *bassia longifolia)* tree, whose base has been plated over with metal on which is a sculptural depiction of Thiruvalluvar's birth. Thiruvalluvar lived here with his wife, Vasuki. According to legend, Vasuki was so virtuous that once, when drawing water from a well, her husband called her, and she let go of the rope holding the container. And the rope did not slip. This well can still be seen.

There is a shrine to Thiruvalluvar, in seated posture, holding rosary beads in his right hand and his immortal work *Thirukkural* in his left hand. *Pujas* are performed morning and evening. The temple also has shrines to Lord Ekambareswar and Goddess Kamakshi, a separate shrine for Vasuki and to the *navagrahams.* Recently, a shrine to Karumariamman has been added. There is a more famous statue of Thiruvalluvar not far from this temple, on Ramakrishna Mutt Road, near Sanskrit College. There, he is depicted as writing his poems.

Marina Beach: When the people of Chennai want relief from the heat, they head to the Marina Beach. The sea breeze, which sets in, in the afternoons provides a change from the sweltering heat, and the pleasure of wetting your feet in the waters of the Bay of Bengal. It is the second longest beach in the world and has a wide sandy foreshore. Memorials to two former chief ministers of Tamil Nadu, C N Annadurai and M G Ramachandran, are located on the beach. Some of the city's most beautiful and historic buildings like the University of Madras, Senate House, Chepauk Palace, Presidency College and Police Headquarters are also on the Marina across the road.

Vivekananda Memorial: An imposing building on the Marina, constructed in 1842 to store ice bars imported from the United States of America by the Tudor Ice Company, it was designed by the great architect R F Chisholm. In 1874, when production of ice began locally, the building was sold. In 1897, Swami Vivekananda stayed here for a brief while after his visit to Chicago. The government took over the building in 1930 and in 1963 it was dedicated to Swami Vivekananda. Today it houses a museum on the Swami. There is also a statue of Vivekananda.

DIVINE DELIBERATIONS ON RIVERBANK

A meeting of the gods, a communion so mystical and magical that the human mind cannot comprehend its significance! The milling crowds gaze with amazement at the bejewelled idols of Lord Varadaraja, Lord Lakshmi Narasimha, Lord Srinivasa with his consorts, Lord Venkateswara and Lord Karumanickar atop their flower-bedecked palanquins. And while the river Palar flows by serenely, fireworks light up the sky to celebrate the coming together of the gods!

The venue for the heavenly conjunction is Thirukoodal, about 25 km from Chengalpattu. The idols of Lord Varadaraja and Lord Lakshmi Narasimha, come from the Lakshmi Narasimha shrine atop a hill at Pazhayaseevaram on the Chengalpattu-Kanchipuram road.

For Lord Varadaraja, it has been a while away from his home at Kanchipuram. He has reached Pazhayaseevaram the previous night and has been giving continuous *darshan* to the devotees who have thronged to the place for the *Parvettai* festival that takes place the day after *Pongal*. The mood is full of festivity as thousands of adults and children, climb to the top of the Pazhayaseevaram hill to have *darshan* of Lord Varadaraja. They come halfway down to pay obeisance to Lord Lakshmi Narasimha, the presiding deity, and then rush down and across the river to Thirukoodal. The riverbed is considered sacred, being the confluence of the rivers Palar, Cheyyar and

Vegavathi, and is generally dry, affording an opportunity for picnicking and frolicking.

The Thirukoodal temple has as its main deity Appan Venkatesa Perumal. What is unique about the idol is that He holds within him the aspects of Lord Vishnu, Lord Siva and Lord Brahma. Vishnu is represented by the conch and the discus, Siva by the matted hair and the third eye and Brahma by the lotus in the hand. The Lord is standing on another beautiful lotus. No wonder then that Thirukoodal is the venue for the divine confluence!

The *utsavar* is Srinivasa with Sreedevi and Bhoodevi, while another important deity in the temple is Karumanickar. From neighbouring Salavakkam has come the deity Prasanna Venkatesar. The deity of the Kavanthandalam shrine also generally participates in the festival.

As to why Lord Varadaraja of Kanchipuram makes this annual visit to Pazhayaseevaram, the legend goes that the original idol being not of stone but of the wood of the fig tree, granite was carved from the Pazhayaseevaram hill to make a stone idol. The Lord visits his birthplace every year to commemorate this fact. Lord Varadaraja is the son-in-law of Lord Lakshmi Narasimha and Goddess Ahobilavalli of Pazhayaseevaram, says another legend.

The ancient Pazhayaseevaram temple has a garland of legends associated with it. One talks of a Gujarati traveller who was beset by unbearable stomachache while on a pilgrimage to Tirupati. The Lord appeared before him in a vision and pointed to a place where He was manifest in *vigraham* form. He asked the traveller to install the idol on the hill and worship him, and drink of the waters of the holy *thirukulam* (holy tank) nearby. The man was cured. His descendants from Gujarat, still continue to administer the temple.

The Kanchi Paramacharya is believed to have once told a devotee who was having a problem with his son, that the remedy was to visit the three *Srivaram*s or abodes of the Goddess, and one among them was Pazhayaseevaram.

The temple at Thirukoodal, of the Pallava period, is preserved by the Archaeological Survey of India and administered by the Government of Tamil Nadu's Hindu Religious and Charitable Endowments Department.

FAST FACTS

How to reach

Air	:	The nearest airport is Chennai, 74 km away.
Rail	:	The nearest railhead is Chengalpattu, 25 km away.
Road	:	Pazhayaseevaram is 25 km from Chengalpattu.
Local Transport	:	There is no local transport available here apart from public buses, which pass on the road.
Season	:	Throughout the year.
Clothing	:	Tropical, light cottons.
Languages spoken	:	English and Tamil.
Accommodation	:	There are no lodging houses here. Accommodation has to be found at Chengalpattu or Kanchipuram.

Kanchipuram

	Tariff (INR)	Phone
MM Hotel	300-800+tax	954112-230023
TM Hotel	550-1000+tax	04112-225250
Shelter Resorts	1450-1900	04114-272424

Chengalpattu

Hotel Ganesh	380-660	954114-22637
Hotel Kanchi	160-420	954114-231019, 226819

Excursions

Singaperumalkoil: Close to Chengalpattu is Singaperumalkoil, a temple to the lion-headed incarnation of Vishnu, Narasimha. It is said that after killing the demon Hiranyakashapu, Narasimha came here in his angry form. He bathed in the temple tank here and became peaceful again. The waters are said to have turned red at the time. The temple is over 1500 years old.

Chengalpattu: This town is located on the national highway between Chennai and Tiruchirapalli. It can be accessed from Mamallapuram through an inner road, the distance being 30 km. It can also be reached from Pazhayaseevaram. The large Kolavai Lake here has boating facilities organised by the Tamil Nadu Tourism Development Corporation. The ruins of an ancient Vijayanagar Fort can also be seen.

Lord Ranganatha of
SRIRANGAM

The island of Srirangam, lying between the Cauvery and its tributary the Coleroon, is unique for its divine ambience. Barely an hour from the bustling city of Tiruchchirapalli, it is an island of peace and serenity. And if one has time to visit only one Vishnu temple in Tamil Nadu, the choice, undoubtedly, should be Srirangam.

All over south India, you can find temples to Lord Ranganatha, who is Vishnu in recumbent posture. Unique among them is *Bhoologa Vaikuntam* (Heaven on Earth), the Ranganatha temple at Srirangam near Tiruchirapalli.

"*Pachchai ma malai pol meni*
Pavazha vai kamala chengann
Achutha amararere ayar tham kozhundhe
Ich chuvai thavira yan poi indira logam aalum
Achchuvai perinum venden Arangama Nagarulale"

"The face as majestic as the verdant mountain
With coral-coloured lips and eyes bright like a bloomed lotus.

Oh Achutha, the immortal; the child of cowherds
I want not power and pelf in Indra loka
But only the proximity to you in this great town
Of Srirangam".

So does the Vaishnavite saint, Thondaradipodi Azhwar describe the beauty of Lord Ranganatha. Not only he, but 11 of the 12 Azhwars (save Madhurakavi Azhwar) have sung hymns on the glory of Sri Ranganatha.

In the *Dasavathara* (10 incarnations of Mahavishnu), the *Ramavatara* (the incarnation of Rama) is special because the Lord appeared on earth as a human being and refrained from using his divine powers to overcome evil. His conduct amidst great suffering is held up as the model for Man to emulate. One of Rama's favourite deities was Lord Ranganatha.

In the fascinating mix of scripture, history and legend that form the backbone of Hinduism, innumerable Gods and Goddesses enter and leave the stage much like Shakespearean drama. Their roles often change. For instance, we have Lord Siva appearing as Hanuman in the epic, the Ramayana, and becoming Rama's most ardent devotee. Ganapathy, whom the Vedas describe as *Pranava* or the primordial, himself worships his father Siva and mother Parvathy. What is incredible is that deities themselves worshipped what may be loosely described as 'principal deities'. We are indeed lucky that we too can pray to the Supreme God to whom Lord Rama himself prayed!

Time almost stands still in the quaint town called Srirangam. It is the temple and its ancient traditions that predicate life here, at the pivot of which is Lord Ranganatha. Even today, one can see people dressed in the traditional styles, their foreheads and bodies covered with the white religious mark of the Vishnu devotee with a streak of red or yellow in between. During the festive month of Marghazhi, the town comes alive with hymn singers and wandering minstrels who go about singing *pasurams* with lilting melody in praise of Ranganatha.

Srirangam is foremost among the 106 Vaishnava *Divya Desas* (temples sung of by the Azhwars). It is one of the eight self-manifested or *swayamvyaktha kshetras* of Vishnu. The others are Srimushnam, Tirumala, Saligrama, Naimisaranyam, Thothathri, Pushkaram and Badrinath.

The temple, situated over an expanse of 156 acres, has innumerable shrines dedicated to myriad Hindu gods and goddesses. Its towering *gopuram*, on the seventh *prakaram*, was consecrated in 1987 and is a landmark that can be seen for miles. One of the tallest temple towers, it stands 236 ft high.

The temple complex itself has seven rectangular enclosures, accommodating residences and shops and a number of shrines with streets separating some of them. This makes it one of the largest temples in the world as no other temple in India has 7 *prakarams!*

If the temple itself is unique, so are the *veedhis* or streets surrounding it. Remarkable examples of old world houses are seen here, with granite *thinnais* (verandas), wooden pillars, long and dark 'halls' and open spaces in the midst of houses. Many of the families here have lived here for generations. Closer to the temple are innumerable shops. Many people go to Srirangam just to pick up an iron pan to make *dosais* (Indian crepe made of rice batter) in, or a brass vessel to store water.

Let us move on to the fascinating legend associated with this temple. Vibhishana, the demon king of Sri Lanka who refused to be a part of Ravana's villainy against Sita, was returning to Lanka after attending the coronation of Lord Rama at Ayodhya. Lord Rama had gifted him the very idol of Mahavishnu – an idol of Ranganatha in recumbent form – that He and his illustrious ancestors of the Ikshvaku clan had worshipped. The condition stipulated by Rama, however, was that the idol should never be placed on the ground. If it was, it would grow to such a size that it could not be removed from that spot!

Vibhishana, however, placed the idol on the ground out of weariness and became disconsolate when he found he could not move it. Seeing Vibhishanas' grief, the Lord is believed to have consoled him saying that he would lie in *yoga nidra* (yogic recumbence) facing Sri Lanka, so that Vibhishana could worship him from his homeland. The Lord in Srirangam faces the south unlike most temples where he faces east. (The Lord is said to have expressed his desire to dwell on the banks of the Cauvery to the King of that region, Dharmavarman). King Dharmavarman is believed to have constructed a temple over the idol. (For another version of this legend, please refer to the chapter on the Uchi Pillayar temple at Rockfort, Tiruchirapalli).

History: It is difficult to fix the antiquity of this temple accurately, as its origins are inextricably linked with mythology. The temple finds mention in the Tamil Sangam classic *Silappadikaram* and in the *Nalayiradivyaprabhandam* of the Azhwars.

The earliest among the inscriptions in the temple date to the 10th century. The most ancient relates to the seventh year of Parantaka I's reign (907-953 A D) that describes the grant by the King for annual upkeep of the temple and for purchase of camphor and cotton wicks.

In the 11th century, the great saint Ramanuja, made Srirangam his base and wrote his learned exegesis on *Visishtadvaita*, which is considered one of the most seminal and profound works on metaphysics. He organised the worship and administration of the temple on sound lines. His embalmed corporeal form is seen in the Srirangam temple complex even today.

The temple stood through the vicissitudes of time and was the beneficiary of the munificence and architectural zeal of various dynasties such as the Pandyas, Nayaks, Hoysalas, Vijayanagara and Mahrattas.

In the 14th century, the temple came under attack from Malik Kafur. During these raids, the idols and jewels were transported to Tirupathi for safekeeping.

Architecture: The Srirangam temple is a virtual museum of south Indian temple architecture. In its precincts, one can see *gopurams*, *vimanams*, pillared corridors, vast terraces, bas-reliefs and exquisite sculptures. The materials used encompass a wide range like stone, brick, mortar, lime and wood of many varieties.

Each of the 7 rectangular enclosures has a towering *gopuram* as its portal. The *gopurams* progressively diminish in height as we approach the sanctum sanctorum. One enters the temple through the seventh *prakaram*, which has a shrine for Vamana. Then follows the sixth *prakaram*, which has the shrine of Jagannatha.

The fifth *prakaram* has a number of shrines dedicated to the Azhwars. There is a bas-relief of a figure said to be the great Tamil poet Kamban, who wrote the Ramayana in Tamil. Some dispute this. In this *prakaram* one can find the Venugopala shrine. There are also sculptures of the Hoysala style. The Chakrathazhvar shrine with its multi-pillared hall is a very popular one. Devotees worship the Discus of the Lord on one side of the idol and Yoga Narasimha on the other. The Andal shrine too is located in this enclosure.

There is also the *samadhi* of Ramanuja. It is said that the *Acharya* was interred here after he attained *samadhi* and he rose after a while to give *darshan* to his devotees in his bodily form. The corporeal form has been embalmed using camphor and some rare herbs. Just outside the shrine is a hall with beautiful paintings depicting the *Krishna Leela* in colour.

In the fourth *prakaram* one can find an imposing structure housing the shrine of Garuda, the mount of the Lord. There is also a shrine of Goddess Ranganayaki, consort of Lord Ranganatha. It also has at the entrance the *vellai* (white) *gopuram*, which was the tallest landmark of the temple before the construction of the *rajagopuram* on the seventh precinct. The *prakaram* has 3 large halls including the 1000-pillared hall, which actually has 953 pillars and the *Seshraya mandapam* and *Thirumani mandapam*, built by Thirumangai Azhwar. In these halls, with the finest examples of south Indian stone sculpture, the work is so fine that stone surfaces are often mistaken to be metal.

Thirumangai Azhwar, who was a bandit before he became a divine poet, is believed to have beautified the temple with the jewels and gems obtained from robbing the rich of the neighbourhood. On one occasion, he and his associates came upon a man and a woman in bridal clothes, bedecked in rich jewels. The Azhwar promptly made them give up every bit of the gold and riches. But when he then attempted to lift up the booty, he found he could not move it! In consternation, he asked the groom "What spell have you cast on this that it cannot be moved?". Whereupon the man beckoned to him and said, "Lend me your ears and I will tell you". When the Azhwar approached the groom, he is said to have uttered the *Ashtakshara mantra – 'Om Namo Narayana'* in his ears. The Azhwar realised that the couple were none other than the Lord and his consort!

Of the stories of the Azhwars, that of Thondaradipodi Azhwar (2814 B C) is also interesting. He grew and nurtured the trees and flowering plants for the *nandavanam* or garden in the temple, took great joy in making garlands to adorn the Lord and spent most of his years in Srirangam. A story about him relates how the Lord, dressed as a servant, took his own gold bowl to the house of a courtesan, so that she would entertain His devotee who was besotted with her. The Azhwar was so ashamed that he spent the rest of his earthly sojourn totally devoted to the service of Ranganatha, impervious to the call of the senses.

Walking around the temple, you come to the third *prakaram* where is situated the *dwajasthambham* or the temple flag post and the *bali pitam* where offerings of rice are made.

These are fully gold-plated. At the centre of the enclosure is the famous *paramapada vaasal* (gate to Heaven). This entrance is opened only once a year on *Vaikunta Ekadasi* day when thousands of devotees wait for hours to pass through the portals. It is believed that those who pass through get salvation.

The second *prakaram*, mainly built by Rajamahendra Chola, has a flight of steps called *padiyetta sevai* (view from the stairs). The innermost enclosure houses the sanctum sanctorum. Here one can see the black-coloured idol of Ranganatha in *yoga nidra* resting on the seven-hooded Adi Sesha. At his feet are Bhoodevi and Sreedevi. His feet are covered with gold and one should pray to his feet to get His grace even though it is virtually impossible to take the eyes away from the sublime and transcendental beauty of his lotus-shaped eyes.

Atop the sanctum sanctorum is a golden *vimanam* or roof with four *kalasams* representing the four Vedas and an intricate carving of the visage of Para Vasudeva. The entire enclosure is full of paintings from the *Vishnu Purana* and of the 108 *Divya Desas* of the Vaishnavaites.

Many *prasadams* or food items are offered to the Lord from dawn to dusk. Strangely, one of them is the north Indian *chapathi* or *roti* (wheat pancakes). How this practice came about in a temple in south India is explained by the following tale.

During the Muslim invasion the festival idol of Lord Ranganatha was taken away to Delhi. The idol was so beautiful that Bibi, the daughter of the Sultan, is said to have fallen in love with it. Meanwhile, a number of ardent devotees set out from Srirangam in search of the idol. One of them, Areyar Swami, (also called Nampaaduvan) recovered the idol from Delhi and brought it back. The grief-stricken Bibi rushed to Srirangam on horseback and pleaded with the Lord that she could not bear to be separated from him. The Lord accepted her devotion and they were united in a 'marriage of minds'. And Bibi is present in the form of a drawing in the temple.

To make Bibi Nachiyar – as she is known today – feel at home, the Lord decided that his breakfast would be *roti* with green-gram and butter. Even to this day, the first offering to the Lord is this. Only later in the day is He offered preparations of the typical cuisine of the south.

One cannot talk of Srirangam without thinking of the River Cauvery. The Cauvery, with its source in distant Karnataka, is the Ganga of south India. Bathing in its waters are believed to wash away sins. While there are several spots on the riverbank which people use to take a dip, a popular one is the easily accessible *Amma Mandapam*, where the waters are believed to be as clear and sacred as the shrine of Lord Ranganatha himself!

FAST FACTS

How to reach

Air	:	Tiruchirapalli, 7 km away, is the nearest airport. Direct flights are available from Tiruchirapalli to Chennai, Madurai, Thiruvananthapuram and Colombo.
Rail	:	Trains are available to Tiruchirapalli from Chennai, Madurai, Bangalore, Rameswaram, Thanjavur, Coimbatore, Tirupathi and Kochi. Direct trains to Kolkatta and Guwahati have also been added. Some trains stop at Srirangam.
Road	:	Buses are available to Tiruchirapalli from all major towns and cities in Tamil Nadu and the neighbouring states of Kerala and Karnataka. There are regular buses from Tiruchirapalli to Srirangam.
Local Transport	:	The local bus service is efficient. Other forms of local transport such as auto rickshaws, taxis and cycle rickshaws are available.

Season	:	Throughout the year.
Clothing	:	Tropical, light cottons.
Languages spoken	:	English and Tamil.

Accommodation

Tiruchirapalli	Tariff (INR)	Phone
Hotel Femina	350-1950	0431-2414501
Hotel Abbirami	270-720	0431-2415128
Hotel Guru	240-840	0431-2415881
Hotel Anand	215-825	0431-2415545

PLACES OF INTEREST NEARBY

Rock Fort: Rock Fort, atop which the Uchi Pillayar Temple is situated, is an attraction in itself. Experts deem this rock to be 3,800 million years old, making it older than the Himalayas and as old as the ancient rocks of Greenland. The rocky outcrop is 83 m high. There are 420 steps leading to the summit, where there are inscriptions dating back to the 3rd century B C. Not much of the fort remains, but the Main Guard Gate is intact. The fort played a crucial role in the Carnatic Wars, and according to an inscription, helped in laying the British Empire's foundations in India. Beside the tank at the foot of Rock Fort is the house where Robert Clive of the East India Company lived while he was in Tiruchirapalli.

Tiruvanaikkaval: This temple, also called the Jambukeswara Temple, is famed for its architectural splendour. It is one of the *panchalingam* shrines of Lord Siva. He is represented in the form of Water here. The *lingam,* installed under an ancient *Jambu* or *Jamoon* tree, is partially submerged by water. The temple is named after an elephant, which is believed to have worshipped Lord Siva here.

Grand Anaicut: An engineering marvel accomplished in the 2nd century A D. The Grand Anaicut, also called Kallanai, is a stone dam built by King Karikala Chola to harness the waters of the River Cauvery. It is 24 km from Tiruchirapalli. The dam is 329 m long and 20 m wide. There is now a road bridge on top of the dam, from where one can have a good vista of the pleasant greenery around and the river waters.

Upper Anaicut: This is another dam, which lies at the head of the Srirangam Island, at a distance of 18 km from Tiruchirapalli. It was built across the river Kollidam in the 19th century. The dam is 685 m long. Its other name, Mukkombu, is derived from the fact that the dam forks into three because of the shape of the island.

Samayapuram: 20 km from Tiruchirapalli, is a famous temple dedicated to Goddess Parvathy, called Mariamman here. It is believed that those who are mentally ill will be cured if they visit this temple.

UCHI PILLAYAR TEMPLE
on Rock Fort

Such is the power and appeal of God that all things pale into insignificance before Him. Take the Rock Fort in Tiruchirappalli, a major city in the state of Tamil Nadu. This fort, atop a hillock, that once defended the throne of the King of Uraiyur is little known today, except among the chroniclers of history. The hillock is now named after the small Ganapathy temple at its summit.

Pillayar is the vernacular name for Ganapathy, the deity worshipped by Hindus before undertaking any endeavour. *Uchi* in Tamil means top, but there is a fascinating legend why this temple is known as the Uchi Pillayar temple.

Before we climb up the steep steps leading to the Ganapathy temple, we first visit the ancient Thayumanaswamy temple, which is carved out of the hill. Thayumanaswamy is none other than Lord Siva, one of the Supreme Trinity of Gods in the Hindu pantheon.

The entrance to these temples is deceptive. The opening is set in the middle of a busy street with small shops vending merchandise ranging from metal vessels to polyester textiles and gold jewellery. As is common in India, the way to the temple is also crammed with shops selling Ganapathy idols, colourful trinkets, cosmetics and what have you. The intense illumination in these shops seems to spill on to the pathway to create a surreal ambience!

Just past the shops is a shrine to Ganapathy called *Manicka Vinayagar*. *Manickam* means ruby. The silver-covered idol faces east. We pray here before beginning the climb up the 420 steps that lead to the shrine. It is at this spot that devotees offer coconuts to the Elephant God, who, legends say, is very fond of the sweet nut.

After a few minutes' climb up the enclosed but well-lit stairway, one reaches the first landing, ahead of which is a fork. To the right is the way to the Uchi Pillayar Koil. We turn to the left to the ancient Thayumanaswamy shrine. The eye-catching hillock, which seems to spring up from nowhere, is 83 m high. Experts estimate the rock to be 3800 million years, even older than the Himalayas in India or the rocks of Greenland!

The two temples hewn out of the rock have some rare inscriptions, which indicate the historical importance of this fort. The oldest of these date back to the 3rd century B C while later inscriptions refer to the Pallava period in the 6th and 7th century A D and the Carnatic Wars during the early British presence in India. Architecturally, they belong to the Pallava cave temple style and have beautiful sculptures, portraying scenes from the life of Siva and his consort Parvathy.

Below the Rock Fort is the temple water tank. Nearby is the house where Robert Clive, the architect of the British Empire in India, lived while he was in Tiruchirapalli. Close by is a church built in the 18th century by a Danish Reverend called Schwartz.

At the Thayumanaswamy temple, the *lingam* in the sanctum sanctorum is represented by an imposing natural projection of rock over 5 ft high. The legend of Mathrubhuteswarar or Thayumanaswamy is a moving illustration of the mother-like compassion God has for His devotees. It is said that when Ratnavati, a great devotee of the Lord, became pregnant; her mother went to help her during childbirth.

Ratnavati lived on the north bank of the river Cauvery, which flows in Tiruchirapalli. As the time for the birth approached, Ratnavati's mother had to go to Tiruchirapalli, crossing the river which was in spate.

A worried Ratnavati prayed to the Lord and was relieved to find her mother by her side. The baby was born safely. Soon the floods receded. Only later, when her mother asked her how she managed to deliver the baby all by herself did she realise the truth. The Lord Himself had come to her aid in her mother's form! And her own mother had actually been able to arrive only after the floods receded. *Thayum ana* in Tamil means 'One who became the Mother'. It has since become customary to pray to this God for safe and easy childbirth by offering a big bunch of plantains. Plantains symbolise fertility and propagation in south India.

Originally the entrance to the temple is believed to have faced east, but now it faces the opposite direction. The story goes that Sage Saramamunivar, a great devotee of Lord Siva, used to grow a special type of flower called Javanti (in Tamil) in his garden, to use in his worship of the Lord. One day he found a guard of King Parantaka Chola's (A D 907-955) palace taking away the flowers. The sage complained to the king about the theft. But when the king learnt that the flowers had been for his own queen, he ignored the complaint. Distraught, the sage cried to the Lord that he could no longer worship Him with the special flowers. And Siva became so angry that He averted his benign glance from the capital city of Uraiyur. This caused a rain of sand to fall on the city, the site of the king's palace. Uraiyur was saved only after the fear stricken King and subjects prayed to Vekkali Amman (a form of Parvathy), who pacified the Lord.

The Lord's consort at the temple is Mattuvarkuzhal Ammai, who is grace personified. In this temple, one can find Brahma in the form of Jureswarar, who cures fever.

An impressive painting of goddess Parvathy can be seen on the ceiling of the forecourt of the temple. The eyes of Parvathy face you whichever angle you look at her, like the painting of Mona Lisa in the Louvre Museum in Paris.

Leaving the precincts of the Thayumanaswamy temple, proceeding towards the east you again catch up with the open stairway. Within a minute, we reach a cave temple called *Kudaivarai Koil* (temple hewn from rock). A protected site of the Archaeological Survey of India (ASI), available records reveal that this shrine was built by the great Pallava King, Mahendravarman, in the 9th century A D.

This cave temple has sculptures of Siva, Parvati and a personification of the river Cauvery as a maiden. The matted locks of Siva are shown bearing the torrents of the river Ganga. The edict in the temple describes Parvati pleading with Siva not to dally with Cauvery as she belonged to King Mahendravarman. Parvati, it is said, was fearful of Siva's fondness for rivers after his encounter with the tempestuous Ganga. The cave temple has a doorway, which is closed. It is said this used to lead to a secret passage to Uraiyur, the royal seat.

Back to the main stairway, which is now open to the sky. To your right the first glimpse of the city lights can be seen. Look up and you see a pinnacle where the Uchi Pillayar sits and surveys the terra firma below. The climb is a little difficult but the breeze is invigorating. From here, Tiruchirapalli looks verdant and the view of the river breathtaking.

An extremely narrow portal leads to the sanctum sanctorum. On this particular day, the idol of Pillayar is decked in sandal paste. There is a 'pit' on the top of his forehead. How it came about is another legend.

According to lore, Vibhishana, the demon king of Sri Lanka who refused to be a part of Ravana's villainy against Sita, was returning to Lanka after attending the coronation of Lord Rama at Ayodhya.

Lord Rama had gifted him the idol of Ranganatha in recumbent form, the same idol of Mahavishnu that He and his illustrious ancestors of the Ikshvaku clan had worshipped. There was, however, a stipulated condition – that the idol should never be placed on the ground. If it were, it would grow to such a size that it could not be removed from that spot!

Vibhishana took enormous care to observe the condition and succeeded in bringing the idol safely, carrying it on his head, till he reached the banks of the Cauvery river flowing near Tiruchirapalli. Tempted by the sight of its pure and flowing waters, he desired to have a dip in it. But eager not to breach the condition, he looked around for someone to entrust the idol to. Spotting a young boy, he gave him the idol after cautioning him not to place it on the ground. The boy's terms were that he would call out thrice and if Vibhishana did not respond, he would put the idol down. Vibhishana then went for a bath in the river.

The swim was so invigorating that Vibhishana did not heed the boys' repeated calls. When he finally emerged, he found that the boy had placed the idol on the ground and it had grown to a massive size. It was immovable. An enraged Vibhishana chased the boy up to the top of a nearby mount and rapped him hard on his forehead. Immediately, the boy turned into the elephant God Ganesha, and gave *darshan* to him. And therefore the 'Uchi Pillaiyar'!

The very idol that Lord Ganapathy placed on the ground is today believed to be the presiding deity at the famous Ranganatha temple at Srirangam, a suburb of Tiruchirapalli.

FAST FACTS

How to reach

Air : Direct flights to Tiruchirapalli are available from Chennai, Madurai, Thiruvanathapuram and Colombo.

Rail	:	Trains are available from Chennai, Madurai, Bangalore, Rameswaram, Thanjavur, Coimbatore, Tirupathi and Cochin. Direct trains to Calcutta and Guwahati have also been added. Tiruchirapalli is 361 km from Chennai.
Road	:	Buses are available to Tiruchirapalli from all major towns and cities in Tamil Nadu and the neighbouring states of Kerala and Karnataka.
Local Transport	:	The local bus service is efficient. Ask for the Main Guard Gate bus stop. Other forms of local transport such as auto rickshaws, taxis and cycle rickshaws are available.
Season	:	Throughout the year.
Clothing	:	Tropical, light cottons.
Languages spoken	:	English and Tamil.

Accommodation

Tiruchirapalli	*Tariff (INR)*	*Phone*
Hotel Femina	350-1950	0431-2414501
Hotel Abbirami	270-720	0431-2415128
Hotel Guru	240-840	0431-2415881
Hotel Anand	215-825	0431-2415545

NEARBY ATTRACTIONS

Rock Fort: Rock Fort, atop which the Uchi Pillayar Temple is situated, is an attraction in itself. Experts deem this rock to be 3,800 million years old, making it older than the Himalayas and as old as the ancient rocks of Greenland. The rocky outcrop is 83 m high. There are 420 steps leading to the summit, where there are inscriptions dating back to the 3rd century B C. Not much remains of the fort ramparts, but the Main Guard Gate is intact. The fort played a crucial role in the Carnatic Wars, and according to an inscription, helped in laying the British Empire's foundations in India. Beside the tank at the foot of Rock Fort is the house where Robert Clive of the East India Company, lived while he was in Tiruchirapalli.

Tiruvanaikkaval: This temple is famed for its architectural spendour. It is one of the *panchalingam* shrines of Lord Siva. He is represented in the form of water here. It is also called the Jambukeswara Temple. The *lingam* is installed under an ancient *Jambu* tree and is partially submerged by water. The temple is named after an elephant, which is believed to have worshipped Lord Siva here.

Grand Anaicut: An engineering marvel indeed! Not a modern one but one accomplished in the 2nd century A D. The Grand Anaicut, also called Kallanai, is a stone dam built by King Karikala Chola to harness the waters of the Cauvery. It is close to the Srirangam Island. The dam is 329 m long and 20 m wide. There is now a road bridge on top of the dam, from where one can have a good vista of the pleasant greenery around and the river waters.

Upper Anaicut: This is another dam, which lies at the head of the Srirangam island, at a distance of 18 km from Tiruchirapalli. It was built across the river Kollidam in the 19th century. The dam is about 685 m long. Its other name, Mukkombu, is derived from the fact that the dam forks into three because of the island's shape.

Samayapuram: 20 km from Tiruchirapalli, Samayapuram is a famous temple dedicated to Goddess Parvathy, called Mariamman here. It is believed that those who are mentally ill will be cured if they visit this temple.

The temple town of
KANCHIPURAM

Most enchanting is the smiling mien of Lord Varadaraja of Kanchipuram. As you enter the shrine, you are struck by the beauty of the *moolavar,* matched only by the perfection of the intricately sculpted *utsavar* idol.

The temple is also called the Devarajaswamy temple, and one of the many names of the Lord is Devathirajan. Unusually, he is facing west, in a standing posture. The goddess is Perundevi Thayar, in seated posture.

Pallava, Chola and Vijayanagara rulers all contributed to the construction. There is a beautiful 100-pillared hall with exquisite sculptures and chains made of stone. The Athivaradar, an idol of Lord Varadaraja displayed for worship only once in 40 years is a unique idol made of the wood of the *Athi* (fig) tree. It was discovered in a pond.

Kanchipuram is also called Athigiri. The name Kanchipuram is believed to have originated from the legend that Brahma once conducted a *yagna* here and was blessed by Lord Varadaraja. The sound *Ka* is unique to Brahma while *Anjitham* means 'that which has been worshipped'.

There is a custom in this temple related to the two engraved 'golden' lizards, which can be seen on the temple ceiling. People reach up to touch them in the belief that they will be cured of disease. Legend says that Asamanjana – the son of Sakara, the King of Ayodhya – and his wife were turned into lizards following a curse. One Upamanyu gave *darshan* of

Lord Varadaraja to the two lizards, on which they attained their true form and went to Heaven. News of Upamanyu's total surrender to the Lord spread far and wide. Lord Varadaraja then gave a blessing that the two lizards would remain in the temple precincts in golden form, and that whoever touched them would be cured of illness.

The *Garuda Seva* – where the Lord is carried around the streets of the town on a statue of the divine eagle, the Garuda – is a very popular festival. This occurs in the Tamil month of Vaikasi (May-June), as does the Annual Car festival during which every inch of space available is filled with locals and visitors. In 2000, the Kanchi Sankaracharya inaugurated a new temple chariot.

This is the birthplace of the great Vaishnavite saints Poigai Azhwar and Sri Swamy Desikan. Saint Ramanuja lived here for a while. Several of the Azhwars have sung of the glory of this Lord. Like Srirangam, it is an important centre of Vaishnavism.

Uniquely, it is a symbol of communal amity. Muslims participate traditionally in the *Brahmotsavam* festival of the temple. The story goes that once, the temple chariot came to a sudden halt when it was being taken in procession. A Muslim saint Auliya, who lived in the area, came forward and provided the ropes that enabled the car to complete the journey. This is recorded in the temple and so the tradition is followed.

In fact, this peaceful coexistence between Hindus and Muslims is unique in Kanchipuram. Near the Ekambareswarar Temple is a 450-year-old mosque built by the Nawab of Arcot. There is another mosque near the Vaikunta Perumal Temple. And both mosque and the temple share a common tank!

Ekambareswarar Temple: Located in Periya Kanchi (*periya* – big) this is one of the most famous temples in south India, in existence even before the 6th century A D. The old temple was pulled down and a new one built by the Pallavas.

The Cholas, who followed, made some additions. The Vijayanagara king Krishnadevaraya completed the main *rajagopuram* that stands 172 ft tall.

The *sthala vriksham* is a mango tree, which is said to be 2500 years old. The Hindu scriptures, the four Vedas, are said to have taken the shape of this tree. The unique feature of the tree is that each of its four branches yields fruit of a different taste – sweet, sour, astringent and bitter. It was under this tree that the Devi, who had to come down to earth because Lord Siva cursed her for closing his eyes, made a small *lingam* out of sand and worshipped Siva. Suddenly, the river Vegavathi, flowing nearby, flooded and threatened to destroy the Siva *lingam*. Goddess Kamakshi, though terrified, embraced the *lingam* to protect it. Her Lord repented, gave her *darshan* and fulfilled her wish to be back by his side. This is represented by a beautiful sculpture.

There are three *lingams* in the temple, worshipped by Brahma, Vishnu and Rudra. They are called Vellakambar, Kallakambar and Nallakambar, respectively. Two other *lingams*, bearing the carvings of 108 *lingams* and 1008 *lingams* on them, respectively, can also be seen. The marriage of Kamakshi Amman to the Lord is celebrated during the *Panguni Uthram* festival.

This temple has a small shrine to Vishnu. The Lord is called 'Nilathingal Thundatthan' here because he assisted Goddess Parvathy during her penance. The shrine is considered part of the 108 Vaishnava *Divya Desas*.

Kamakshi Amman Temple: This is one of the important *Shakthi sthalams* (place of goddess worship) in the country. The main deity is in a sitting posture. Known as *Parabrahma-roopini*, she is seated on Brahma, Vishnu, Rudra, Iswara and Sadasiva. The Devi was originally in *ugra* or angry form here. Adi Sankara, the founder of the Advaita school of Hindu philosophy (see chapter on Sringeri for explanation of

Advaita), made her the embodiment of *shanta* (peace) by installing a *Sri Chakra* (a cosmological diagram representing the powers of the goddess) in front of her. In most temples, the *Sri Chakra* is embedded in the earth and the goddess rests on the *Sri Chakra,* accounting for the *pujas* done at Her feet. Here, as the *Sri Chakra is* in front of the goddess, the *pujas* are done there.

The festival idol of Goddess Kamakshi, along with idols of Goddess Lakshmi and Goddess Saraswathi, are in standing posture. The Cholas in the 14th century A D built the temple in its present form. The temple has beautiful *gopurams,* pillars, *mandapams* and tanks. Close to the temple lies the Kanchi Kamakoti Peeta established by Adi Sankara.

Inside the Kamakshi temple there is a shrine to Lord Vishnu. He is called Adi Varaha Perumal here. After a quarrel between Siva and Parvathy, Siva directed Parvathy to do penance to Vishnu, standing on one leg. Vishnu appeared here for this purpose. After the penance, Siva forgave Parvathi. Vishnu appears in three postures – standing, seated and recumbent. This Vishnu shrine is considered one of the Vaishnava *Divya Desas.*

Vaikunta Perumal Temple: This is one of the oldest temples in Tamil Nadu, built by the Pallava king Nandivarman II, in the 8th century A D. Later Chola rulers constructed the entrance to the temple. This temple is noted for its sculptures and inscriptions, particularly relating to battle scenes. The presiding deity is Vaikunta Perumal (Lord Vishnu), who is in seated posture. His consort is Vaikuntavalli. The *vimanam* here is special, with 3 storeys. On the first, the deity is in sitting pose, in the second in recumbent posture and in the third in standing pose. Saint Thirumangai Azhwar has sung of the glory of this temple.

Ulagalanda Perumal Temple: Lord Vishnu, in his incarnation as the dwarf Vamana, subdued the pride of King

Mahabali. Mahabali was known for his munificence and boasted that he would never turn down a request. Lord Vishnu appeared before him in a dwarf form and asked for three stretches of land, to be measured by his strides. Mahabali readily agreed. The Lord then assumed his full, awesome size. With one stride he covered the earth and then with another the Heavens. Mahabali realised his error and offered his head for the Lord to place his foot on, for the third stride. After this, the Lord gave him salvation. *Ulagalanda Perumal* literally means one who measured the universe. In commemoration of this legend, Jayamkonda Chola built this temple. There is a stone inscription in the inner *prakarams* of the temple, mentioning this.

The awe-inspiring idol is 35 ft in height and 24 ft in breadth. It is believed that the lord gave *darshan* to Anjaneya here as Trivikrama with the conch and the discus, and also as Vamana. Parimela Azhagar, a priest of this temple, wrote a commentary for the immortal Tamil poem, the *Thirukkural*. A Tamil and Sanskrit scholar, his statue is found in the northern wall.

In the precincts of this temple, three other idols of Lord Vishnu are found. They are considered part of the 108 Vaishava *Divya Desas,* meaning that the Ulagalanda Perumal Temple actually houses four *Divya Desas.*

Govindavadi Temple: This is a Siva temple around 15 km from Kanchipuram off the Kanchipuram-Arakkonam Railway Line. The nearest railway station is Tirumalpur. The temple belongs to Pandya times. The main deity is Lord Dakshinamurthy, who is Siva in meditative form. The *Kanchipuram Sthala Puranam* of 1887 records this. There is also an inscription on the walls of the inner *prakaram* of the temple. Lord Kailashanathar, in the form of a *lingam,* is also present in the sanctum sanctorum. The *lingam* is 2½ ft in height and 3 ft in breadth. A 5 ft high Vishnu idol and

2 idols of Goddess Parvathy were dug out of the earth recently. There is a distinctive *gopuram*.

Ashtabuja Perumal Temple: The remarkable feature of this deity is that it has 8 arms. Lord Vishnu is in standing posture, facing west. His consort is Sri Pushpavalli, in seated posture. The temple is ancient, and has stone inscriptions. It is located in Reddipet. Saints Peyazhwar and Thirumangai Azhwar have visited this shrine.

Pandavudhootha Perumal Temple: This temple in Pillayarpalayam is dedicated to Lord Vishnu, and built by King Rajakesari Varman about a 1000 years ago. The sanctum sanctorum contains 2 stones with inscriptions. According to legend, Lord Krishna came to Hasthinapur as the ambassador of the Pandavas. King Duriyodana decided to do away with him. He dug a trench in his *durbar* (court) hall and hid some wrestlers inside. He then covered it with bamboo and carpets and placed a throne on it. When Lord Krishna entered the hall, Duriyodana asked him to sit on the throne. He did so, and the false floor collapsed. The Lord assumed *Viswaroopa* (universal form) and killed all the wrestlers in the trench. The saints Boothathazhwar, Peyazhwar, Thirumangai Azhwar and Thirumazhisai Azhwar have visited this temple and composed songs in praise of the deity. The temple is located in Pillayarpalayam.

Yadhothakara Perumal Temple: The origin of this temple goes back to prehistoric times. The ancient Tamil literature *Tholkappiam* and *Silappadikaram*, mention this temple. The *moolavar* Sri Yadothakara is in recumbent posture with his head towards the south. His consort is Sri Komalavalli Thayar.

The story goes that the Lord was initially lying with his head to the north. Kanikannan, a disciple of Saint Thirumazhisai Azhwar, was greatly attached to the deity. There was another person, an old woman, who was doing service at the temple. So that her services could be prolonged,

Kanikannan requested the saint to make her a young woman. The saint did so. Seeing this, the Pallava king of the times asked Kanikannan to work a similar miracle for him. When he refused, he was banished from the kingdom. Both he and the saint left Kanchipuram. The Lord followed suit, and the city became dark! The ruler, realising his error, pleaded with Kanikannan to return and asked for his forgiveness. Only when he came back, did the Lord! This time, He lay down, facing south.

The saint philosopher Vedanta Desika took instructions in this temple. Sri Manavalamamunigal gave religious discourses here. Among the many *vahanams*, the gold palanquin deserves mention. The temple is located in Thumbavanam. Poigai Azhwar, Boothathazhwar, Thirumazhisai Azhwar, Thirumangai Azhwar and Nammazhwar have sung of this deity.

Kailasanathar Temple: An ancient temple, the construction was begun in 700 A D by Raja Simha, the father of Mahendravarman III, who later completed it. It has all the characteristics of the Pallava style – the pyramidal tower, a pillared hall and a vestibule, all enclosed by a wall. The temple is famous for its exquisite carvings and attracts devotees and tourists alike. There are 58 small shrines situated around the main shrine, as a compound wall. Paintings of fresco style adorn the inner walls of the shrines. Sandstone was used in the construction of the temple. The presiding deity is in *lingam* form. There is a figure of Ardhanareeswarar, which represents the male and female forms of divinity in one idol. The feminine aspect has a *veena* in her hand while the masculine aspect is seated on a bull.

FAST FACTS

How to reach

Air : The nearest Airport is Chennai, which is 71 km away.

Rail	:	Kanchipuram is connected to Chennai by rail.
Road	:	It is well connected to Chennai and other parts of south India.
Local Transport	:	Taxis, auto rickshaws and cycle rickshaws.
Season	:	Throughout the year.
Clothing	:	Tropical, light cottons.
Languages spoken	:	English and Tamil.

Accommodation

	Tariff (INR)	Phone
MM Hotel	300-800+tax	954112-230023
TM Hotel	550-1000+tax	04112-225250
Shelter Resorts	1450-1900	04114-272424

Nearby Attractions

Kanchi Mutt: The Kanchi Mutt is one of the mutts or *peetas* established by Adi Sankara, who lived from 788 to 820 A.D. Similar to the pontiffs of other *peetas* like Puri or Dwaraka, the heads of this mutt are called Sankaracharyas. Adi Sankara revived Hinduism when it was going through a dull period. His philosophy is called Advaita. He established a *Sri Chakra* at the Kamakshi Amman temple at Kanchipuram. In recent times, the Paramacharya of Kanchi, Sri Chandrasekarendra Saraswathi, brought great fame to this mutt with his learning and humanitarian approach. He lived nearly for a 100 years before leaving this earth. The present pontiffs are Sri Jayendra Saraswathi and Sri Vijayendra Saraswathi. All the pontiffs of this mutt belong to the *Sanyasi* (ascetic) tradition. In keeping with the reputation of Kanchipuram as a great centre of learning, the mutt undertakes educational activities in many spheres. It has established a modern centre of learning, which has been given deemed university status. Located at Enathur, this university has a library with ancient books and palm leaf manuscripts. There are plans to set up an informational technology park. Apart from this, the mutt teaches traditional learning and administers various temples. It has also taken up the task of providing medical care to the people.

Thiruparuthikundram: This is a suburb of Kanchipuram, on the southern banks of the Vegavathy river. It was a centre of Jainism. It is also known as Jaina Kanchi. Two temples dedicated to Vardhaman Mahavira and Chandra Prabha can be seen here. The first was built in the 6th century

A D. The earliest Pallankoil copper plate records land donation by King Simhavarman Pallava to the temple and the monks of Nandhisangha in 556 A D. The temple was enlarged during the Chola period. A *sangeetha mandapa* or music hall was built by Irugappa, a minister in the Vijayanagara courts. It has a series of paintings belonging to the 14th and 17th centuries. The Chandra Prabha temple is said to have been built during Raja Simha Pallava's reign in the 8th century A D. Both the temples come under the Tamil Nadu Archaeology Department. There was a series of pontiffs here till the 16th century, when the seat shifted to Melchittamur near Dindivanam.

Uthiramerur: An ancient Siva temple bearing inscriptions about village administration in past times is found here. There is also an ancient and massive Vaishnavite temple. It is multi-storeyed with an *asthanga vimanam*. This village, 28 km from Kanchipuram, also has a pretty lake.

Thiruthani: At a distance of 42 km, it is one of the 6 abodes of Lord Muruga. The temple is atop a hillock. It can be accessed by a *ghat* road or by steps. The 365 steps are said to represent the 365 days of the year. This temple attracts a large number of pilgrims. It is here that Muruga is believed to have married Valli. It is also the birthplace of Dr S Radhakrishnan, former President of India and a philosopher-statesman.

Silk weaving: All the colours of the rainbow and a few more. Borders shining bright with *Zari* or silk thread, woven with traditional *yalis*, elephants, houses and trees. *Pallus* (the decorated end of a sari, which is worn over the shoulder) shining even brighter. That is the Kanchipuram silk *sari* for you. These magical creations are a part of weddings in Tamil Nadu. The weaving and dyeing tradition is hundreds of years old. In Kanchipuram alone, there are over 30,000 looms engaged in this industry. It provides livelihoods for 50,000 people. It is believed that the weavers came to Kanchipuram in the 12th century A D during the Chola period. There is another version that they came at the invitation of the Vijayanagara ruler Krishnadevaraya. It used to be a family effort, with all members doing their bit. Weaving used to be done by certain communities. The Kanchi cotton, which is in fact older than the Kanchipuram silk, is equally popular.

Shakunthala Jagannathan Museum of Folk Art: This is located near the Ekambareswar Temple. The 400-year-old house belonging to the landowners of Damal, the maternal ancestors of Sir C P Ramaswamy Aiyar, has been converted into a museum. Shakunthala Jagannathan, the eldest grand daughter of Sir C P, conceived the idea and gifted her own collections and inheritance. Some of the museum's attractions are the *Thinnai* or front veranda, now adapted as a craft shop; the *Kalyana Kudal* or main hall, which has traditional furniture, a doll collection and ancient palm leaves (the history of Kanchipuram from 300 B C to the British period is painted on one wall); the *Vadyashala,* where musical instruments are displayed; the *Nadumitham,* where stone sculptures dated from the Pre-Pallava to the Vijayanagara period are housed, a *Chitrashala* which has a collection of south Indian paintings and *Aindu Tinai,* which depicts the five ecological divisions of ancient India. There are also displays of lamps, *puja* items, utensils, textiles, jewellery and traditional games. The airy rooftop room houses a terracotta image of goddess Kamakshi, which faces the tower of the Ekambareshwarar temple. There is a nominal entrance fee.

The Divine Temple at
SRIVILLIPUTHUR

Srivilliputhur is a temple that you will want to visit again and again. The atmosphere of sanctity represented by Goddess Andal's divine love for the Lord, the absolute devotion of Her father Periazhwar, to the Lord, the stupendous sight of Lord Vatapatrasayee in recumbent posture, and the magnificent *gopuram* – all these make the temple unique.

Traditionally, one should visit the Vatapatrasayee shrine first, before seeing Goddess Andal in all her glory with her consort Rangamannar, who is none other than Lord Krishna. To the Lord's left side is his vehicle Garuda, in a rare position. Usually the shrine to Garuda will be placed exactly opposite the Lord's sanctum sanctorum.

Not aware of the traditional practice, we went straight into the Andal shrine. The annual festival during the Tamil month of Margazhi had come to its conclusion. It was the day of *Kanu pidi*, which falls just after *Pongal*, the harvest festival. The priests performed a special benediction for us reciting a verse from Andal's *Thiruppavai*, that describes the benefits of observing the *Pavai nonbu*, the austerity that Andal and her young friends observed to reach the feet of Lord Krishna.

'*Ongiulagalanda uttamanperpadi*
Nangalnampavaikku satrineeradinal
Theengindrinadellam thingal mummaripeithu
Ongu perunchennellodu kayalugala

Poonguvalaippodhil porivandukanpaduppa
Thengadhepukkirindu seerthamulaipattri
Vaanga. Kudam neraikkum vallalperumpasukkal
Neengada selvam neraindailorempavai.'

The verse translates to 'If one observes the *Pavai nonbu* by singing the praise of the Lord who strides the universe, the world will be free of harm, there will be good rains, the paddy will flourish and the cows will yield abundantly. Everywhere prosperity will reign.'

Among all the shrines associated with the Azhwars, Srivilliputhur can be said to be the most sacred because it is the birthplace of not one, but two Azhwars – Periazhwar and his daughter Andal, who is none other than an incarnation of Goddess Lakshmi herself. There is a beautiful *nandavanam* (garden) in the temple precincts where a spot near a *tulsi* plant is marked out as Andal's birthplace. It was here that Periazhwar found her, goes the legend. Touching the soil here is said to confer many blessings.

After visiting the Periazhwar and the Chakrathazhwar shrines, we climb up a flight of steps to the Vatapatrasayee *sannidhi* (sanctum sanctorum), where the sight of the Lord in *sayana* (recumbent) posture is truly beautiful. There is a silence and stillness here and the presence of Godhead is supreme. The literal meaning of the Lord's name here is 'One who is recumbent on the *vata* leaf'. Adi Sesha too is present here. From the navel of the granite idol emerges a lotus with Brahma, Sreedevi, Bhoodevi and two local chieftains, called Villi and Puttan. It is said that the place derived its name from these chieftains.

The story of Andal is well known for its beauty, and the message that total surrender and faith in God always yields results. Her father Vishnuchitta, or Periazhwar as he came to be called, is believed to have lived in the 8th century A D. He once attended a conference of scholars summoned by a Pandya king in the kingdom's capital, Madurai. His exposition of the Vedas so astounded the audience and he was given a cash award for his accomplishment. He used the money to make improvements to the Vatapatrasayee temple in Srivilliputhur. He was named 'Periazhwar' because he sang a verse blessing the Lord. This is a hymn, in the *Nalayira Divyaprabhandham*, which begins *Pallandu pallandu*, which is chanted after every temple *puja* and is believed to protect the Lord himself from *'drishti'* or 'the evil eye'.

Periazhwar used to string a garland everyday for worship of Lord Vatapatrasayee. One day he found that the child Andal wearing it round her neck and admiring herself in a mirror. He remonstrated with her, but God appeared to him in a vision and said he would only don the garland worn by Andal. One of Andal's names is *'Chuudikodutha Sudarkodi'* (Maiden who wore the garland and presented it to the Lord). Andal's immense faith and daily worship culminated in her wedding to the Lord and her merging with the idol of Lord Ranganatha. Since Rangan came to her in the form of a *mannan* (king), he is called 'Rangamannar'.

This account indicates that the Vatapatrasayee temple existed in the 8th century. However, the earliest of the epigraphs in the temple dates it to the 10th century. This matter has not been resolved. As for the Andal temple, it is believed to have been constructed in the 14th century A D.

After renovations, the *mahasamprokshanam* of this temple was conducted in February 2000. The important festivals here are the *Margazhi* festival and *Panguni Uthiram* festival, when *Andalkalyanam* is celebrated. The birthday of Andal falls in the Tamil month of Adi, on the star Pooram, a time of great celebration. Andal not only composed the *Thiruppavai*, but also the *Nachiar Thirumozhi*, whose powerful poetry and musical verse depict bridal mysticism in all its intensity.

She conceived of Lord Krishna as her husband, much as Radha did, and the Nachiar Thirumozhi is an outpouring of her feelings for the Lord in all their sanctity and purity.

From an architectural point of view, the 60 m tall *gopuram* is the most impressive feature. Inscribed on the *gopuram* is a Tamil verse believed to have been penned by the great Tamil poet Kamban, which says that this *gopuram* 'should be compared to Mount Meru, and to Mount Meru alone'.

Another striking feature is the large number of pillars, with sculptures in the Baroque style on them. Look out also for the copper-plated portraits of King Tirumalai Nayak and his consorts. Embossed with gold, the portraits can be seen in the small *mandapam* in front of the main shrine. The king made a lot of contributions to the temple, and was the recipient of temple honours during his lifetime. This tradition is still carried on and his image is honoured with *parivattam* (headband). His descendants also organize special worship to his image every year. Apart from the Pandyas, the Chola and Travancore kings also made gifts to the temple.

The Srivilliputhur temple is truly a shrine that is timeless.

FAST FACTS

How to reach

Air	:	The nearest airport is Madurai, which is 100 km away.
Rail	:	There is a weekly express train from Chennai to Srivilliputhur via Madurai. There is a daily link from Madurai by passenger trains.
Road	:	There are good roads to Madurai and Tirunelveli. The distance to Virudhunagar is 45 km.
Local Transport	:	Tourist taxis and auto rickshaws are available.
Season	:	Through the year.

Accommodation

Srivilliputhur	Tariff (INR)	Phone
Sashidharan Lodge	110-700	04563 265109
Thangam Lodge Rajapalayam Bypass Road	90-195	04563-260337
Raja Lodge Madurai Road.	225-520	04563-264474

Clothing : Tropical, light cottons.
Languages spoken : English and Tamil.

NEARBY ATTRACTIONS

Thiruttangal: This temple is located on a small hillock. There are convenient steps, which the devotee can climb up to reach the entrance. The presiding deity, in standing posture and facing east, is Lord Narayana. The festival idol is called Thirutthangalappan. The consort Sengamalanayaki, has a shrine to herself. In the main sanctorum sanctorum, there are three goddesses – Sreedevi and Neeladevi on the right of the Lord and Bhoodevi to his right. As the deities have been painted over, there is no *Thirumanjanam* or ritual bath. Garuda can be seen here in unique form with his traditional enemy, the serpent, and a vessel containing ambrosia. This temple, one of the 108 *Divya Desas,* is said to have got its name from the fact that Lord Muruga stayed here awhile. It is also said that Lord Krishna's son Aniruddha got married here and the Lord was present at the festivities. The temple can be approached from both Srivilliputhur and Virudhunagar. The drive takes around half an hour.

Badrakali Amman temple: This famous temple is situated in the heart of Sivakasi, 20 km from Srivilliputhur. It is spread over a sprawling campus. Apart from the main shrine, there is a unique idol of Vinayaka with five heads. Vinayaka in this form is called Heramba Vinayaka, and is a fierce manifestation. Usually the five-headed Vinayaka has the lion as the vehicle—he gets his five heads from his father Siva and the lion from his mother Parvathy. In this temple, however, he has his customary vehicle, the bandicoot.

Grizzled Squirrel Wild Life Sanctuary: This is 15 km off Srivilliputhur town, and is a combination of deciduous forest and grasslands that offer sanctuary to giant grizzled squirrels. Apart from these squirrels, one can sight the flying squirrel, tree shrew, lion tailed macaque, mouse deer, barking deer and an occasional elephant. The sanctuary can be visited throughout the year. For details, contact: Wildlife Warden, Srivilliputhur, Phone: 04568-260565.

Rama the Saviour
MADURANTAKAM TEMPLE

God is omnipotent, omniscient and omnipresent. He is also eternal. His grace is not only for those holy people who lived in ancient times. It is for us modern, sceptical folk too. The story of *'Eri Katha Ramar'* ('The One who protected the tank') of Madurantakam, a village in Tamil Nadu, is an emphatic testimony of the gracious ways of the divine. Even more fascinating is that the central character is a British official. Is this not proof that Godhead is one, whatever name it is known by or worshipped as?

During the period 1795–99, the Collector of Chengalpattu District was a British officer named Colonel Lionel Place, who had witnessed the devastation caused by two breaches to a huge water tank – that still exists – in Madurantakam taluk. With an area of 13 square miles and a depth of 21 ft, the length of the tank bund is 12,960 ft. As it is rain fed, the danger of a breach becomes all too real during the monsoon season.

In 1798, the wise Collector decided to be prepared, camping in Madurantakam to handle any emergency. Coming upon a large store of granite stones in the precincts of the local Rama temple, he immediately instructed his subordinates to use them to strengthen the tank walls. Hearing this, the temple priests told him that the stones were actually meant for building a separate shrine for Goddess Janakavalli (Sita), but work had not begun for want of funds. The collector then asked in jest, "Why does your Lord, who is not able to save the tank each year, need a separate shrine for his consort?" The priests replied that the Lord 'always answered a prayer from the heart'. Soon after, the Collector left saying that he definitely would not be wanting in prayers to the Lord. Such was his desire to save the tank!

The rains came and filled the tank to the brim, and a breach seemed imminent. That night the worried Collector camped near the tank, hoping that the walls would hold. Suddenly he saw a wondrous sight. He saw two warriors bearing a bow and quiver of arrows, guarding the tank. The British officer went down on his knees and prayed, for he realized that the figures were none other than Lord Rama and his brother Lakshmana.

When those who were accompanying him saw Colonel Place on his knees, they rushed to his side assuming he was ill. And it was then he described the amazing sight he had seen! The tank was saved and the people were safe. Colonel Place took it upon himself to build a shrine for goddess Janakavalli. Thus did Lord Rama in Madurantakam come to be known as *'Eri Katha Ramar'*! The edict with the Collector's name, citing him as a benefactor, can be seen even today in the temple.

The *Ramayana,* the epic poem by Sage Valmiki, recounts the heroic deeds of Lord Rama, an incarnation of Lord Vishnu. Rama appeared on earth as a human being and right from his youth, assisted the forces of good to overcome evil. The eldest son of King Dasaratha of Ayodhya, he was about to be coronated when his stepmother invoked a boon given by the king and had him exiled. The *Ramayana* describes Rama's stay in the forest; the abduction of his beautiful young wife Sita by the demon king of Sri Lanka, Ravana; Rama's victory against the demons in Lanka and the rescue of his wife. Rama then assumed the throne of Ayodhya, which lies in north India. There are many tales of the valiant deeds he performed on the path from Ayodhya to Sri Lanka and on his return from Lanka to Ayodhya.

According to legend, Lord Rama visited the hermitage of sage Vibhandaka during his exile. The sage requested him to return there on his way back to Ayodhya from Sri Lanka. When he was returning home on his *Pushpaka Vimana* (aeroplane) it landed at this spot, to Rama's puzzlement. Sita reminded him of the sage's request. Lord Rama alighted from the carrier, lending a hand to Sita to help her down. And that is why one sees the rare sight of Rama holding Sita's hand in this shrine. This heart-warming sight is called *hastavalambana* (hands held together).

Originally, Madurantakam was known as Vaghularanyam (forest of sweet smelling *vahula* blossoms). A legend relates how the *Brahmaputras* (sons of Brahma) asked Lord Vishnu how to achieve salvation. He gave them an image of himself in the form of *Karunakaramurthy* (The All Merciful) and advised them to meditate upon it at a place called Vibhandakasram in Vaghularanyam, which is the modern Madurantakam. As bidden, the *Brahmaputras* installed the idol of Karunakaramurthy in the hermitage of sage Vibhandaka, who attained salvation after worshipping the idol. This took place in *Krita Yugam*.

This place was also the site where the great Vaishnavite saint Ramanuja, received initiation from his guru Peria Nambi. Upon the death of Pontiff Alavandar in the great temple town of Srirangam, Saint Peria Nambi went towards Kanchipuram in search of Ramanuja to anoint him as the successor. It so happened that the two met at Madurantakam, which lies *en route*. It was under the *Vaghula* tree that Peria Nambi initiated Ramanuja in the *pancha samskaras* (five practices) – *Taapam* (branding the conch and the discus on the shoulders), *Pundram* (donning the Lord's feet on 12 parts of the body), *Namam* (submitting to the guru) *Mantram* (learning sacred 'strings' of words and uttering them) and *Yagam* (doing pujas to the Lord everyday).

King Uttama Chola, who ruled these parts before King Raja Raja Chola (12th century A D), granted this land as a gift to Vedic priests. The Cholas were famous for their munificence towards temples and they built many a grand temple in Tamil nadu.

The beautiful temple has a shrine to Lord Kothanda Rama bearing the *kothandam* (bow), accompanied by Sita and Lakshmana. The festival idols of Lord Rama and Lord Karunakara can also be seen. There are separate shrines to Goddess Janakavalli and Goddess Andal.

Lord Karunakara is Lord Vishnu, accompanied by his consorts Sreedevi and Bhoodevi. Lord Rama himself is said to have worshipped Lord Karunakara at Madurantakam. Madurantakam means 'a spot possessing springs that spout water as sweet as nectar'. The temple has shrines to Goddess Lakshmi, Lord Narasimha and various Vaishnavite saints. There is a shrine for Anjaneya, in the south eastern corner of the temple tank. Some of the most beautiful songs on Lord Rama, composed by Saint Thyagaraja, are inscribed on the walls near the sanctum sanctorum

In another more recent occurrence, Seth Maganlal Banker of Calcutta discovered an underground cave in 1937, when he was renovating the temple. In this cave were found a small idol of Navaneetha Krishna and some copper *puja* utensils that could have been used by a great sage.

Madurantakam is now a busy, dusty little township off the Grand Trunk Southern highway and the temple is close to the bazaar. The miracle of Madurantakam reinforces faith in the Almighty's limitless compassion. As you behold that massive sheet of water and picture in your mind God with his mighty bow, you can sense for a second the awesome nature of divinity and feel empowered beyond imagination.

FAST FACTS

How to reach

Air	:	The nearest airport is Chennai, 81 km away.
Rail	:	Madurantakam is situated on the Chennai-Triuchirapalli Broad Gauge rail route. As all trains do not halt at Madurantakam, you can get off at Chengalpattu and hire a taxi. The distance is 25 km.
Road	:	The temple is situated 81 km from Chennai on the Grand Southern Trunk road leading to Tiruchirapalli. Chengalpattu is 25 km away.
Local Transport	:	Auto Rickshaws.
Season	:	Throughout the year.
Clothing	:	Tropical, light cottons.
Languages spoken	:	English and Tamil.

Accommodation

Chengalpattu	*Tariff (INR)*	*Phone*
Hotel Ganesh	380-660	954114-22637
Hotel Kanchi	*160-420*	*954114-231019, 226819.*

PLACES OF INTEREST NEARBY

Singaperumal Temple: Situated close to Chengalpattu is the 1500-year-old Singaperumal temple. Singaperumal is none other than Lord Narasimha. Legend goes that after slaying the demon Hiranyakashapu, Narasimha came here in his angry form. He bathed in the temple tank here and became peaceful again. The waters are said to have turned red at that time. The distance from Madurantakam is 32 km.

Chengalpattu Lake: This is a vast expanse of water, which is also known as the Kolalavai lake. It can be seen as you go by on train or by road southwards from Chennai. This lake with scenic hills providing a picturesque backdrop, is a popular picnic spot. While it can be easily approached from NH4, the adventurous can also try the route that passes through an old fort, which lies on one side of the lake. The Tamil Nadu Tourism Development Corporation provides boating facilities here.

Chanmundi Hill Mahishasura

Temples of
KARNATAKA

Mysore, Dusserah

Udipi Fest

Melkote Temple

Somnathpur

Talacaud

Queen's Bath - Hampi

Ugranarasimha Hampi

Srirangapatnam

Belur

Hampi ruins

BELUR, HALEBID AND SOMNATHPUR –
Marvels of Architecture

The finest expression of the artistic consciousness of humankind is what you see in the temples of Belur, Halebid and Somnathpur in Karnataka.

How many years did this romance between the chisel and the stone take to produce these rhapsodies in sculpture that transcend their muteness and speak volumes about the age, its culture, civilization and most importantly its relentless pursuit of perfection? How many editions had to be discarded before the final products were deemed ready to stand up for scrutiny thousands of years hence? What goaded such toil? What motivation gilded such art? Whose aesthetic sense found such collective expression? How did beauty find so many manifestations? These are questions that buffet you as you meander through these jewels that sprang from the Kingdom of the Hoysalas.

These temples are different from the colossal Thanjavur Big Temple, the stately Srirangam *rajagopuram* or the vast spaces of the Nataraja temple of Chidambaram that impress you even from afar. But as you gaze at sculpture after sculpture, frieze after frieze and relief after relief, theirs is a spell that enthralls you forever.

To call this wonderful result of earnest endeavour even human seems somewhat inappropriate. Much as one would like to attribute these wondrous works of art to the divine architect Viswakarma, the truth is that they were built by sculptors like Chikka, Hampa, Dasoja, Chavana, Malliyana, Nagoja and others who lived and worked during the reign of the Hoysalas from the early 12th century to the late 13th century in the area that is now Karnataka.

Belur: The temples at Belur were constructed in the early 12th century by a Hoysala king Vishnu Vardhana, as a commemoration of his victory over the Cholas at Talakad. He also constructed a shrine for Lord Vishnu at Thondanur near Mysore after coming under the influence of Saint Ramanuja and embracing Vishnavism.

Belur is a town nestling on the banks of the river Yagachi. It is verdant country with bright sunshine and a salubrious climate. An ideal setting for the ornate temples of the Hoysalas, it was the capital of the Hoysalas after the fall of Halebid and also the last bastion of the Vijayanagar Rayas.

The most important temple is the Chennakesava temple, set in a large and wide *prakaram* enclosed by high walls. At the entrance, you see a lofty *gopuram*. It is as you enter the courtyard that you come under the spell of Hoysala art. The arresting frontage of the temple with its multidimensional façade and geometric symmetry of a star-shaped configuration is breathtaking. On either side of the steps leading to the interior of the temple, are conical mini *gopurams* with a figurine in each. The first few steps take you to the platform, which runs round the main edifice, from which you can feast on layers and layers of variegated sculpture. They include human forms, gods, celestial beings and depiction of scenes from social life. Such is the intricacy of the carving that no justice can be done to its beauty by merely describing the motifs and themes. It would be similar to describing the fragrance of a jasmine flower and attempting to convey its gentle yet heady scent.

The next few steps take you to the level of the doorway to the interior. Here too you find conical miniature *gopurams* on either side. In between is the highly decorated doorway with pillars and *toranams* (festoons) with forms of celestial and mythical beings as sculpture. On either side of the doorway at a higher level, are windows carved out of stone with myriad holes, each one a gem of perfection and symmetry. The *vimanam* is missing, destroyed during the Muslim invasions. According to archaeological reports, it was star-shaped and ornately carved.

The main shrine of Kesava, known also as Vijaya Narayana, is in the centre of the enclosure on a pedestal. The temple has an arched doorway to the shrine. The image is 2 m high. You can only see the outlines of the idol, as the Archaeological Survey of India (ASI), under whose protection this monument is, does not permit bright illumination for fear of the damage it might cause. There is no worship conducted here as the idol is mutilated. This also means that non-Hindus can freely enter the shrine.

Unlike other temples in south India, the Hoysala temples are built not of solid granite but what is called 'soft chloristic schist or talc, which permits fine and minute carving' writes the renowned archaeologist, K R Srinivasan in his *Temples of South India*. This stone, while being more malleable, is not as hardy and durable.

The massive domed ceiling in the centre, supported by four pillars, is a *tour de force*. A lotus bud carries bas-reliefs with scenes from the *Ramayana* and pillars contain various figures of women. The guide flashes his torchlight off and on quickly for visitors to get a glimpse of the grandeur.

To the south of the main Kesava shrine is the Kappe Chennigarya shrine, which also contains an image of Venugopala. There is a touching legend about this idol. A great sculptor called Jakanacharya, who had left his native village near Tumkur even before his son was born, sculpted the idol. The father and son had never seen each other. One day a young man came to Belur and said there was a flaw in the Chennigarya idol. Jakanacharya, confident about his work, promised to cut off his hand if the charge was proved. The idol was covered with sandal paste and it was noticed that the sandal dried everywhere except around the navel. On examination, it was found that this was due to a cavity at that spot, which contained water, sand and a frog! (*Kappe* frog, in Kannada). As he had sworn, Jakanacharya cut his hand off. He later discovered that the critic was none other than his own son. Jakanacharya later had a vision in which the Lord asked him to build a shrine in his native village Kridapura. When he did so, his hand was restored and the village was re-christened *Kaidala*, meaning 'restored hand' in Kannada.

Among the other shrines in the temple, there is the Vira Narayana shrine, to the west of the Kesava temple. The Sowmyanayaki shrine and the shrine of Andal, the Azhwar from Srivilliputtur, can also be found inside the enclosure.

This temple is also famed for its figures of women in various poses, numbering 42. Known as *madanikas* they can be seen both on the façade and in the *mukha mandapam* of the main shrine. Don't miss the one depicting a woman with a beard and a moustache!

Halebid: Halebid, the original capital of the Hoysalas, was known as Dwarasamudra as it had a huge lake. It flourished for many years and witnessed the construction of a number of temples, the chief among which is the Hoysaleswara temple built by Ketamalla, an officer of King Vishnu Vardhana.

The temple is slightly older than the Chennakesava temple at Belur. The main deity is Siva in the form of two *lingams*, named Hoysaleswara and Santaleswara. A huge *Nandi* (bull and vehicle of Siva) is seen outside the shrine housed in a *Nandi mandapam*. In Halebid too, there is no worship.

The temple is the acme of Hoysala temple architecture characterised by a chiselled base platform displaying a soapstone structure that is wrought to perfection. The star shaped *vimanam* sans the superstructure presents a spectacle of beauty, ravished but unconquered.

James Ferguson – the Indologist, has compared – or should we say contrasted, Halebid and the Greek Parthenon. He wrote 'They form the two opposite poles – the alpha and omega of architectural design; but they are the best examples of their class and between these two extremes lies the whole range of art........... All the pillars of the Parthenon are identical, while no facet of the Indian temple are the same; every convolution of every part exhibits a joyous exuberance of fancy, scorning every mathematical restraint. All that is wild in human faith or warm in human feelings is found portrayed on these walls'. Wonderfully appropriate words!

The temple's walls are replete with the most richly sculpted friezes. There are scenes from the epics, the *Mahabharata, Ramayana* and the *Bhaghavata*. In the upper parts of the temple, there are perforated windows and bas-reliefs on pedestals with canopies above. On the beautifully sculpted south door, there is a Kannada inscription. Hoysala kings used this doorway to enter the temple and offer prayers. Like Belur this temple too boasted of a number of *madanika* sculptures, only a few of which have survived. There are also a few Jain shrines reflecting the religious inclination of the Hoysalas before their conversion to Vaishnavism.

The Muslim general Mallik Kafur sacked the temples of Halebid in the 14th century with disastrous results. Many temples here are today in ruins that can only be appreciated for the great artistry they once displayed. The Kedareswara shrine is an example. The vast expanses that surround Halebid vest it with an air of suspended animation far removed from the bustle of cities.

The temples that now lie in decrepit majesty can best be described as some of the finest works of the human hand and mind.

Somnathpur: Somnathpura was the last hurrah of the Hoysalas before the Muslim invaders overran them. Less well known than Belur or Halebid, a visit to Somnathpur, which is just 36 km away from Mysore, is rewarded as soon as one enters the portals of the Kesava temple here.

Situated on the bank of the Cauvery in what is even today a slumbering hamlet, the temple virtually transports one to the early chapters of mediaeval Indian history. Being a temple where no worship is conducted, as the idols have been mutilated, it is also primarily a monument under the care of the ASI.

The entry into the enclosure brings immediately into view a structure with remarkable artistry. It has 3 *vimanams*, all positioned on a multi-faceted base shaped like a star. The walls, ceilings and pillars bear the imprimatur of the masters of sculpture who lived in Hoysala times. Sculptures galore on pillars, walls, doorways and every conceivable inch of space, of such perfection, make this relatively small sized temple, just 10 m high, stand on par with an edifice of monumental proportions. This aspect, one must reiterate, is the cornerstone of Hoysala temple architecture – that size is not the lone criterion for greatness or immortality in the realm of art.

The temple was built by Somanatha, a general of Hoysala Narasimha III (1254-1291), who was given funds for the purpose by the king. The shrine was completed by 1269. The main shrine, now bare, contained an image of Kesava. In the northern and southern directions of the main shrine are images of Janardhana and Venugopala of about 2 m height. They have minor mutilations. In the *prakaram* are 64 cells, each of which contained an image in the past, but are empty now.

The flagstaff, which is usually right in front of the entrance, is located a little to the northeast. There is a story behind this. It seems when the great sculptor Jakanacharya, built this temple, it was so flawless that the *devas* decided that such perfection had no place on earth. They began transporting it to *Indra loka*. Just as the structure was rising into the air Jakanacharya mutilated some images on the walls and the edifice fell back on terra firma, a little askew, so much so the flagstaff was misaligned with the entrance!

It is both sadness and happiness that fill the mind as we leave the magnificent monuments of the Hoysalas to their hard-earned peace.

FAST FACTS

How to reach

Belur

Air	:	The nearest airport is Mangalore, 154 km away. Bangalore is 220 km away.
Rail	:	The nearest railhead is Hassan, 38 km away. However, Mysore, 155 km away, is more convenient.
Road	:	One can approach Belur by road from Hassan, 38 km away. Mysore, 155 km away, is more convenient. Bangalore is 220 km away. The Jain monument of Sravanabelagola is 90 km away.

Halebid

Air	:	The nearest airport is Mangalore, 148 km away. Bangalore is 216 km away.
Rail	:	Hassan is 31 km away and Mysore 149 km away.
Road	:	The distance between Belur and Halebid is 16 km. Hassan is 31 km away and Mysore 149 km.

Somnathpur

Air	:	Bangalore is the nearest airport, 137 km away.
Rail	:	The nearest railhead is Mysore, 35 km away.

Road	:	Mysore is 35 km away.
Local transport	:	There is no local transport here. Taking a tourist taxi or a tourist bus from Mysore is best. Most buses cover the circuit of Belur, Halebid and Sravanabelagola in a day.
Season	:	Throughout the year.
Clothing	:	Cottons in summer, light woollens in winter.
Languages spoken	:	Kannada and English.

Accommodation

Mysore	*Tariff (INR)*	*Phone*
Lalith Mahal Palace Hotel	5000-30,000	0821-2470470-76
Paradise	50-1200	0821-2410366, 2515655
Hotel Roopa	400-750	0821-2443770
Maurya Palace	465-635	0821-2435912
Railway Retiring rooms		
Belur		
Mayura Velapuri	135-200	08177-22209
Halebid		
Mayura Shantala	100-250	08177-73224

PLACES OF INTEREST NEARBY

Sravanabelagola: One of the most important Jain pilgrim centres in India is Sravanabelagola. It has a huge 17 m high monolithic statue of Lord Gomateshwara, also called Bahubali, over a thousand years old. Climbing up to the top using the steps provided is well worth the effort. Sravanabelagola is 93 km from Mysore and usually the first stop for tourist buses on the Sravanabelagola-Belur-Halebid circuit.

SREE CHAMUNDEESWARI
of Mysore

The female Trinity of Mahalakshmi, Parvathi and Saraswathi, complements the male Trinity of Hindu theology – Lord Vishnu, Siva and Brahma, and represents Wealth, Strength and Knowledge respectively. All of them symbolize the mother figure and often the 'garland of names' in their praise find the same attribute ascribed to all three.

In Parvathy or Ambal, the maternal and the powerful aspects are accentuated. Followers of the Sakthi cult hold Parvathy to be the main force in the universe. In her beneficent form, Parvathy appeared in the world as Kamakshi, Meenakshi, and Visalakshi and others. In her fierce form, she manifested as Kali, Mookambika, Chamundeeswari and others.

Goddess Chamundeeswari, who represents a fierce form of Eswari or Eswar's (Lord Siva's) consort, can be found in a small but famous hill shrine in Mysore. The legend of Chamundeeswari is recounted in the *Markandeya Purana*. (ancient Indian lore, which tell the stories of divine and semi-divine beings).

Indian mythology is rife with tales of how demons can acquire powers by performing rigorous penance and asking boons of the deities, they prayed to. One such was Mahishasura. Lord Brahma granted him a boon that no man or deity would be able to kill him. He began his reign of terror over both Earth and Heaven. The merciless Mahishasura went about killing and rampaging. He audaciously took out a strong army of demons and besieged the abode of the *devas* (celestials). In the form of a green-skinned buffalo, he led his army to victory against the God of the celestials, Indra. He also usurped Indra's throne and drove out all the *devas.*

The celestials went to Brahma, Siva and Vishnu and pleaded for help, but the supreme Trinity could not help them immediately because of Brahma's boon. The gods became angry, and according to one version, fire came forth from their faces. This fire coalesced to form a young woman, who was none other than Parvathy. Called Durga, Her face was from the light of Siva, her ten arms were from Lord Vishnu and her legs from Brahma.

Durga was given a trident with a spear-shaped tip by Siva, the disc by Lord Krishna, an incarnation of Vishnu, the conch by Varuna, the God of rain, and a missile by the God of Fire. From Vayu, the wind, she got arrows, the dispossessed Indra gave her the thunderbolt, and his white-skinned elephant Airavata, a bell. From Yama, the god of Death, Durga received a rod, and from the Ruler of the Waters she obtained a noose. And the god of the mountains gave her a majestic lion to ride on.

Soon she came to be noticed by Mahishasura, who wanted to wed this wondrous maiden. When his emissaries approached her, she said she would only marry the person who defeated her in battle. Amused, Mahishasura sent another emissary with promises of luxuries and a rich life. When she refused again, this demon Dumralochana, tried to drag her away by force. She burnt him with her powers. Then came the mighty demons, Chanda and Munda. She defeated them and earned the name Chamundeeswari. Then followed the demon kings Sumba and Nisumba, who were vassals of Mahishasura, with their armies. But they were no match for the maiden.

Mahishasura's pride was hurt, and exactly as planned by the Gods, he himself came out to battle. He thought his boon from Brahma would protect him, but had forgotten that it did not shield him from death at the hands of a woman. When he found his army exterminated by Durga, the demon entered the fray, changing his form frequently to bewilder his opponents. Durga soon realised the trick he was playing. She beheaded him in his form as a buffalo, from which emerged his original form. She then pierced his chest with the trident to rid both Heaven and Earth of the fearsome demon.

It is in this form, armed with dagger and serpent, that Mahishasura is seen outside the temple precincts in Mysore. The brightly painted statue can be seen as soon as you climb the hill on which the main shrine is located.

Chamundi Hill is a landmark in Mysore and can be seen as soon as the train pulls into the beautiful city. The drive up the 1000 foot high hill takes about 15 minutes. Others choose to climb up the 1000 steps that have been cut into the hill.

The hill houses many temples and small shrines. Chief among these is the Chamundeeswari temple and the Mahabaleswara temple alongside. The latter temple is said to be older, built by the Hoysala king Vishnu Vardhana, in the 12th century. Mahabaleswara is the name given locally for Lord Siva.

The exact date of the Chamundeeswari temple has not been ascertained. It is however known that the goddess is the presiding deity of the Wodeyar kings, who ruled the princely state of Mysore before India became independent. In 1573, King Chamaraja Wodeyar IV was struck by lightning while worshipping at the temple. He had a miraculous escape, only losing some of his hair! As a gesture of thanksgiving, he erected a *gopuram*. This tower stood till the early 19th century, when Maharaja Krishnaraja Wodeyar III decided to build a more ornate one, which is the tower we see today. The king also renovated the temple, completing the work in 1827. He and his consort stand as devoted sentinels outside the sanctum sanctorum.

The architecture is typically Dravidian with a pyramidal structure. It highlights fine sculpture and fretwork. Wooden pillars support the roof. Parapets with balustrades and cusped arches add to the beauty of the temple. The whole ambience is unique, with a breathtaking view of the city below.

The Wodeyar kings lavished their wealth to decorate the deity with gold ornaments, a golden lion throne, and gold armour. The goddess also wears a necklace of golden stars called *nakshatramalige,* inscribed with 30 *slokas* (verses) in Sanskrit.

The Muslim kings of Mysore, Haider Ali and Tippu Sultan were also said to have been devotees of Goddess Chamundeeswari.

On the way down, do not miss the small Siva temple in front of which is the famous 16 ft high and 23 ft long granite *Nandi* with exquisite carved bells around its neck. There is a deep cave near here. The bull was sculpted in granite during King Dodda Devaraja (1659-72)'s reign. One version says he also built the 1000 steps.

The erstwhile Wodeyar kings still carry on the tradition of honouring Chamundeeswari. During the 10-day festival of *Dusserah* in the month of September-October, the idol of the Goddess is taken in a grand procession on specially chosen elephants. This is also the most pleasant time to visit Mysore. The whole city is decorated with bright lights and festoons and you can actually see a real king taking part in the celebrations!

FAST FACTS

How to reach

Air	:	The nearest airport is Bangalore, 140 km away. The airport is on the other side of Bangalore, which means an extra few kilometres.
Rail	:	There are trains running through the day linking Bangalore, the capital of Karnataka to Mysore, 139 km away.
Road	:	Mysore can be easily accessed by road from Bangalore, 140 km away.
Local transport	:	Public transport is available. Taxis, auto rickshaws and quaint horse drawn carriages can be seen in Mysore in large numbers.
Season	:	Throughout the year.
Clothing	:	Cottons in summer. Winters can be a little chilly, calling for light woollens.
Languages spoken	:	Kannada, English, and Urdu.

Accommodation

	Tariff (INR)	Phone
Lalith Mahal Palace Hotel	5000-30,000	0821-2470470-76
Paradise	750-1200	0821-2410366, 2515655
Hotel Roopa	400-750	0821-2443770
Maurya Palace	465-635	0821-2435912

Railway Retiring rooms

PLACES OF INTEREST NEARBY

Mysore Palace: This palace is a fine example of the Indo-Saracenic style of architecture with domes, sprawling colonnades, arches and turrets. It was built in 1912. It has an exquisite collection of paintings and carvings. The Royal Golden Elephant Throne and the Durbar Hall should not be missed.

Brindavan Gardens: The Brindavan Gardens, which abut the Krishna Raja Sagar Dam on the River Cauvery, lie 19 km from Mysore. The specially installed fountains in different shapes and styles are illuminated in the evenings and on festival days. The dancing fountain is a pretty sight.

Mysore Zoo: Laid out with beautiful natural vegetation as a backdrop, the zoo has a good collection of animals. The lions are a sight for sore eyes, in their natural habitat with the barrier from the human visitor suitably far away.

Nagarhole: *Naga* means snake and *Hole* means stream. Nagarhole has streams snaking through it. The flora and fauna in the national park comprise teak, rosewood, sandal, silver oak, and elephant, panther, antelope, mouse deer, gaur and the giant flying squirrel. The best season to visit is June – October. It is 140 km from Mysore. The Kabini River Lodge, run by Jungle Lodges (a Karnataka government venture), offers visitors a unique experience of travelling in the jungle in jeeps organised by the resort. When there is water in the Kabini, boat rides are also offered. The package includes stay and food.

Biligirirangan Hills: Jungle Lodges runs a similar facility in the Biligiri Rangan Hills, but these are tents rather than cottages. These hills are more pristine in their lack of encroachment by humans. A rare visitor can spot a tiger, as we did, during a trip to Biligirirangan. There is a temple to Lord Ranganatha here, who is deemed the god of the local tribals, the Soligas. BR Hills are 90 km from Mysore.

Coorg: Known as Kodagu in Kannada, Coorg is a fascinating hill station in the Western Ghats. Situated at an elevation of 1525 m, it is the coffee county of India. It has cardamom and pepper plantations as well. The inhabitants of this region are called Kodavas. The nearest airport is Mangalore, 136 km away. The nearest railhead is Mysore, 120 km away. It is well connected to Bangalore, which is 270 km away. On the way to Kodagu, one should visit Talacauvery, the source of the river Cauvery, which is 47 km before the hill station on a branch road.

Nanjangud: The stately Nanjundeswara Temple is situated on the banks of the Kapila River. It is dedicated to Lord Siva, who consumed the poison (*nanju* in Kannada), which the serpent Vasuki spat out while the ocean was being churned by the *devas* and *asuras* in their quest for nectar. The temple is in the Dravidian style and is notable for its striking architecture. It is 23 km from Mysore.

HILLY ABODE OF NARAYANA

About two hours drive from Mysore, through narrow roads and up a hill, lies Melkote, a sacred Vaishnavite shrine that takes its name from the hill on which it is situated. The locals call it Yadugiri. It is more well known as Thirunarayanapuram. On the way upwards one can see more than 40 sacred ponds or *kulams*, most of which are dry now. In ancient times, however, bathing in all these *kulams* was said to confer salvation.

The ancient temple is very large and breathes history. The Hoysala king Bittadeva, built the temple in the 12th century. A Jain who embraced Vaishnavism after coming into contact with Saint Ramanuja, he built five shrines for Vishnu, known as the *Panchanarayana* temples. He later assumed the name Vishnu Vardhana. The temple also enjoyed the patronage of the Mysore Wodeyar kings and Tippu Sultan.

The temple has a pink coloured *gopuram* and lion's heads facing north, south, east and west. The pillars in the *mandapams* have ornate stone carvings, conforming to the Hoysala style of architecture.

Vishnu is said to have worshipped here before his *Dasavatara* incarnations. Rama too is believed to have offered prayers here. The main deity is Thirunarayana. The *utsavar* is called Sampathkumar, Chelva Pillai and Ramapriya as well. The goddess is Yadugiri Nachiyar or 'Goddess of the

Yadu Hill'. At the feet of the Lord are Bhoomidevi and Varanandhini.

Other *sannidhis* are for Ramanuja, who spent a good portion of his life on earth here, and Paramapadanada. Outside the temple are shrines to Desika, Manavala Mamuni and other *Acharyas*. On a hill overlooking the town is a separate Yoganarasimha temple of great antiquity, that you can reach after a climb on worn steps.

While none of the Azhwars or Vaishnavite saints have sung of this temple, Nammazhwar mentions Lord Thirunarayana in one of his *pasurams*. Ramanuja interpreted this as referring to Thirunarayana of Melkote. The town is peaceful and calm, almost like a village. The same family has been serving as chief priest at the shrine for many generations.

After *darshan*, the aged chief priest takes us to his home and gives us delicious *prasadam*. The cuisine of Melkote is quite unique. Unlike the rice *pongal* usually offered in other Vaishnavite shrines, *Ulundurai*, a savoury made from Black Gram is the speciality here. Another delightful sweet is the *Melkote Manoharam*.

Only once a year, during the famous *Vairamudi Seva*, do crowds congregate in Melkote. This festival, when the *utsavar* is adorned with a diamond-encrusted tiara, falls in the Tamil month of Panguni. The Mysore royal family is the patron for the festivities.

The legend behind this *Vairamudi Seva* says that once, Lord Narayana was lying on his serpent bed Adi Sesha, on the ocean of milk in Heaven. Virochana, the son of Prahlada, snatched the crown and vanished. Lord Narayana's divine vehicle Garuda, was despatched to recover it. Garuda waged war with Virochana, recovered the crown and planted it on the head of Lord Krishna, an incarnation of Narayana. Krishna found the crown did not fit him, and in turn, placed it on the head of the Rama idol he was worshipping. Garuda went to

Heaven and got permission for this from Lord Vishnu. As Garuda, who is also called Vainatheya, recovered the crown, it got the title *'Vainamudi'*. In time, this became *Vairamudi*, probably because of the diamonds encrusted in it.

Other fascinating stories say that Brahma gave Lord Rama an idol of Narayana for worship. The idol was passed on to Rama's son Kucha, who gave it as a wedding gift to his daughter Kanakamalika. Later, Raja Yadushekhara and his descendants, Vasudeva, Balarama and Krishna worshipped the idol.

Many other sacred associations are also mentioned. Lord Narayana is believed to have given *darshan* to Chandilya Maharishi here in the form of Lord Badri Narayana of Badrinath in the Himalayas. So, this place got the name Dakshina Badri. Those unable to go to Badrinath can worship here, contemplating the idol as Lord Badri Narayana.

Thirunarayanapuram with its serene and sacred atmosphere, is a temple that is truly special.

FAST FACTS

How to reach?

Air	:	The nearest airport is Bangalore, which is 150 km away.
Rail	:	Pandavapura, on the Mysore-Bangalore line, is 20 km away
Road	:	Mysore is 40 km away.
Local Transport	:	There is no local transport available here. Taking a tourist taxi from Mysore is the best option.
Season	:	Throughout the year.
Clothing	:	Cottons in summer and light woollens in winter.
Languages spoken	:	Some English and Kannada.

Accommodation

Mysore	*Tariff (INR)*	*Phone*
Lalith Mahal Palace Hotel	5,000-30,000	0821-2470470-76

Paradise	850-1200	0821-2410366, 2515655
Hotel Roopa	400-750	0821-2443770
Maurya Palace	465-635	0821-2435912

The unimaginable wonder that is
HAMPI

At some spots, there is a total sense of loss. In others, there is a sense of unbridled wonder. In yet others, a feeling of emptiness. And in many, a colossal feeling of the futility of human effort – the unstoppable cycle of creation and destruction. Where else can one experience this gamut of emotions except at Hampi?

Pillars and arches, carvings and niches, towers and trenches– are they ruins? Or relics? No, because, here your mind's eye can see a bejewelled queen emerging from her lotus-shaped home, or the saint poet Purandaradasa meditating on the banks of River Tungabhadra. King Krishnadevaraya worshipping at the 'Gram Dhal Ganesh' meant for the royals, or even a commoner praying at the 'Mustard Ganesh' meant for ordinary folk!

The ruins of Hampi are real. Any doubts and make your way straight to the musical pillars at the Vitthala temple. Your guide (yes, in Hampi it is better to have one!) will strike the pillars and ask you to put your ears to the cold stone. You will hear the seven notes of music *'sa re ga ma pa da ni'* the clang of the *kanjira*, the tinkle of the lute and the beats of the *mridangam*. Or proceed to the Virupaksha temple, the only major temple in the whole complex that is still in worship. Go to the spot where the temple builders have made a hole so that the shadow of the temple tower falls on the opposite wall upside down! "All those years ago they even knew the technique of the pinhole camera," the guide says, his tone still reflecting wonder after all the numerous tourists, students and visitors he must have taken around. Over 800 years ago, the architects of the pretty Lotus Mahal, had even devised a system of air conditioning for queens by installing pipes through the whole construction and running water through them!

There is only one thing to fear! By the time you reach the jewel of Hampi, the Vitthala temple, you are likely to be so tired that your bones might creak louder than the musical pillars! So take some time to study what there is to see and insist on your guide following the route suggested.

The best place to get knowledgeable guides, who will charge standard rates is at the Archaeological Survey of India Office at Kamalapura, a few kilometres from Hampi. Everyone in Hampi, from the guides to the ubiquitous guidebook vendors, the women selling fresh plantain fruit and the Lambadi tribals who spread out their beautiful mirror work handicrafts on the roadside, knows English! They also know Tamil and Telugu apart from their native Kannada!

Since Hampi has such plenty to offer, one option is to follow the path suggested by the ASI to visit its attractions.

Hampi is a short drive from Hospet in Bellary District of Karnataka. History tells us that it was the glorious capital of the Vijayanagar Empire, while legend identifies it thousands of years earlier as Kishkinta, the capital of the monkey kings who helped Lord Rama rescue Sita from her abductors. In the former incarnation, Hampi is known as Vijayanagara, while in the latter it is called Pampa. The ancient name for the Tungabhadra which lies on one side of Hampi, was Pampa. The word 'Hampi' is believed to be derived from the word 'Pampa'. Hampi is also called Vidyanagara, after the Sage Vidyaranya who played a major role in founding the city.

Legend says that when the monkey kings Vali and Sugriva, ruled Kishkinta, trouble arose between them and Vali drove his brother out. Sugriva took shelter along with Hanuman or Anjaneya in a hill called Matanga Parvatam, identified as a steep hill to the east of Hampi village on the south bank of the Tungabhadra.

Rama and Lakshmana, searching desperately for Sita, came to Kishkinta. Rama killed Vali, restored the kingdom to Sugriva and then stayed on the Malyavanta Hill while the monkeys went in search of Sita. This hill is located on the road to Kampili and has a Raghunatha temple with a large image of Rama. A mound of ash in the nearby village of Nimbapuram is believed to be the cremated remains of Vali, while a cave on the Tungabhadra's southern bank is believed to be the spot where Sita's jewels were hidden. With its numerous associations with the *Ramayana,* little wonder that Hampi is an important pilgrim centre to this day. In fact, many of the temples and other structures in Hampi communicate the story of the epic.

The story of Hampi is fascinating, especially the way it was built, literally stone by stone, by various rulers and kings stretching over a considerable period. Based on the discovery of neoliths and handmade pottery in excavations near the Vitthala temple, the ASI dates the history of the Hampi region to the Neolithic/Chalcolithic times. It is also surmised that the region was within the Asokan Empire, based on the recent discovery of some rock edicts in Bellary District. Excavations have also revealed a Brahmi inscription and a terracotta seal belonging to the 2nd century A D.

Among the dynasties, which ruled Hampi at various times were the Kadambas, the Chalukyas of Badami, Rashtrakutas, Chalukyas of Kalyani, the Hoysalas and the Yadavas. It is believed that feudal chiefs called Kampilis ruled Hampi before the ascent of the Vijayanagara dynasty. In the early 14th century, Kampili was the seat of an independent principality ruled by Kampiladeva. This king was defeated by Muhammadbin-Tughluq and the kingdom became a part of the Delhi Empire. Two brothers, Harihara and Bukka, who were treasury officers of Kampila, were taken to Delhi as prisoners. It is said they embraced Islam there. After a few years, when the Muslim governor of Kampili asked Delhi for help to control the many uprisings in the area, Harihara and Bukka were sent there. They restored order, gave up Islam, and broke off with Delhi, going on to establish the mighty Vijayanagar Empire.

At the instruction of their guru Vidyaranya, the 2 brothers set up the wonderful city of Vidyanagara or Vijayanagara and made it their capital. The city was completed by 1343 A D. Their crest was the boar and their signage was 'Virupaksha' since they considered themselves the deputies of God Virupaksha. The early Vijayanagara rulers belonged to the Sunga dynasty. Some of the earliest monuments in the capital city date back to the times of Bukka's son, Harihara II. The fortifications and irrigation works were built during the reign of Bukka himself and later his grandson Devaraya I. Devaraya II also made a notable contribution by way of sculpture and architecture, but his successors were weak. The Saluva dynasty took over and later the Tuluva dynasty, to which the famous king Krishnadeva Raya belonged.

The Krishna Temple, the massive Narasimha figure, parts of the Pampati temple, and the embellishments to the Vitthala and Hazara Rama temples – these were some of Krishna Deva Rayas' magnificent achievements. Many foreign travellers who visited Vijayanagara during his reign have described the glory of the capital. The king's successors also made additions to existing structures, besides building new ones. This continued till the kingdom was taken over by the Aravidu dynasty.

One of Aravidu kings, Rama Raya, antagonised the Deccan sultanates and this resulted in war in 1565. Rama Raya was defeated and the Muslims plundered and looted Hampi. Most of its buildings and monuments were left in ruins, and others defaced in parts. It is said that it is the moon in the insignia that saved the Virupaksha temple, which alone seems to have survived the Muslim onslaught (as the crescent moon was sacred to the Muslims).

Most of the monuments in Hampi belong to Vijayanagara times, while some are of earlier origin. The ASI classifies the architecture in Hampi and surrounding areas into three types – religious, civil and military buildings.

On the way to Hampi from Hospet, the first feature that strikes the eye is the **Domed Gate.** Around 18 m high, it was one of the main entrances to the city from the east and the south. Square in appearance, it has 4 large four-centred arches. There is scrollwork, in stucco on the edge and apex of the arches and medallions in the spandrels. Above the arches, there is a cubical portion, then a round drum, which supports a large dome (from which the name is derived). To the right of the entrance, on the fort wall, there is a guardroom shaped like a pillared veranda. There is also a large bas-relief depicting a chief or king worshipping a *lingam*.

You then pass through **Bhima's Gate,** its name derived from a sculpted 17 m tall figure of Bhima that is complemented by a bas-relief of Bhima killing Kichaka. In this whole area, one can see **Citadel Walls.** Next comes the southeast entrance gate in the citadel wall, through which you enter a large open space in front of the Palace Buildings.

The Queen's Bath looks plain from the outside, but go in and you can marvel at the ornate corridors and balconies inside. The bath itself is 1.8 m deep and 15 m square. On the ceilings are vestiges of stuccowork.

Among several in the **King's Palace Enclosure,** the most striking monument is the **Mahanavami Dibba,** which used to play a major role in the 9 day *Navaratri* festival celebrations. Believed to have been put up after Krishna Deva Raya's victorious campaign in Orissa (therefore also called Throne Platform or House of Victory), records say that it was a beautifully painted and decorated pillared hall of several storeys. What you see now is a huge granite-faced base in 3 tiers, whose walls are covered with carved, horizontal friezes of horses, elephants, warriors, dancers and musicians.

The western side has steps, which the king used to ascend the platform. Dark green chlorite can be seen on parts of the western side. On the east side, there is a small chamber projecting from the platform. The chamber walls are filled with friezes and panels of animals and clowns. With conical caps, plaited hair and swords, there is also a group of people believed to be members of a visiting Chinese embassy at the Vijayanagara court. There are also Arab horse dealers and exotic animals.

Other monuments of note in this enclosure are a **Large Tank**, **Base** of the **King's Palace, Underground Chamber** and **King's Audience Hall.**

To the northwest of the King's Palace Enclosure lies the **Hazara Rama Temple**. As there is no idol in the sanctum sanctorum, this temple is not in worship. The striking feature is the ornate *ardhamandapam*, whose outer walls are richly carved with bas-reliefs depicting scenes from the Ramayana. Four black stone pillars with intricate carvings stand at the centre of the *ardhamandapam*. On these can be seen bas-reliefs of Ganesa, Mahisasuramardhini, Anjaneya and several forms of Vishnu.

There are two sancta sanctorum, one to the Lord and another to the goddess. The former has a *vimanam* in three storeys. The projection of the super structure is deemed to be in typical Chalukyan style. The two-storeyed shrine to the goddess, though smaller, is more ornate. The different parts of the temple were built over a period, starting from the early Vijayanagara period to the time of Krishna Deva Raya.

There are two explanations offered for the name of the temple. One is that *Hazara Rama* refers to the 'temple of the thousand Ramas' (*Hazar* in Hindi means 1000). This is a reference to the numerous bas-reliefs of Lord Rama in the temple complex. The other explanation is that the name is *Hajara Rama,* because it was the palace temple. *Hajaramu* in Telugu, means audience hall or entrance hall of a palace. Either way, this temple should not be missed!

From this temple one can enter the royal **Mint**, a large walled area with several entrances and impressive fortifications. There has been a lot of excavation here in recent times, revealing structures belonging to three phases of the Vijayanagara period. Of note are some fragmentary Brahmi inscriptions of the 2nd century A D. The excavations have also thrown doubt as to whether it is accurate to describe this whole area as the King's Palace, since indications are that it was not a residential area.

To the north of the above area is the **Danaik's enclosure**, with evidence of several partitions. Danaik is believed to be an adaptation of the word *Dandanayaka* meaning Commander-in-Chief. Among the structures of note here is a huge and ornate palace base constructed in 3 tiers to the southwest. To the southeast is an interesting structure that is known as a mosque. A large, high-pillared hall open on one side, its ceiling has 9 large inverted apsidal domes. The ornamental motifs are, however, Hindu in type. The Danaik's enclosure has imposing watchtowers built around it. Two of the towers still stand though damaged. One of these, a massive square tower, is called the Muhammadan watchtower.

Striking features of this women's enclosure or **Zenana Enclosure** are the Lotus Mahal, the women's guards' quarters and the elephant stables. The women's guards' quarters is interesting because it is low-ceilinged and has no windows or other doors apart from the entrance. The interior comprises a large rectangular space with a pillared corridor on all four sides. Arches and pillars are the only relief in this otherwise bare structure.

The **Lotus Mahal,** known locally as the Chitrangi Mahal, is a pretty structure from which royal women used to witness celebrations and processions. The two-storeyed building has intricate work with sharp edged awnings, crenellated arches and tiered facades. The base is elaborate and the top comprises three-tiered *shikaras*. The interior today seems comparatively plain, with clear spaces. At the centre, the roof has a lotus bud as decoration, giving the *mahal* its name. The finish of the walls is smooth and the stuccowork has remnants of paintings undertaken centuries ago for the joy of the queen. With a number of arched balconies and windows, the edifice is a good example of the blend of Islamic, Hindu and Jain architecture styles. The structure is once believed to have had an elaborate network of pipes to carry water to keep the interiors cool!

Just outside the Zenana enclosure, to the south, lie the **Elephant Stables.** The massive structure extends from one end to another with a number of arched entrances each crowned with a domed ceiling. The ribbed domes which resemble cupolas, are reminiscent of the Muslim style of architecture. There are 11 huge stalls for the elephants. The interiors are bare with sandy floors and chain hooks from the roof. One can almost visualise a looming elephant swaying from side to side in the large caverns!

Some of the marvellous structures that lie on the road from Kamalapuram to Hampi include the **Uddhana Virabhadra Temple,** one of the few temples where worship is still carried on. The four-armed Virabhadra, with arrow, bow shield and sword, stands 3.6 m tall. A small idol of Daksha can be seen to the right of the God. There is an inscription in the temple, which dates the Virabhadra idol to 1545 A D.

Walking through a green patch, you suddenly come upon the fierce mien of the God who incarnated on earth as a man-lion, **Lakshmi Narasimha**. The idol is mutilated but no less impressive for that. Carved from a single boulder by a Brahmin under the patronage of Krishnadeva Raya in 1528, the figure is 6.7 m high. The arched canopy over the figure and the seven-hooded sculpture of Adi Sesha are arresting. It is said that the idol in its original form had Goddess Lakshmi seated on Narasimha's lap.

The **Krishna Temple** originally had an image of Balakrishna brought from Udayagiri by Krishnadevaraya in 1513. It does not have an idol in worship now, but is an excellent example of the Vijayanagara style of temple architecture with large halls and *prakarams* and elevated shrines. The temple has a number of sub-shrines. There is a remarkable carving of the *Dasavataras* (10 incarnations) of Vishnu on a pillar. Unlike other depictions where the last incarnation, Kalki is seen riding a horse, here He is shown in a seated posture with the head of a horse. There is also a stucco figure of Subramanya in this temple, noteworthy since this is a Saivite idol in a Vaishnavite temple. To the northwest of the sanctorum is a shrine to the goddess. Close to the temple there is a stone with a carving of a fish, which indicates the presence of a water source nearby. Its size is also said to indicate the proximity of the tank or well.

Remarkable for their majestic sculpture and beauty are the two images of Ganesha, called **Mustard Ganesha** or *Sasivekalu* and **Gram Ganesha** or *Kadalekalu*. The images are massive, 2.4 and 4.5 m high respectively. Both however bear the scars of mutilation. The *Kadalekalu* is said to be the largest Ganesha in India. The Mustard Ganesha is said to have been worshipped by the common folk and the Gram Ganesha by royal personages (since the price of gram dhal was high compared to mustard, which was associated with the economically weaker class).

The most important shrine in Hampi is the **Virupaksha Temple** and it bears the insignia of the royal rulers of Vijayanagara. The main deity is Virupaksha (Siva) or Pampapathy. He is the Lord of Pampa (the original name of the Tungabhadra river, the daughter of Brahma).

The temple has an imposing appearance with its white hued, 9 storeyed 52 m high *gopura*. The base and the first tier are made of stone while the superstructure is of brickwork. The temple has a large outer court with a number of sub-shrines housed in pillared *mandapams*. The Hampa or Pampa Devi shrine is important as it is after her that the name Hampi was derived.

An outstanding feature is that a narrow channel of water from the Tungabhadra flows along the terrace of the temple to descend to the temple kitchen. The sanctum sanctorum of Virupaksha faces the east and the *mandapam* around it has a number of paintings from the life of the Vijayanagara kings. The sanctum enshrines the well-known Virupaksha *lingam*. There are also images of Narasimha, Mahishasuramardhini and sage Vidyaranya. You can also see the inverted image of the *gopuram* falling through a hole on the wall behind the Hampa Devi shrine.

Just outside the Virupaksha temple, is the broad **Hampi Bazaar** with its large collection of hotels and restaurants, which not only offer vegetarian delicacies of north and south India but also Lebanese, Tibetan and Mediterranean cuisine. In this busy road, you can visualise how the many bazaars of Hampi, the features of the Vijayanagara kingdom's thriving economy, must have functioned in olden times. Today, these are all just ruins.

In this area, one can also see the **Octagonal Water Pavilion**, which is an octagonal hall with an octagonal dome shaped roof. It has a fountain basin at the centre and a massive monolithic trough. Outside the pavilion, there are remains of earthen water pipes, which were used to supply water to the tank.

Adjacent is the **Bhojana Shala,** (communal dining hall). It is an L-shaped channel paved with granite stones and inlaid with chlorite slabs. There are also depressions, which act as table cum plate for a diner.

The **Siva Temple** next to the walled enclosure of Lakshmi Narasimha, is ancient. It has an enormous 3 m high *lingam* with its base permanently immersed in water.

Finally we come to the structures and shrines along the banks of the Tungabhadra. There are numerous temples dedicated to a number of Hindu gods and goddesses. Apart from the famous Vitthala temple, this part of Hampi is notable for its many temples to Lord Rama and places associated with the *Ramayana*.

Among them are the **Kondandarama Temple,** the **Rama Temple** and the **Malyavanta Raghunatha Temple.** The first has a huge relief of Rama, Sita and Lakshmana carved on a boulder. There is also a shrine with a figure of Hanuman, who is known as Yantrodaraka Anjaneya. This is because the idol is surrounded by a circular *yantra*. Just opposite is the *Chakratirtha*, considered the most sacred bathing ghat in the river. Nearby is a temple to Suryanarayana. The deity here is Sudarshana with 16 hands.

The Rama temple is the only Vaishnava shrine in Hampi in the Kadamba style with a pyramidal super-structure. There are bas-reliefs of Garuda, Gajalakshmi and Dwarapalas. Opposite is the Sugriva cave where Sita's jewels were said to have been stored. The Malyavanta Raghunatha temple is situated on Malyavantha hill, to the east of the Vitthala temple and has large seated images of Rama and Sita, with a kneeling Hanuman.

The **Vitthala Temple** stands on the southern banks of the Tungabhadra and belongs to the 15th century A D. This temple is the apogee of Vijayanagara architecture, and it is no exaggeration to say it has no comparison in its exquisite combination of the art of sculpture and the science of auditory acoustics. Sited within a large rectangular enclosure, it has a number of pillared *mandapams*. The temple is dedicated to Vishnu as Vitthala (Krishna) and faces east. There are conflicting views whether this temple was ever completed and consecrated. However, epigraphic evidence suggests that this temple was in worship for some time.

As you enter the temple, your eyes are riveted to a stone chariot that is so beautifully carved that it looks life-like. The chariot is the virtual trademark of Hampi, and the stone wheels still rotate, a standing testimony to the level to which Vijayanagara civilization had raised the craft of sculpture. It houses an image of Vishnu's mount Garuda, who faces the temple. The brick superstructure which forms the pyramidal top of the chariot, is absent.

The temple has a large *mahamandapam*, based upon an intricately sculpted platform. It has 56 musical pillars with figures of dancers and musicians sculpted on them, which produce sounds or notes of distinct musical instruments when they are tapped upon. There was even a time when the sound of the music could be heard upon the hilltop a mile away! It is said that all the pillars were sculpted out of one block of stone and thus form a monolithic sculptural group. While the pillars on the outer periphery are slender, those inside are of the *yali* type and stouter. One of the pillars is broken, apparently because an English collector of the area wanted to see if there was any musical instrument hidden inside the pillars!

The *mandapam* houses the *garba griham* or the sanctum sanctorum and has a number of other shrines. There are many exquisite carvings on the roof. The shrine is a treasure trove of sculpted forms that include reliefs of animals and humans.

Here too one can find a bas-relief of the *Dasavatara* of Vishnu, with Kalki being depicted as a standing figure with the head of a horse. Behind the Vitthala temple is the **Purandaradasa Mandapa**, commemorating the great composer who, seated by the river, wrote many a song in praise of Lord Krishna.

Hampi is indeed the Horn of Plenty!

FAST FACTS

How to reach

Air	:	The nearest airport is Bangalore, 339 km away.
Rail	:	The nearest railhead is Hospet, on the Bangalore-Hubli route. One can also approach Hospet from Guntakal.
Road	:	Hampi is 15 km from Hospet. State transport buses are available from Hospet to Hampi.
Local Transport	:	Cycles can be hired to go around Hampi. Tourist taxis and auto rickshaws are available.
Season	:	Through the year. It is better to visit when temperatures are cooler as extensive outdoor activity is involved.
Clothing	:	Tropical, light cottons.
Languages Spoken	:	English, Kannada, Telugu and Tamil.

Accommodation

Hospet:	*Tariff (INR)*	*Phone*
Hotel Malige, Hospet 583201 E-mail: *malligihome@hotmail.com*	400-2250	08394-428101
Shan bag Towers International Hospet E-mail: *shanbhagtowers@yahoo.com*	450-550	08394-425910 to 425917
Hotel Nagarjuna Residency	400-1000	08394-429009
Hotel Priyadarshini	550-750	08394-427313
Hotel Karthik	250-1200	08394-425639

At Hampi

Hotel Mayura Bhuvaneswari (KSTDC hotel)
Kamalapura, (Near Hampi)   350-825   08394-441574
Bellary District.

A number of dharamshalas are available at Hampi.

Nearby Attractions

Tungabhadra Dam: This massive dam built by the great engineer Visveswarayya is a magnificent sight. Standing 49 m high, the 2 km long dam stores a huge expanse of water, which extends for miles and miles. Beneath is a beautiful garden with fountains that are illuminated by power generated from the hydroelectric power project. It is 6 km from Hospet and one requires special permission from the Superintending Engineer, Tungabhadra Dam, Hospet, 583201, to go up to the dam. It has two lovely guesthouses, 'Vaikuntam' and 'Kailasam'.

ASI museum, Kamalapuram: This museum has 4 galleries. Two of these are devoted to sculptures of Siva and Vishnu. The other two depict armaments and recent additions. The museum also has a colourful map depicting the whole of Hampi and it would be useful to study it for a while before embarking on a tour.

Anegondi: This is on the north bank of the Tungabhadra, opposite Hampi. It has a fort and can be accessed by crossing the river on basket boats. The birthplace of Hanuman is said to be nearby. The ruins consist of temples in the Chalukyan and Vijayanagara styles. There is a road route too, around 45 km long.

Anantasayanagudi: Located 1.6 km from Hospet, this is a huge Vishnu temple.

Mookambiga at Kollur
TRISHAKTHI

The first thing that is visible as one enters the sacred shrine of Mookambika at Kollur is the golden *vimanam* of the temple. More reminiscent of the Kerala style of architecture though located in Karnataka, the temple is unique as the Goddess here represents all the three forms of *Shakthi* — Lakshmi, Saraswathi and Parvathi.

The vision of the goddess resplendent in her silken apparel and adorned in the most rare and purest of gems serene is dazzling. In front of the *vigraham* is the *swayumbhu swarnarekha lingam,* where the male Trinity of Hinduism is said to be in *arupa* (formless) form. *Abhishekams* (oblations) are performed only to the *lingam.*

The *vigraham* is decorated daily for the various *pujas*. It is a matter of good fortune to have *darshan* of goddess Mookambika who is in *padmasana* posture on a lion. She bears the *shankhu* (conch) and the *chakra* (discus), unique in a Devi *vigraham* because they are the insignia of Lord Vishnu. Her other two hands are in the *abhaya* and *varada* postures. On Her right is a gold sword in a silver scabbard, (endowed to the temple by the late Chief Minister of Tamil Nadu, M G Ramachandran).

After *darshan*, the *prakaram* is to be circled thrice and the devotee should then pray to the goddess again for her blessings. After the initial *darshan*, devotees are asked to sit along with family members to do *sankalpa* (determination) for the noon *puja*. The priest utters the sacred names of the goddess and the devotees repeat this. The rice given in the hands is then poured into a common plate. The *puja* is performed and *prasad* is given.

Devotees with small children perform *vidyarambam* or *aksharabyasam* (ritual commencement of learning) in the Saraswati *mandapam* on the northern precincts of the temple. This is an initiation ritual, where Goddess Mookambika is said to bless her devotees with good skills of learning and writing and speech. It was in this *mandapam* that Adi Sankara composed the immortal *Soundarya Lahari*.

On the northern side of the temple are the shrines of Prana Lingeswara, Pratheswara, Panchamukha Ganapathy, Chandramouleeswara and Nanjundeswara. On the eastern side behind the main sanctum sanctorum is the Sankara Peetam with a seated figure of Adi Sankara. There are also shrines to Vishnu and Anjaneya.

On the western side of the temple courtyard is seen the awe-inspiring Kudajathri hills, on which Adi Sankara is said to have performed penance. The hills can be seen in the distance from the undulating single road, which takes you from National Highway NH17 to Kollur. There are thick forests on either side of the road, periodically giving way to clearings with small collection of dwellings.

It was Adi Sankara who had a vision of Mookambika and translated it into the *moolavar* and *utsavar* idols with the aid of a sculptor hailing from the lineage of Viswakarma, the divine architect. The flooring of the outer *prakaram*, the sanctum sanctorum's walls, halls, pillars and roof are all in granite, the contribution of the Salivahanas. The tower and interiors are in the Kerala style of architecture, built by one Benganna Samandar of the Bengi lineage. Various kings from Kerala endowed the temple with lands, gold and diamonds.

According to legend, the goddess is called Mookambika as she struck the demon Kamhasura *muka* (dumb) when he was about to ask for the boon of immortality from Siva. She also vanquished the powerful demon Mahishasura, nephew of Kamhasura, who had obtained a boon from Siva that no male could kill him. He disrupted the penance of Kola Munivar, who was performing *pujas* to the *lingam*. The sage prayed intensely to Ambal (Parvathy), who incarnated as Thrisoolanayaki. With Veerabhadra's assistance, the battle began and the demon was vanquished.

The village of Kollur is, named after Kola Munivar who was shown the *swarnarekha lingam* by none other than Isvara. When the saint asked Siva how he could worship Isvara without Devi, He is supposed to have said that on the left side of the *lingam* were all the three manifestations of Devi – Lakshmi, Saraswati and Parvathi.

Every day, following the noon *puja*, there is free feeding of devotees. After the last *puja* at night, devotees are given a concoction called *kashayam*, which is beneficial to one's health.

There are a number of rivers on the way to Kollur, of which the most important are Souparnika and its tributary Agnitheertham, which lie close to the temple. Along the route from Mangalore, there are beautiful rivers with beautiful names – the Seetha, Haladi, Tallur, Netravathi.

There is another temple on the left of the narrow road leading to the Mookambika temple from the national highway – the Lakshmi Venkatramana Temple. The shrine, located in Kechanaru village, cannot be seen from the road and comes into view as you walk down a tree-lined avenue. Here, the *vigraham* is in black stone with a *Dasavatara* frame. The temple has a beautiful chariot with intricate carvings. The priest and his family who live in a house adjoining the temple, offered us lunch in a spontaneous gesture. Their simplicity and warmth amazed us city folk.

FAST FACTS

How to reach

Air	:	The nearest airport is Mangalore, 147 km away.
Rail	:	The most convenient railhead is Mangalore, though there are other small stations closer such as Udupi on the Konkan railway.
Road	:	Mangalore is 147 km away. Kollur can be reached using NH17, which extends from Kochi to Mumbai. Mulki, Padubidri and Kaup are some towns en route apart from the famous temple town, Udupi. There is a signboard at a place called Vanse, where one turns right for Kollur. The distance from the turn is 38 km.
Local Transport	:	There is no local transport in Kollur. It is best to take a tourist taxi from Mangalore. Other choices are tourist buses and public buses.
Season	:	The road to Kollur becomes difficult to navigate during the monsoon from July to end August if there is very heavy rain. Otherwise the climate is pleasant.
Clothing	:	Cottons with a shawl in case the weather turns chilly. Carry an umbrella.
Languages spoken	:	English and Kannada.

Accommodation

Mangalore	*Tariff (INR)*	*Phone*
Taj Manjarun	1200-2500 (+10%)	0824-2420420
Moti Mahal	450-1800 (+10%)	0824-2441411
Pooja International	500-950 (+10%)	0824-2440171

NEARBY ATTRACTIONS

Anegudde: On the way to Kollur from Mangalore, before Udupi, an impressive arch announces the entrance to the Vinayaka temple of Anegudde at Kumbhashi. *Anegudde* means 'elephant hillock' and the idol here is said to be a *swayambhu* who manifested in *Dwapara Yugam*. The temple is like a note of music — subtle yet strong, soothing yet powerful. The sanctum sanctorum with the majestic figure of Vinayaka resplendent in silver armour, in standing posture, can be seen from the entrance. Most striking is the very large head of the God with huge ears. Two of the four arms are *varada hastam* indicating his quality of granting boons. Two hands point to his feet, as a means to salvation. *Tulabharam* (offering made with a physical balance) is frequent here. This is a *Parasurama kshetram*. The *prasad* here, as in most temples in this area, is the *panchyagajya* – a mixture of pulses, sugar, copra, milk and honey. All around the shrine there are sculpted depictions from the *Bhargava Purana*. There is a guesthouse for pilgrims. At noon the temple provides food.

Serenity in
SRIRANGAPATNAM

Srirangapatnam is a place that never palls. Whether it is the beatific idol of Lord Ranganatha or the beautiful and serene Cauvery river flowing by, it draws the devotee time and again. Even more wonderful is the fact that the Muslim king Tipu Sultan, used to pray here. Both Tipu and his father Hyder Ali, had great faith in Lord Ranganatha and the temple witnessed significant growth during their reign. Seringapatam, as the British called it, was their capital before Tipu had to submit to the British in the late 18th century.

Shrines of Lord Ranganatha are invariably found on islands on the Cauvery. Srirangapatnam, which lies closest to the origins of the river at Talacauvery, is known as *Adhi Ranga*. Near Sivasamudram is a little known temple called *Madhya Ranga*. The idol here is different from the others as it is small and painted. *Anta Ranga* or the 'final' Ranganatha is found in Srirangam. Known as Srirangapuri or Lathoshyanapuri in Sanskrit, Srirangapatnam is enclosed by the river on all four sides.

Mother Cauvery is said to have sought and obtained three boons from Lord Ranganatha here, according to legend. First, that she should be equal in praise to the river Ganga, second that the place should become an acclaimed shrine, and third that devotees should be granted whatever they wish for when they pray at the temple. According the *Puranas*, the Ganga, in whose waters people bathe to rid themselves of their sins, mixes with the Cauvery once a year to regain her purity.

The legend says that Sage Gautama, who was known for his hospitality, was living on the banks of the river Godavari with his disciples, when some sages who came from a drought-stricken area hatched a plot against him. They hoped to drive him away. With their powers, they created a cow. When Gautama's disciples drove away the cow from the paddy fields, it fell at the sage's feet and died. Immediately the sages who wanted to supplant him raised a hue and cry that he had killed the cow. Gautama, who, in his wisdom knew what had happened, cursed the sages and embarked on a *theerthayatra* (visiting pilgrim centres). After praying at several places, he came to worship at Thennarangam (Srirangam).

The Lord appeared before him and bade him pray at Adhi Ranga, where Vibhishana had worshipped. After a long search, Gautama arrived at Srirangapatnam. He conducted a big *yagna* there. Mahavishnu appeared before him and said that he was residing in a huge anthill in a *tulsi* garden.

As per the sages' pleas, the divine cow Kamadhenu dissolved the anthill with it's milk. The idol of Ranganatha was found! That day was in the month of Chitrai (April 15th – May 15th), *sukla paksham, saptami thithi* (seventh day of the waxing phase of the moon) and it continues to be celebrated as *Sriranga Jayanthi*.

The Gangas built the original temple in the 9th century A D. The majestic *gopuram* is dated around 849 A D. The *gopuram* and *vimanam* have features of the Pandya style too. Three hundred years later, the temple was embellished. The architecture became a combination of the Hoysala and Vijayanagara styles. Timmanna, a viceroy of Vijayanagar, enlarged the temple in 1454. Vishnu Vardhana, the great Hoysala king, invited Saint Ramanujacharya to settle at Srirangapatnam.

Saint Ramanuja has a major presence in this area, as Thondanur, where he built a huge tank and stayed for some years, is only about 20 km away.

The goddess here is Ranganayaki. There is also a beautiful idol of Lord Srinivasa to the right of the main shrine, while facing the latter. The granite idol of Lord Ranganatha reclining on Adi Sesha is awe-inspiring. As always, the *pada darshanam* is all-important. On a festival day, the idol is smeared with butter and decorated with tutti-fruity, delighting the devotees.

On the express train route from Bangalore to Mysore, Srirangapatnam is what is known as an operational halt. Those in the know can quickly jump off the train and make their way to the temple, which is close to the railway station.

FAST FACTS

How to reach

Air	:	The nearest airport is Bangalore, 125 km away.
Rail	:	Srirangapatnam lies on the rail route from Bangalore to Mysore.
Road	:	Srirangapatnam is 14 km north of Mysore.
Local Transport	:	Tourist taxis, auto rickshaws and cycle rickshaws are available.
Season	:	Throughout the year.
Clothing	:	Cottons in summer, light woollens in winter.
Languages spoken	:	English and Kannada.

Accommodation

Mysore	*Tariff (INR)*	*Phone*
Lalith Mahal Palace Hotel	5000-30,000	0821-2470470-76
Paradise	50-1200	0821-2410366, 2515655
Hotel Roopa	400-750	0821-2443770
Maurya Palace	465-635	0821-2435912

Railway Retiring rooms

Places of interest nearby

Thondanur: Thondanur, 20 km away, is where the Hoysala king Vishnu Vardhana built two temples in the early 12th century. Originally from the

Jain Community, he became a Vaishnavite after Saint Ramanuja cured his daughter of a terrible ailment. Actually a complex of two temples, the deities are Nambi Narayanar, Parthasarathy, Kannan and Yoga Narasimhar. The goddesses are Aravindavalli, Rukmini and Mahalakshmi. Saint Ramanuja built a huge tank here. Any autorickshaw or taxi driver in Srirangapatnam will take you here.

Monuments related to Hyder Ali and Tippu Sultan: Tippu built a large mosque here called the Jama Masjid. He also constructed an ornate summer palace. The mausoleum where Hyder Ali and Tippu are interred is called the Gol Gumbaz. Srirangapatnam is a fort town.

Ranganthittu Bird Sanctuary: On the backwaters of the Cauvery river, this sanctuary is a delight for bird lovers. The mangrove forests are an ecological delight. There are arrangements to take a pleasurable cruise in the waters on country boats for a small fee, and take a closer look at the birds perched on treetops. The white ibis, open bill stork, night heron and egret are some of the birds that can be spotted here. Many of them come from Siberia. The season is June – February. The sanctuary is 4 km from Srirangapatnam.

Mysore: Mysore and all its delights are near Srirangapatnam. See the chapter on Chamundeeswari Temple for details.

Sri Saradambal of
SRINGERI

The rain beat down on the sides of car and the driver had to navigate the narrow ghat road with all his skills. Very little could be seen on either side except for the swinging branches of huge trees silhouetted against the darkening sky. It was monsoon time and perhaps the wrong season to go to Sringeri, which lies on a valley in the Western Ghats. But it had been decided to leave cracker-smoke filled Madras for the Diwali festival and it was too late to turn back.

As the road twisted and turned, the distant Kudremukh hills, that had dominated the horizon a few minutes ago, were hidden from the view by a thick blanket woven by the waters of the monsoon. The taxi driver, who was a local and quite unfazed, guaranteed that he would take us from Mangalore to Sringeri in four hours flat. Four hours seemed an eternity in that situation.

Sringeri is the place where where Adi Sankara lived for 12 years and set up his first *matha* or seat. To pray at the shrine of Goddess Saradambha and take a dip in the holy waters of the Tunga is the wish of many devotees. *Sringeri* in Sanskrit, actually means 'snake and frog'. It is believed that it was here that Sankara saw the rare sight of a hooded King Cobra giving shade to a pregnant frog, saving it from the burning rays of the sun. He therefore chose this mountain location for establishing a *Peeta* (Seat), for he felt that a place which makes the worst of enemies help each other is where a temple for the Goddess should come up.

We had seen a King Cobra flash across the road on our drive to Sringeri. The taxi driver, who brought the vehicle to a halt, told us, "It is very lucky to see a King Cobra in this area. Sringeri is the place where the cobra and the frog lived together in peace".

Sringeri is also interpreted as *Shrnka Giri*, which means 'mountain shaped like a question mark'. In the vernacular, the word *Sringeri* is derived from the Rishyasringa Hill nearby. The story of the *rishi* called Rishyasringa is told in the *Mahabaratha*. The son of *rishi* Vibahndaka, he lived with his father in Sringeri. He brought rain to the parched lands of king Romapada. King Dasaratha of Ayodhya is believed to have invited Rishyasringa to officiate in the ceremony he performed to beget progeny. There is a temple dedicated to the *rishi* in Kigga near Sringeri. The Siva *lingam* here has a horn at the top.

Sringeri is a small town and the Sankara Mutt is its pivot. From the window of the rest house at the Mutt, you can see the river and behind the waters, the unbroken rain forest forming a dark green backdrop. A bath in the refreshing and clean waters of the Tunga is said to be equivalent to *Ganga snanam* (bathing in the holy river Ganges).

The temple is very ancient, set on a huge expanse. It is said that Adi Sankara built the temple virtually single-handed. The first shrine as you enter is the one dedicated to Lord Siva. Then you go on to the shrine of Goddess Saradamba, who is both beatific and beautiful. She represents *Sowkhyam* (bliss) and *Shantham* (peace).

On the way out, you can see the *samadhis* of the various *Peetadipathis* (pontiffs) of Sringeri. At the dining hall all visitors are given divine-tasting food. We spent the afternoon having *darshan* of the present Sringeri

Sankaracharya, Sri Bharathi Theertha Swami. The walk to his quarters *Narasimha Vana* across a lovely garden, and the sight of a new suspension bridge across the Tunga which rises high in the hills and flows through Sringeri was memorable.

The Sri Saradha temple in Sringeri, a striking example of south Indian temple architecture, was originally a simple structure erected by Adi Sankara in which the sandalwood *vigraham* of the goddess was installed and worshipped. It was Sri Vidyaranya, the 12th *Acharya*, who renovated the temple and installed the gold *vigraham* of Sri Saradhambhal that abides in the temple at present. The tiled roof that he established in the 14th century stood till 1907 when the 33rd *Acharya* decided to put a more substantial edifice in place. The work he began was completed by his successor who performed the *kumbhabhishekam* (ceremonial cleansing performed by pouring holy water on the finials or *kumbhas*) in 1916.

Adi Sankara originally installed the image of Goddess Sarada over a *Sri Chakra* engraved on a rock on the left bank of the river Tunga. Sarada here represents the aspect of the Supreme Absolute. She displays in her hands a jar full of nectar, symbolising immortality, a book signifying the highest knowledge, a rosary with the beads denoting the *bijas* (seeds) from which the gross forms of the universe emanated and the *chinmudra* displaying the identity of the *jiva* (the soul) with *Brahman* (Godhead). You can have *darshan* of the eight-armed Mahishasuramardhini and Rajarajeswari inside the temple hall. The three-tiered *gopuram* was added by Sri Bharathi Theertha Swami.

On the southern *prakaram* of the temple is the Silver *Peeta* also known as the *Vyakyana Simhasanam* (throne of discourse). While normally the seat is adorned by the *vigraham* of Sri Saradha, on the day a new *Acharya* becomes the disciple of the *Mahasannidhanam*, the disciple is seated on the *Simhasana* and is said to represent Vidyadevi.

The complex also houses the temple of Sri Vidyasankara or Lord Siva. Known for its architectural excellence, it was built in 1346 A D in a confluence of Dravidian and Hoysala styles. It contains, on finely carved stones, the essence of the Yoga *sastras*, astronomy and every other subject of practical interest. The *gopuram* of the temple resembles a recumbent elephant with a raised trunk. This is also the *adhishtanam* (final resting place) of the tenth *Acharya* of Sringeri.

The main hall of the temple has 12 pillars on which are marked the 12 signs of the zodiac. A unique feature is that the rays of the sun fall on them in the order of the solar months with only one pillar being lit up by the sun's rays each month.

The Mutt compound, which houses these temples, also has a shrine to Maha Vishnu or Janardhana. The temple of Adi Sankara is located in the quadrangle of the old mutt building. The smaller temples are mostly *samadhis* of previous *Acharyas* in which *lingams* have been installed and worship is carried out. The wide quadrangle in front of the various temples is airy and spacious and bespeaks peace and quiet.

When Sankara established his *matha* at Sringeri, he first built 4 guardian temples on the surrounding hillocks, to protect the village from dangers, disease and forces of evil. On the eastern hillock he built a temple for Kala Bhairava, on the west for Anjaneya, on the south for Durga and on the north for Kali. Pujas are being continued at these temples.

Adi Sankara, who was born on earth at a time when the people were beginning to forget the teachings of the Vedas, was the exponent of the Hindu philosophy called Advaita or Monism. This system states that the individual (*atman*) is one with the Universal (*Brahman*). His writings are simple yet extremely profound. One *sloka* on Lord Siva resembles the undulating movement of a serpent while the *Maneesha*

Panchakam talks of the oneness of every human being. He wrote it after Siva appeared to him in the form of a *chandala* (a person of the suppressed class). The short *Dakshinamurthi Slokam*, in praise of Siva, actually contains the essence of Advaita. It has been explained and commented on at length by Adi Sankara's chief disciple, Sureshwara.

Today the Sringeri mutt is a great institution propagating ancient values and religious and philosophic knowledge. It has a strong philanthropic aspect to its functioning, which can be seen in the service of the poor and the sick. The Mutt runs a number of educational institutions and a big hospital. The preservation of ancient Hindu culture through the *guru sishya parampara* (the student learning directly from a teacher) is another signal service of the Sringeri mutt.

Sringeri is a place, which beckons the visitor to come again and again! A good time to visit is *Navaratri* (Dussehra) when Sri Saradambal is decorated in different *alankarams* (adornments) every day and there are grand celebrations.

FAST FACTS

How to reach

Air	:	The nearest airport is Mangalore, 190 km away.
Rail	:	The nearest railheads are Birur and Shimoga about 100 km from Sringeri. But Mangalore is more convenient.
Road	:	Sringeri is about 340 km from Bangalore and 175 kms from Mangalore.
Local Transport	:	The town is small and walking is the best way to get around.
Season	:	Sringeri experiences heavy rainfall during the months of June, July, August and September. Throughout the year there is intermittent rainfall. This should not put off the visitor, as the sight of the ghats in the rainy season is breathtaking.

Clothing	: Light woollens at night. Winters are cold. An umbrella is essential.
Languages spoken	: English and Kannada.
Accommodation	: The Sringeri Mutt has three guesthouse complexes where accommodation is available for a nominal rental. The Mutt provides free lunch to visitors and dinner is available from small eateries, which serve Kannadiga style vegetarian food.

For accommodation, write well in advance to
The Administrator, **Sri Sringeri Matham**
Dakshinamnaya Sri Sringeri Sarada Peetam, Sringeri, Karnataka - 577 139.

Accommodation in Mangalore
Luxury
Hotel Manjarun, Old Port Road, Bundar, Mangalore 1.
Ph: 91-824-420420   DR A/c Rs.1400 plus tax
                         Standard Room Rs.2300 plus tax
                         Suite Rs.2995 plus tax.

Summer Sands Beach Resort, Chota Mangalore, Ullal, Mangalore: 574159 Ph: 91-824-467690
                         Cottage Double Bed a/c   Rs.1665/-
                         Cottage non-a/c   Rs.1175/-
                         Standard non-a/c   Rs. 960/-

Moderate
Hotel Mangalore International, Aysha Tower, K.S.Rao Road, Mangalore –1 Ph: 91-824-444860
            DR a/c Rs. 850/- plus tax non a/c Rs.630/- plus tax
            SR a/c Rs. 750/- plus tax non a/c Rs.530/- plus tax

Budget
Hotel Poonja International, K.S.Rao Road, Mangalore 1. Ph; 91-824-440168
            DR a/c Rs.900 plus tax non-a/c Rs.600 plus tax
            SR a/c Rs.800 plus tax non-a/c Rs.500 plus tax

PLACES OF INTEREST NEARBY

Kudremukh: On the road to Sringeri from Mangalore is a fork leading to Kudremukh. This mountain range is so named because of the unique shape of the Kudremukh peak (*Kudremukh* means horse-face, in Kannada). With the Arabian sea to the West, these hills with their lush valleys, waterfalls and rivulets, are a refreshing retreat from crowds and cities. A paradise waiting to be discovered, it is at an elevation of over 1800 m above sea level. Kudemukh has rich iron ore deposits. The Kudremukh Iron Ore Limited mines the hills for iron ore and transports the slurry through pipelines to Panambur Port near Mangalore.

Agumbe: 27 km from Sringeri, Agumbe is the highest point in the Western Ghats. The road is difficult, with a number of hairpin bends but the effort is worth it, particularly the sight of the sunset. The golden rays bounce off the waters of the Arabian Sea into the horizon. Look out for the Lion Tailed Black Macaque and the endangered Yellow Ringed Krait.

Mangalore: As Mangalore is the starting point for a trip to Sringeri, it is worthwhile to spend a few days in this charming city. Apart from the many temples and churches, the Ullal beach is a good place for relaxation. There is accommodation available here. Mangalorean cuisine is famous for its seafood and curries. A vegetarian specialty is the Mangalore *Halwa*, a sweetmeat made of a special variety of banana, jaggery and ghee. Other good buys are nut filled homemade chocolates and raw and roasted cashew nuts. Attractive handicrafts are also available.

UDIPI SRI KRISHNA -
ever benevolent to his devotees

Krishna, the ninth *avatara* of Mahavishnu, is the manifestation of the supreme and awesome omnipotence of Godhead. From the very moment of his birth, he gave evidence of his divine powers, which made mortals acknowledge him as Vasudeva or Jagannatha.

Few Krishna temples are as popular as the one in Udipi, an hour's drive from Mangalore in south Karnataka. Here the Lord is in the form of a child, because Yashoda, his adoptive mother, wanted to see him in that form. The idol is believed to have been made by the divine architect and sculptor Viswakarma, and worshipped daily by Lord Krishna's wife Rukmini. When Krishna left the earth after his sojourn here in Dwapara Yuga, during which he defeated evil forces and assisted the Pandavas to defeat the Kauravas in the battle of Kurukshetra, the Pandava king Arjuna is said to have hidden the idol.

Eventually it came to be loaded as a lump of clay on a ship as ballast. When the ship was approaching Udipi, Madhwa, a great Krishna devotee and the proponent of the Dwaita (Dualism) philosophy, sensed the presence of the Lord. Simultaneously, a fierce tempest arose. Madhwa quietened the sea with his spiritual powers. He waved his saffron robe and all was calm. The grateful captain of the ship offered him the entire cargo but Madhwa took only the lump of clay. Scraping the soil off, he revealed the beautiful image of Balakrishna and installed the *vigraham* in a temple. Some versions say it was not a lump of clay but a ball of holy sandalwood in which the idol was hidden.

Sri Raghuvarya Thirtha, one of the noted mutt heads of Udupi, relates a different story. Of how a ship was wrecked when it hit a rock in the storm, and all the cargo sank. A few days later, Madhwacharya came to Udupi on his travels to spread his philosophy. One day, while meditating, he had a vision and rushed to Malpe on the coast. Recovering a Krishna idol from the depths of the ocean, he took the idol to Udupi, composing and singing on the way, the hymn *Dvadasa Stotram*.

He placed it in a pond near the mutt, which later came to be called the *Madhwa Sarovar*. On *Sankranthi* day, he installed the idol in the mutt's sanctum sanctorum and organised daily *pujas*. According to Sri Raghuvarya Thirtha, this was in the 13th century A D. Today Balakrishna can be viewed from a window, which has 9 silver sheeted square holes, and so is called the *Navagraha* window (*nava*-nine). Twenty-four different images of the Lord are embossed here.

There is another beautiful story, that shows how Krishna holds all his devotees close to his heart. In the 16th century, poet Kanakadasa, a great *bhaktha* of Krishna, was not allowed to enter the temple because of his caste. The idol was facing east at that time. Kanakadasa went and sat at the back of the temple in distress. Suddenly, the idol turned around and faced west! The temple priests were astonished and understood Krishna's love for his devotees and universal treatment of all. The window through which Lord Krishna gave *darshan* is called *Kanakana Kindi* (window of Kanakadasa).

Apart from religious work, Udipi is also a centre for educational and social activities. Madhwacharya himself is said to have begun this tradition. Born in a village a few kilometres from Udupi in the year 1236, Vasudeva as he was named, was credited with many miracles right from a young age. He studied the scriptures at the Anantheshwara temple and then became an ascetic. He was given titles such as *Poorna Pragna*, *Ananda Theertha* and *Madhwacharya*. He became the preceptor in the Anantheshwara temple, following the footsteps of his teacher.

His *Dwaita* philosophy holds that *Atman* and *Brahman* are distinct entities. That is, soul and godhead are different. To quote Swami Prabhavananda of the Ramakrishna Mission, Madhwa's philosophy is based on the idea of difference or distinction. There are five such distinctions – God is distinct from individual souls; God is distinct from non-living matter; Each individual soul is distinct from every other; individual souls are distinct from matter; in matter, when it is divided, the parts are distinct from one another. Similarly, the soul is dependent, whereas God is independent. Souls are divided into classes and only those who are moral and devoted to Lord Vishnu can attain salvation.

Madhwa wrote commentaries on the *Bhagavad Gita*, *Upanishads* and *Brahma Sutras*. He ordained 8 young men to perpetuate the tradition of daily worship to the Krishna idol. With these youths as heads, 8 mutts called the *Paryaya* Mutts were set up the Palimar, Admar, Krishnapur, Puthigee, Shirur, Sode, Kaniyur and Pejawar. Every alternate year, the responsibility of looking after the Sri Krishna Temple at Udipi shifts from one mutt head to the other in a specified order. Originally, each pontiff was to officiate for two months at a time. This was changed during the tenure of Sri Vadiraja, one of the most respected among the mutt chiefs.

Born in 1480 in a village north of Udipi, Sri Vadiraja was the 18th head of the Sode Mutt. A great philosopher and teacher, he was the guide of several kings of the Vijayanagara dynasty, including Krishnadeva Raya. He was awarded the title *Sri Gururaja* (King of Preceptors), and is the author of many learned works.

Each of the 8 mutts has an idol for worship. While Palimar has an image of Sri Rama presented by Madhwacharya to the first incumbent, Admar and Krishnapur have idols of Kaliyamardhana Krishna. Puthigee, Shirur and Pejawar, have a Vitthala icon while Sode has Bhuvaraha. Kaniyur has an idol of Narasimha.

The Krishna temple is small in size, but very famous. There are *pujas* throughout the day. It has a beautiful golden chariot, which was offered to the Lord, along with a diamond-studded crown for the Lord and a golden cradle, through the efforts of Sri Vidyamanya Theertha, a famous pontiff of the 20th Century. Like in most temples in Dakshina Kannada district of Karnataka, a fascinating repast is served for devotees at lunch time.

Every alternate year, in January, there is a festival called *Paryayothsava* marking the transfer of the administration of the Sri Krishna temple from one mutt head to another. Preparations for the *Paryaya* begin a year in advance with the planting of plantain shoots. Two months later, there is a ceremony when the rice for the grand feast on *Paryaya* day is stored. Three months hence, firewood is stacked in the shape of a chariot. A month before the celebration, a dome is erected over the temple chariot.

The incoming mutt head goes on a pilgrimage from his mutt and returns a week before the festivities. The day before the milestone, he visits all the other 7 mutts, invites the heads to take part in the ceremony and requests them to help him in conducting the affairs of the Krishna temple smoothly.

On the *Paryaya* day there is a spectacular procession, which reaches the temple after the incoming mutt head worships at the Chandreshwara and Anantheshwara temples. The outgoing *peetadipathi* welcomes him and then all of them are seated on special thrones made of puffed rice. There is a public assembly and the new incumbent is welcomed. *Prasad* is distributed to all and as night falls, there is a feast where thousands are fed. The event culminates with a fireworks display and a procession by the temple chariot.

Just before *Makar Sankaranthi,* is another important festival called *Sapthotsava* when grand ceremonies are held for 7 days. On the eighth day, *Churnothsava,* lakhs of people congregate in Udipi.

Other important festivals are *Madhvanavami, Ramanavami, Nrisimha Jayanthi, Bhagirathi Janmadina, Krishna Leelothsava, Ganesh Chathurthi, Anantha Chathurdashi, Subrahmanya Shashti, Dusserah, Holi, Vasantha Puja, Jagarana Seva, Tulsi Puja, Laksha Deepothsava* and *Dhanur Puja.*

FAST FACTS

How to reach

Air	:	Mangalore is the nearest airport, 60 km away.
Rail	:	Udupi station is on the Mangalore-Mumbai Konkan railway.
Road	:	It is easily accessed from Mangalore, 60 km away.
Local transport	:	Tourist cabs.
Season	:	Throughout the year.
Clothing	:	Tropical, light cottons.
Languages spoken	:	Kannada, English.

Accommodation

Mangalore

	Tariff (INR)	Phone
Taj Manjarun	1200-2500 (+10%)	0824-2420420
Moti Mahal	450-1800 (+10%)	0824-2441411
Pooja International	500-950 (+10%)	0824-2440171

At Udupi

Karavali Hotel	265-5000	08252-2522862
Hotel Kediyoor	200-900	08252-222382
Mallika	150-350	08252-221121

Places of Interest Nearby

Chandreshwara Temple: This temple is said to have been built on the spot where Chandra, the moon, did penance to overcome the curse of Daksha Prajapathi. The town gets its name from this legend (*Udu* – star, and *pa* – follower).

Anantheshwara Temple: Legend has it that an ardent follower of Parasurama, King Rama Bhoja, installed the statue of Anantheshwara. It is believed that Parasurama appeared in the form of Padmanabha here.

It is a custom that one should worship at these two temples in Udipi before offering prayers at the Sri Krishna temple.

Sandy *darshan* at
TALAKAD

Talakad, 45 km from Mysore, is on the way to the Ranganatha temple at Sivasamudram. It is one of the most unique groups of temples ever. As you go from shrine to shrine, some partly buried by the sand dunes, some completely covered and others visible in their entirety, you will be truly amazed. It seems to be the scene of a constant battle for superiority between Nature represented by the sands, and Man symbolised by his creations, the temples. It is an unequal battle, and every few years when the famous *Panchalinga Utsav* comes around, a massive effort is undertaken to remove the sand and reveal the shrines.

Though Science will attribute this phenomenon to deforestation, soil erosion, the building of a reservoir on the river Cauvery nearby, the monsoon and so on, this annual occurrence lends itself to the imagination, and is the stuff of legends. A story goes that Alamelamma, wife of Tirumalaraya of the Vijayanagar kingdom, fled to Malingi on the opposite bank of the river Cauvery from Talakad, following the defeat of the Vijayanagaras by the first Wodeyar king at Srirangapatnam. A pious woman, she used to send jewels to the temples at Talakad frequently, to adorn the image of the goddesses. When the Raja Wodeyar tried to arrogate these jewels which she was carrying with her, she cursed him saying *"Talakadu Marulagi"* ("Let Talakad be covered by sand."). She then drowned herself in the river.

The other legend, from which the *Panchalinga* festival originates, is related in the *Puranas*. The name Talakad is said to be derived from two brothers Tala and Kada, who were hunters. In the jungle, they saw a strange sight. Some elephants were worshipping at a tree near the river, offering lotuses. Curious, they struck the base of the tree with an axe to find blood flowing. The *lingam* found there is believed to have formed when Siva himself had visited the place.

The hunters were dismayed till an ethereal voice told them to bind the 'wound' caused by the axe with juice from the fruit and leaves of the tree. As soon as they did this, the blood turned into milk. The voice then directed them to drink the milk. They did so and went to heaven. So did the elephants, who were none other than the Sage Somadatta of Kasi, and his followers. They were killed by wild elephants in the Vindhya mountains on their way to Talakad (called Siddharanya Kshetra in those days) at the instance of Lord Siva to gain liberation. In their last mortal breath in their previous birth, they had thought of wild elephants and so, it is believed, were born as elephants.

The 5 *Panchalingam* shrines are called Vaidyeswara, Arkeswara, Vasukiswara, Saikateswara and Mallikarjuna, and date back to Chola times. They have features of the Hoysala and Vijayanagara styles of architecture too. The first is deemed the most important. Siva is called Vaidyeswara (Doctor) here as He cured the injury to the *lingam* himself. The 5 shrines are said to represent Lord Siva's 5 faces. The festival usually occurs in November-December, on particular years when there is a specific astronomical combination. It is held on New Moon day, in the Karthigai month. Observing the ritual correctly during the festival involves a 30 km walk in a single day.

The Western Ganga rulers (350 to 1050 AD) were in power at Talakad for nearly 500 years. It came into Chola hands during the final years of the 10th century and was with them till 1116, when the Hoysalas captured the area. King Vishnu Vardhana who built the Kirthinarayana temple here in 1117, assumed the title Talakadu Gonda. In mid 14th century, the Vijayanagaras took over, after whom came the Wodeyars.

Fortunately, thanks to the brick walls surrounding the Kirthinarayana temple, the sanctum sanctorum has largely withstood the onslaught of the sand. In the dim light, we can see the image of Lord Vishnu in standing posture. The temple has some Chalukyan features.

There is an inscription which says a golden idol of goddess Lakshmi was presented to the temple. Recent excavations have revealed a flag post emblazoned with Garuda, a carved stone *mandapam* with a depiction of Narasimha and a structure meant for growing the sacred *tulsi* plant.

The Vaidyeswara temple is notable for its granite structure. It has a combination of Dravidian and Hoysala features. Some versions say that the temple was erected around 1360 to cover the *lingam*, which is of the Chola period. There are some intricate sculptures which can be seen at this temple. Another temple worth a visit here is the Kapileshwara temple. It has a *navaranga mandapam* (nine-coloured *mandapam*) with pillars, stone windows with apertures, carvings of dancers and vines.

Another interesting temple is the Vasukiswara Temple, also called Pataleswara temple. The latter name comes from the fact that the temple is below ground level. The locals say that the *lingam* here changes colour from red in the morning to black in the afternoon, to white in the evening! A good reason to visit Talakad, if the uniqueness of the place is not in itself enough attraction.

FAST FACTS

How to reach

Air : The nearest airport is Bangalore, 130 km away.

...Temples of Karnataka

Rail	:	The nearest railhead is Mysore, 45 km away.
Road	:	Talakad is 45 Km from Mysore.
Local Transport	:	There is no local transport. It is advisable to hire a tourist taxi at Mysore.
Season	:	Throughout the year.
Clothing	:	Tropical, light cottons.
Languages Spoken	:	English and Kannada.

Accommodation

Mysore	Tariff (INR)	Phone
Lalith Mahal Palace Hotel	5000-30,000	0821-2470470-76
Paradise	50-1200	0821-2410366, 2515655
Hotel Roopa	400-750	0821-2443770
Maurya Palace	465-635	0821-2435912

Railway Retiring rooms

PLACES OF INTEREST NEARBY

Kunjala Narasimha temple: This temple is 30 km from Talakad in a place called T.Narasipur. There is a small but potent image of Lord Narasimha here. The goddess is Mahalakshmi. The local belief is that this temple is more powerful than Kasi.

Sivasamudram: Called Madyaranga, the presiding deity here is Lord Ranganatha. Unlike other shrines, the idol is quite small. It is said that visiting this temple will rid one of *Sarpa Dosham* – negative influences caused by serpents. There is a shrine here to a sage who was rid of such a *dosham* here. He is present in half-serpent and half-man form.

The famous Sivasamudram Falls and hydro-electric project are located here, on the river Cauvery. Sivasamudram is 70 km from Mysore.

Guruvayur

Temples of
KERALA

Boat Race

Napier Museum

Vadakkunnathan Temple

Sri Krishna Temple, Ambalappuzha

Guruvayur Temple

Sri Anantha Padmanabhaswamy Temple

Sree Ananthapadmanabha Swamy of
THIRUVANANTHAPURAM

The environs are dark and one has to wait for the eyes to get accustomed to the dim light. Three doors slowly come into focus and then you suddenly see the grand recumbent form of Lord Vishnu. Craning your head from right to left so that you can have *darshan* of the Lord's beauteous face, majestic torso and sacred feet, you then move aside reluctantly to make way for the next devotee. Your heart tells you that you can never have your fill of the divine sight of Lord Ananthapadmanabhaswamy of Thiruvanthapuram. Here is one of the most sacred and powerful images of Vishnu anywhere in India!

There are references to this temple in the *Puranas* as Syanandoori and in literary works as Anantapuri. The Vaishnavaite saint poet Nammazhwar composed 11 *pasurams* or hymns on this deity. It is one among the 108 *Vaishnava Divya Desas*.

This temple, in the heart of the capital of Kerala, has origins in both mythology and history. According to legend, a sage called Divakara Muni was constantly engaged in performing *puja* to Lord Vishnu. Pleased with his intense devotion, the Lord appeared before him as a charming child. The *rishi* requested the child to stay with him, and he agreed. On one condition, though – the moment he was chastised, he would leave!

The child was quite naughty but the *rishi* was indulgent. Once when he was worshipping, he saw the child putting a

Saligrama stone into his mouth. The *Saligrama* is the most sacred object to Hindus as it is considered God Himself. Unable to control his anger, the *rishi* remonstrated with the child. Immediately, the child left, crying, "If you want to see me, go to the Anantha forest."

Realising the child was none other than Lord Narayana, the *rishi* became distraught and set out to find the forest of Anantha. He travelled for some days and one evening, he came upon a hut, where he heard a woman telling her child, "Stop screaming or I will throw you into the forest of Anantha!" The sage asked her to tell him the way to the woods and borrowing a lamp, reached the forest. In the early hours of the morning, he saw a mighty tree crash to the ground and transform itself into the divine form of Ananthasayana, 18 miles long – His head in Thiruvallom, His body in Thiruvananthapuram and His feet in Thiruppadapuram! Awed by this spectacle and unable to see the entire figure of the Lord, the *rishi* begged Him to be no bigger than three times the length of his staff, so that he could behold the entire form. The merciful Lord, ever willing to comply with the wishes of devotees, obliged. This is the story of Ananthapadmanabhaswamy.

You enter the temple through a multi-tiered *rajagopuram*, which is a mix of the Kerala and Dravidian style of architecture. While the shape is pyramidal, the angle of eminence is less sharp, resulting in a *gopuram* which is notable more for width than height. Though work on it was begun in 1565, the *gopuram* was completed in the year 1753 during Raja Marthanda Varma's reign. Between the *Sivelipura* or the four-sided corridor (*prakaram*) and the main temple, a number of shrines dedicated to other gods can be seen.

Particularly remarkable is the Ampaty Krishna temple, for its antiquity and origin. It is said that members of the *Vrishni* sect brought the granite idol of Krishna from Gujarat. The deity here has two arms, one holding a whip and the other placed on the thigh.

Before we enter the precincts of the main shrine, we can see the idol of Hanuman. It is said that the butter applied on Hanuman, as per custom, never melts or turns rancid.

The *Kulashekhara Mandapam*, on the way to the main shrine has 36 exquisite *deepalakshmi* sculptures and intricate friezes depicting scenes from nature. You will also cross the *Naalambalam* or *Chuttambalam*, (*prakarams*) before approaching the *Cherchuttu*, which houses the sanctum sanctorum.

The main deity is Ananthapadmanabha, recumbent on the coils of the five-hooded snake Anantha facing east. His recumbent pose is called *bhujanga sayana*. The 3 doors to the shrine symbolize the shrinking of the Lord's form to 3 times the size of Divaraka Muni's staff. It also gives you an opportunity to pay obeisance to the Lord, 3 times!

The main idol is made of a type of wood known as *Kaatu sarkara yogam* (in Malayalam). The idol is 18½ ft long and is studded with 12,008 *saligrama* stones brought from Nepal. The idol was made in the early 18th century and consecrated in 1739. The Lord's recumbent posture with eyes half shut is significant. Scholars call it the *yoga nidra*, where Vishnu as the Preserver of the universe, contemplates his multifarious tasks and performs them through *yoga*. There is also the concept of *Bhoga nidra* where the Lord is thought to be taking a much-needed rest!

The idol has two arms, with one in a *Chin Mudra* pose over a Siva *lingam* and the other holding a lotus. Here, Siva is represented by a *lingam* and Brahma by a lotus. From the navel you can see a lotus projecting skywards, on which is seated Brahma. This has given the name Padmanabha to the Lord, as 'One from whose navel sprouts a lotus'. An amazing frieze in the background depicts '30 crore' celestials praying to the Lord. The real number may be far less, but the artiste's work is no less impressive!

The entire Hindu Trinity can be seen in the confines of the sanctum sanctorum. This concept is very popular in this region of south India (another example is the Sthanumalayan temple in Suchindram). It enables devotees to pray to all three major deities at once.

Inside the *garbha griham* are the *vigrahams* of Sreedevi and Bhoodevi, the consorts of Vishnu, Sage Markandeya and Sage Divakara. One can also find standing idols of Vishnu and his two consorts and a Vishnu image in seated posture. It is believed that the final resting place of Sage Agastya is under the main idols' feet.

No oblation is offered to the *moolavar*. It is offered to the idol of Vishnu in seated posture. The *pujas* in the temple are performed by *Namboodiris*, originally from Irinjalakuda near Thrissur, and disciples of Lord Parasurama.

The temple is famous for its festivals. The *Alpasi Utsava* in October-November and the *Panguni* festival in April-May are very special. The god is taken around on various *vahanams*. The *Arat* festival is another special event when members of the royal family accompany the *vigraham* of the Lord to the Arabian Sea to bathe the idols. This is done after the *vetta* or hunt is successfully completed, with the slaying of a demon representing evil. The images are bathed in the Arabian Sea to purify them after the 'bloody battle'. The *Arat* procession culminates in the temple premises with fervour and gaiety.

Most outstanding is the spectacular sight of the *lakshadeepa* when the entire temple is lit up with one-lakh lamps. An event that takes place once in 6 years, the last was held in 2002.

Another important record pertaining to this temple is its association with the royal house of Travancore. In 1750 A D, Maharaja Marthanda Varma placed the entire state of

Travancore, his family and his kingly powers and privileges in the charge of the Lord. He received them back as a fief to be ruled in the name of the Lord. Duly placing his sword in front of the sanctum sanctorum, he called himself *Padmanabha dasa*. He even wrote out a legal document to this effect. From that day onwards, the Lord Himself is believed to have ruled over Travancore with benign grace.

It is also notable that the famous royal composer Swati Thirunal, used to sign off his songs in praise of various deities as 'Padmanabha'.

Sri Ananthapadmanabhaswamy is not only the potentate of the divine and the spiritual, but the temporal too. What a relief in this *Kali Yugam!*

FAST FACTS

How to reach

Air	:	Thiruvananthapuram has an international airport served by most major airlines. It is 20 km from the city.
Rail	:	Thiruvananthapuram is a major terminal of the Southern Railway with direct trains to most major cities of India.
Road	:	National Highway 47 links it to the rest of the country.
Local transport	:	Auto rickshaws, tourist taxis and public buses.
Season	:	Throughout the year. There can be heavy rain during the south west monsoon from June to end July. An umbrella is necessary.
Clothing	:	Tropical, light cottons.
Languages spoken	:	English, Malayalam and Tamil.

Accommodation

Thiruvananthapuram	*Tariff Range (INR)*	*Phone*
Mascot Hotel	2400-6000	0471-2318990
E-mail: hotelmascot@vsnl.net		

Muthoot Plaza E-mail: *muthoot@eth.net*	2300-8000	0471-2337733
South Park E-mail: *mail@southpark.com*	2200-3645	0471-2333333
Ariya Nivas	500-1000	0471-2330789
Chaithram E-mail: *chaithram@vsnl.com*	600-1000	0471-2330977
Pallava	200-550	0471-2454540
Siver Sand E-mail: *hotelsilversand@hclinfinet.com*	300-800	0471-2460942

Kovalam

Surya Samudra E-mail: *suryasamudra@vsnl.com*	5000-12000	0471-2267124
Kovalam Hotel	4000-12500	0471-2480101
Coconut Bay E-mail: *cocobay@vsnl.com*	1400-4600	0471-2480566
Santhatheeram	900-2000	0471-2481972
Golden Sands	450-900	0471-2481995
Sreevisakh	500-2000	0471-2840445

PLACES OF INTEREST NEARBY

Kuthiramalika Palace Museum: Maharaja Swati Tirunal of Travancore built this palace, which has been turned into a museum. It has a priceless collection of the royal family's paintings and woodcarvings. It is very close to the Padmanabhaswamy temple. Open from 8.30 a.m to 12.30 p.m and 3.30 p.m to 5.30 p.m and closed on Mondays.

Art Gallery: The Sree Chitra Art Gallery displays paintings of the famous painter of Kerala, Raja Ravi Varma and the Russian couple, Svetlana and Nicholas Roerich. It is open all days from 10 a.m to 5 p.m except on Monday and Wednesday forenoons.

Zoo: One of the first zoological parks to be set up in India, it is open on all days except Monday between 10 a.m and 5 p.m.

Shankhumugham Beach: Close to the airport, this is a popular beach.

Kovalam Beach: Located 16 km from the city, the beach has a striking promontory. The waters of the Arabian Sea are inviting and the beach is popular with foreign tourists. There are good lodging facilities here.

Ponmudi: This is a verdant hill resort, 61 km from Thiruvananthapuram. It is 915 m above sea level and has a deer park and excellent walking trails.

Neyyar Dam: 32 km from the city, this dam is a popular picnic spot. It has a crocodile farm and a lion safari.

Varkala Temple: There is a temple to Lord Janardhana (Krishna) here. Varkala is a well-known seaside resort 40 km from the city. Look under the chapter on Varkala for details.

Padmanabhapuram Palace: An exquisite palace of the Travancore Kings built entirely of wood, it is a repository of the finest in the Kerala style of architecture and craft. Located 63 km from Thiruvananthapuram at a place called Thuckalay, it is open on all days except Monday.

Suchindram: Very close to Thuckalay and 6 km from Nagercoil, this is the place where the famous Sthanumalayan temple is located. It is noted for the large Hanuman statue and some incredible sculpture including musical stone pillars.

AYYAPPA at SABARIMALA –
the universal deity

The Ayyappa shrine atop the Sabarimala hills in Kerala is the most sacred and special of all the shrines of the *Dharma Sastha*, as Lord Ayyappa is called. Devotees from all over India make a beeline to this shrine in the winter months of November, December and January. The climax of devotion is the sighting of the *Makara Jothi* in the sky on *Makara Sankranthi* day. This divine light is said to be Lord Ayyappa himself.

Hariharasudhan, which means the son of Hari and Hara, is the divine symbol of the synergy of Siva and Vishnu, whose combined might was required to vanquish the demon Mahishan. Vishnu took the female form of Mohini and the union between Mohini and Siva resulted in the birth of Ayyappa. The Raja of Pandalam, who found the infant on the banks of the River Pamba, brought him up.

The fascinating legend about how Ayyappa was sent by the queen of the Raja of Pandalam to the forest to fetch the milk of the tiger is well known. The story goes that the queen wanted her son and not Ayyappa to ascend the throne and so she hatched a conspiracy to get him out of the way. A cabal of the queen, the court physician and the minister decided that it would be best to send Ayyappa to the jungle on the pretext of getting 'tiger's milk' to cure the queen of her headache.

Ayyappa, a mere child, went forth into the forest and was challenged by Mahishi, the sister of Mahishasura. Ayyappa redeemed Mahishi by slaying her and she became a beautiful maiden. Seeing this, the *devas* showered roses on Ayyappa and transformed themselves into tigers. In a short while Ayyappa returned to the kingdom riding a tiger, followed by hundreds of others. The terrified queen realized her grave error and begged forgiveness. It is believed that Ayyappa gave up the empire and decided to do *yogic tapas* in sitting posture with a *chinmudra,* for the welfare of mankind.

There is a quaint story associated with this god. A young maiden wanted to marry the beautiful and effulgent youngster. To her pleas, Ayyappa replied that he would marry her the year no *Kanni Ayyappan* (first-time visitor) visited him. But that, however, does not seem to be. Each year the numbers of new devotees drawn to this shrine only swells!

Sabarimala, situated on the thickly forested slopes of the Western Ghats, can be reached only after an arduous trek. Devotees clad in black, blue or saffron, bearded and barefoot, walk through hill and dale to have *darshan* of the Lord, who is in seated posture. The vibrant chant of *'Swamiye Saranam Aiyappa'* in chorus suffuses the air. It is said Parasurama consecrated the deity of the temple at the foot of the Sabari hill, which has been mentioned in the *Ramayana.*

The temple's most distinct feature is the sacred 18 steps that lead to the sanctum sanctorum. Called the *ponnu pathinettam padi,* this steep flight signifies the 18 hurdles that have to be crossed to attain salvation.

A pilgrimage to Sabarimala entails the observance of certain austerities. One is enjoined to strict vegetarianism and celibacy for 41 days. Intoxicants are totally banned and praying twice a day to the Lord is a must. The whole process culminates with the tying of the *irumudi,* which is a bag containing a coconut filled with ghee. When the devotee crosses the 18 steps, he breaks the *irumudi* and offers the ghee to the Lord. Women of menstruating age are not permitted to visit this temple.

While there are two routes to Sabarimala known as *periya padhai* and *siriya padhai*, meaning the long and short route, most devotees take the short route from Pamba, which is 4 km of sheer climb over *Neeli malai*. Since one has to walk bare foot, some practice in walking without footwear before the pilgrimage is advised. Since the gradient is very steep, physical toning up before the pilgrimage is a must. There are many devotees who visit the hill shrine every year, individually or in groups.

It is a popular belief that Ayyappa is a fierce god, who gets angry with his devotees if they do not fulfil their vows properly. In contrast is the cherubic and childlike mien of the deity, signalling that anyone with faith has Ayyappa's blessings.

The Annamalai Ayyappa Temple in Chennai: Anyone who has seen the cherubic and sublime mien of the god of Sabarimala will want to see that visage again and again. A pilgrimage to Sabarimala is arduous and the shrine itself is open only during certain seasons. To make worship continuous and right through the year, a leading industrialist of Chennai constructed a replica of the hill shrine at Raja Annamalaipuram. Also, while women of a certain age group are not permitted to visit the Sabarimala shrine, these restrictions are not there in other Ayyappa temples.

Maheswara Tantri consecrated the temple in 1982 in the presence of the Sringeri Sankaracharya. The temple conforms to the Kerala temple architecture in the use of granite and metal roofing. The *vigraham* is made of *panchaloha*. The *utsavamoorthy* of Lord Ayyappa is in a standing posture with a bow and arrow.

Pujas are conducted in Sanskrit. The holy 18 steps are open only on Tamil and English New Year's day, 41 days from the first day of the month of Karthigai, the first day of other Tamil months and from January 1st – 20th.

Ayyappan Temple at Anna Nagar, Chennai: The Ayyappan temple at Anna Nagar grew out of a community's need for a space to conduct the *mandala pujas* for Lord Ayyappa during the *makara vilakku* season. What began as a small effort is today an impressive edifice, which stands testimony to the faith of devotees.

This temple built with a grand *natamandapam* was consecrated in 1984 and has shrines to Ganesa, Subramanya, Sree Durga and Krishna. The *pujas* are performed by *melshantis* here, just as in Sabarimala. The *deeparadhanai* in the evening is the high point when devotees gather in large numbers to witness the effulgence of the seated Lord, who is the repository of divine power.

To conclude, one can say that Lord Ayyappa, though so powerful, is the God of the common man and woman. His appeal is universal and prayers to Him never go without reward.

FAST FACTS

How to reach

Air	:	The nearest airport is Thiruvananthapuram, 191 km away. Kochi is 210 km.
Rail	:	The most convenient railhead is Kottayam, 123 km away.
Road	:	The climb uphill has to be begun at Pamba, which is 123 km from Kottayam.
Local Transport	:	Not available.
Season	:	The temple is open from November to mid-January and on the first day of all Tamil months.
Clothing	:	Light woollens.
Languages spoken	:	English and Malayalam.
Accommodation	:	Contact: Dewaswom authorities at Pamba: 04735- 592048.

The glory of
GURUVAYURAPPA

Numerous indeed are the shrines dedicated to Lord Krishna but few can match the history, antiquity and grandeur of Guruvayur where he presides as Guruvayurappan. Guruvayurappan is so beloved of his devotees, as he grants great gifts to his supplicants. The popularity of the shrine at Guruvayur near Thrissur in Kerala is ever ascendant.

Krishna himself is said to have given the idol found in the sanctum sanctorum of this shrine to Uddhava, his foremost disciple. The Lord commanded Uddhava, just before his ascension to heaven, to establish the idol in a proper place in consultation with Guru, the Preceptor of the Gods, so that people could worship it in *Kaliyugam* and derive great good.

Such is the greatness of the *vigraham*, which was worshipped by a string of divine beings ranging from Brahma the Creator, to Kasyapa, Sutapa, Vasudeva and Sri Krishna himself. The *vigraham* is called a *chaitanya* (an idol that has powers of its own), as it has been worshipped for so long and as a result is vested with immense potency.

It is said that when 5 people worship an idol at a time, its power doubles. This goes up by an incremental factor of two for every 5 new devotees. No wonder then that Sri Guruvayurappan or Sri Venkatachalapathi in Tirumala possess such powers.

A playmate, sweetheart, an incurable prankster, supreme among counsellors, compassionate, a God who evoked emotions as varied as desperation, indulgent anger, numbing love and supreme awe among his coevals and devotees! Who but Krishna would fit this description? He was a playmate of the impecunious Sudhama whom he blessed with riches. He was the sweetheart of Radha and the tormentor of a hundred *gopikas* (dairy maids). He drove his mother and the residents of Vrindavan to the limits of despair with his butter and curd brand of mischief. He could enchant with his beguiling smile and inspire awe by dancing on the dreaded snake Kalinga or by lifting the Govardhana Mountain with his little finger.

His *leelas* (divine escapades) as a child god and later as a man and his great gift to mankind in the form of the *Bhagavad Gita* constitute as it were, the bedrock of Hinduism. In the incarnations of Lord Vishnu, Krishna is deemed Godhead in its maximal form.

Let us return to the Guruvayur temple. Legend says that after Uddhava's request, Guru accompanied by Vayu, the God of Air, essayed far and wide to select a spot. Finally, they came upon a beautiful lake full of lotuses where Siva and Parvati were residing. Seeing them with the *vigraham*, Siva told them to install the idol there, while He and Parvati moved to nearby Mammiyur.

It is believed that the divine architect Viswakarma then built a temple at this spot, which came to be known as Guruvayur as Guru and Vayu set it up. Such is the construction that on the day of *Vishu* (Malayalam new year) the sun's rays touch the feet of the Lord, symbolizing the obeisance of the Sun God to Guruvayurappan!

Another version says that it was none other than Parasurama, another incarnation of Vishnu and the creator of the land mass called Kerala today, who advised Guru and Vayu to install the idol at its present location.

Parikshit's son, King Janamejaya, is said to have worshipped here and bathed in the lotus tank to be cured of leprosy.

Another story narrates how a Pandya king who was cursed to die of a cobra bite came to Guruvayur and obtained a reprieve from death by praying to the Lord. He built the temple here as a gesture of thankfulness.

Lord Guruvayurappan is said to have appeared as a child to His devotees Kururamma and Vilavamangalam, and as a buffalo to a humble Varier attendant of a Namboodiri. These incidents are said to reiterate the fact that the Lord is ready to accept the *bhakti* of a devotee in its most simple and straightforward form, even holding it higher than the highest levels of scholarship. This was illustrated through none other than Adi Sankara himself.

One day, Adi Sankara (8th century A D) was passing via Guruvayur while the Lord was being taken out in a procession. Adi Sankara did not pray to the Lord, as he believed that *gnana* (knowledge) was more important than *bhakti* (devotion). Suddenly he swooned and found himself in front of the elephant carrying the Lord. He at once realised his folly and composed the *Bhajagovindam* and the *Govindashtakam*. He then devised the entire timetable for *pujas* to be performed daily at the temple.

The temple is in the typical Kerala style, with a lot of wood work, a low roof and a number of *vilakku madams* (niches where lamps are kept). In fact, the innumerable number of twinkling lamps is the first sight that attracts the eye as you enters the temple. Imagine the labour that goes into lighting these oil lamps everyday!

The temple or *Srikoil* as it is called locally, is square and two-storeyed. It has a gabled roof made of sheet metal very similar to other renowned temples in the area such as the Vadakkunatha temple at Thrissur. The idol of Balakrishna or Guruvayurappan is made of the *patalanjana sila,* a stone which is considered very rare and sacred. There are shrines to Ganapathy, Ayyappa and Goddess Bhagavathy.

The temple *prakaram* is replete with pillars and carvings. Notable among these is a pillar with a carving of Lord Narasimha, which is supposed to have appeared when Melpathur Narayanan faced difficulties in visualizing the man-lion form of Vishnu in his fourth *avatara* while composing the divine poem, *Narayaneeyam*. This story of Melpathur Narayanan exemplifies the kindness and compassion the Lord has for his devotees.

Narayanan, a youth who led a dissolute life went on to become a devotee of the Lord. Even when he was afflicted with severe rheumatism, he did not flinch from his service to the Lord. It was while serving Him that he composed the famous *Narayaneeyam*, in Sanskrit. It is said that the day he completed the work in the year 1586, his ailment vanished miraculously and the Lord appeared to him in a vision. Daily chanting of the *Narayaneeyam*, a collection of hymns on the glory of Lord Narayana, is said to confer *Ayur, Arogya, Sowkhyam* (Longevity, Health and Happiness.)

Poonthanam was another Malayalam poet who composed the *Gnanappana* in Malayalam. After composing it, he took it to Melpathur Narayanan for his opinion and Melpathur contemptuously brushed aside the work written in a language other than Sanskrit and asked Poonthanam to develop *Vibhakti*, (Sanskrit grammar). The heartbroken Poonthanam could do nothing other than turn to the Lord. Then something strange happened. A small boy went to Melpathur as he sat composing the Narayaneeyam and started finding one fault after another in his metre. Melpathur immediately realised the great injustice he had done to Poonthanam. He blessed the work acknowledging that Guruvayurappan valued *Bhakti* (devotion) more than *Vibhakti*! Several poets, including contemporary ones, have composed songs on Guruvayurappan.

This temple is famous for its myriad *pujas*. The temple opens every morning at 3 a.m with the famous *Nirmalya-darsanam* of the Lord decked in the garlands and vestments of the previous day. This *darshan* is considered most auspicious.

A series of other *pujas* are performed throughout the day vesting the temple with a festive look that climaxes with the *deeparadhanai* (worship with lamps) in the evening. A riot of light mingling with holy chants and the music of drums and cymbals imbues the place with an ambience that transcends the terrestrial.

Devotees have marriages conducted here. They also perform *thulabharam* to offer the Lord various commodities equal to their body weight. Another popular custom, which devotees observe at Guruvayur, is *annaprasnam* — the ritual of giving a child its first grain of rice.

The temple has over 60 elephants donated to the Lord by various people and they are housed in a sanctuary at Punnathur Kotta, 3 km from the temple. It is a beautiful sight to see the elephants being cared for like little children.

Any description of Guruvayur is incomplete without a note on two of its great elephants, Guruvayur Padmanabhan and Gajarajan Kesavan. These two huge elephants were known for their unflinching devotion to the God and their tremendous compassion and concern for devotees. Once Padmanabhan stood still for hours when a small child was playing near its legs. On another occasion during the annual festival, Padmanabhan ran round the temple 12 times as though he had prayed to the Lord to do so. He did this without hurting any pilgrim or devotee.

The story of Gajarajan Kesavan is even more remarkable. Called 'Lunatic Kesavan' in his younger days. This noble elephant spent more than 50 years in the service of the Lord. The golden jubilee of his services was celebrated in Guruvayur in 1973 and he was given the title 'Gajarajan' (King of Elephants).

On one occasion, Kesavan's mahout was taking him to the Nilambur forest to help in the logging. Unaware of this, he went along quietly, till a devotee who recognised Kesavan stopped his car and asked the mahout where they were going. The mahout replied that they were proceeding to Nilambur for logging. The moment Kesavan heard this, he refused to budge from the spot. He stayed there for six months getting his feed from a local landlord. Only after the mahout convinced him that he would be taken back to Guruvayur, did he move!

Gajarajan took ill suddenly on the day of *Guruvayur Navami* in 1976 while the *Navami Vilakku* procession was going on with God on his majestic frame. The stand carrying the *vigraham* was transferred to another elephant and Kesavan stood still for over a day as if contemplating the Almighty. The next day he suddenly filled his trunk with water and sprayed it towards the direction of the sanctum sanctorum. On the dawn of the holy day of *Guruvayur Ekadasi*, when the Lord is said to have appeared in his *Viswaroopa* to Arjuna and the very day he appeared before the poet Melpathur, Gajarajan Kesavan breathed his last, lying with his trunk stretched out to the Lord.

The important festivals include an annual *Utsavam* in February–March for 10 days with an elephant race. *Vishukani* is celebrated in April–May. There is an *Ashtami Rohini* festival in August–September and a *Shukla Paksha Ekadasi* celebration in November–December.

In Guruvayur, worship is at the level of the heart filled with devotion, leaving little room for the quibbles of scholarship and philosophy.

FAST FACTS

How to reach

Air	:	Nedumbassery is the nearest airport and is 58 km from Thrissur.
Rail	:	Direct trains connect Chennai, Tiruchirapalli, Madurai, Tirunelveli, Thiruvananthapuram and Ernakulam to Guruvayur.
Road	:	Thrissur is 28 km away. Shoranur is 41 km away.
Local Transport	:	Tourist taxis.
Season	:	Throughout the year.
Clothing	:	Tropical, light cottons.
Languages spoken	:	Malayalam, English.

Accommodation

Guruvayur	Tariff (INR)	Phone
Sreekrishna Inn	1200-1600	0487-2551723
Hotel Sopanam	700-1850	2555244
Vanamala	550-1300	2555504
Yadava Tourist Home	290-885	2555462
Anjanam	150-400	2552408

Guesthouses of the Dewaswom: There are three guesthouses. For reserving rooms, reservation charges have to be sent in advance to the Administrator, Guruvayur Devaswom, Guruvayur, 680101. Thrissur District, Kerala, India. Contact Phone Nos: Sree Valsam Guest House: 0487-2556335,2556799 Extn: 330

Panchajanyam Guest House: 0487-2556335,2556365 Extn: 300
Kousthubam Guest House: 0487-2556538,2556672 Extn: 500

PLACES OF INTEREST NEARBY

Punnathoorkotta: 2 km from Guruvayur, this place is home to the temple elephants, numbering over 40. Tourists are permitted to visit and see the elephants.

Thrissur: The Vadukkunatha temple is a big attraction in Thrissur. Look up that chapter for details.

LORD JANARDHANA
at Varkala

The waves of the Arabian Sea hit the beach gently as a few tourists linger, some standing apart so as to keep themselves dry and others revelling in the feel of water on their feet. The beach is not too clean, with black smudges on the sand. Yet, Varkala is a popular resort in Kerala with accommodation ranging from thatched huts to five star hotels.

A different group of people also come to Varkala. These are the pilgrim tourists, who come to worship at the beautiful Krishna temple set atop a small hill.

It can be said without doubt that Lord Krishna, the ninth incarnation of Lord Vishnu, is the most popular deity in Kerala. Temples dedicated to Him are found all over the small coastal state, many of them known only to the locals. Varkala is among the better known among these, as it is a *Purana Sthala* (temple mentioned in the *Puranas*). It is mentioned in both the *Brahmanda Purana* and the *Skanda Purana*.

There are two entrances to the temple, with steps leading to both. The main entrance leads to the carved portals of the temple and one can see a massive banyan tree just beyond. There is also a granite Krishna idol.

The other, to the right of the main entrance, has on its path a *Nagalinga* tree – a scented tree, which has pink flowers shaped like the hood of a cobra. These flowers are considered sacred.

The copper covered flag mast stands majestically in front of the shrine, bearing an inscription that it was put up on the orders of King Rama Varma of Travancore. There is another inscription on the outer walls of the sanctum sanctorum, which credits King Marthanda Varma with embellishing the temple in the 13th century A D.

The temple itself is in typical Kerala style of architecture, with intricate carved wooden pillars, roofing plated with copper sheets, and shining brass lamps. The *prakaram* around the main shrine is paved with granite. The sanctum sanctorum is circular in shape with carvings and granite lamps on its circumference.

As dusk falls, the twinkling lamps lend a magical atmosphere to the whole place. The idol of Krishna we see is bedecked in sandalwood paste and flowers and he is holding the flute, in the form of Venugopala.

In the original form, the idol is of Janardhana (The Oppressor of evil-doers) in standing posture with four arms. The lower right hand is of special significance, as a legend says. Krishna in this temple is variously decorated as Venugopala, Narasimha and Mohini. Only on *Janmashtami*, the birthday of Lord Krishna, is the granite idol left in its own form.

The circumambulation of the temple brings us to a small shrine to the right of the main shrine, where there are idols of Lord Ganapathy and Lord Ayyappa. There is no female goddess in this temple.

There are several representations of *Deepalakshmy* (woman holding a lamp) seen in the temple precincts. Innumerable typical lamps in the Kerala style, polished with caring hands, have been placed on the *Thinnai* (raised veranda) just outside the main shrine. Two metal bells also draw attention.

According to the book, *Thulasi Garland* by Aswathi Thirunal Gowri Lakshmi Bayi, the erstwhile Princess of Travancore, there is a legend behind the larger of the two bells. A Dutch ship sailing on the Arabian Sea came to an inexplicable halt close to Varkala. The ship captain was advised by the locals to take a vow to donate a bell to the Janardhana temple. The moment he did, the ship started moving. He kept his promise and endowed the temple with the bell. Some English inscriptions can be seen on its surface.

If you come down by the main steps, you can worship at a small Ayyappa shrine in the courtyard below. Nearby is a Siva temple.

According to legend, Sage Narada once visited Brahma in Heaven. Behind him came Lord Vishnu. When Brahma saw Vishnu, he prostrated before him. Vishnu then vanished. The nine *prajapathis* (progenitors), who were with Brahma, did not see Vishnu and mocked the Creator because they thought he had fallen at Narada's feet. When Brahma told them the truth, they became distraught and wanted to redeem themselves. Brahma asked them to go back to earth to a spot marked out by Narada and do penance there.

Narada then removed his *Valkalam* (garment made of bark) and threw it down. The garment fell on a Banyan tree. The *prajapathis* reached the place and then started wondering where they would get clean water to bathe before beginning their penance. Narada, who had come with them, prayed to Lord Vishnu. Vishnu sent his powerful *Sudarshana Chakra* to create a pond there. Called *Chakra Theertha* it is still the pond of the temple.

Lord Vishnu then manifested as Ananthakrishna, below the banyan tree. This is the form of the idol seen even today. The *prajapathis* built a Vishnu temple here at Narada's instance. After finishing their penance, they returned to heaven. The name Varkala is said to be derived from the word *Valkalam*.

Some time later, Brahma decided to conduct a *yagna* (sacrifice) at this same spot. He became egotistical at the thought of the *yagna* he was conducting. Vishnu decided to remove his ego, so that Brahma could derive full benefit from the *yagna*. In the guise of an old man, he came and sat down for a meal along with the Brahmins assembled there. The rice was served. As per tradition, he asked for water to be poured into his right hand before beginning the meal. He circled the plantain leaf with the food thrice with his right hand and everything disappeared from it! Hearing of this, Brahma rushed to the old man, and on seeing him, immediately realized that he was none other than Lord Vishnu.

Vishnu revealed himself as Janardhana and said, "When my hand reaches my mouth to drink this sacred water, it will signal the *Maha Pralaya*". *Pralaya* is the great flood, which Hindus believe will come when *Kaliyuga* ends and this cycle of creation closes. Legend has it that every 12 years the hand of Lord Janardhana at Varkala rises by half an inch. To counter this, an *Ashtabandha Kalasam* (reinstalling the idol on the base) is organized every 12 years.

According to the *Brahmanda Purana*, the original temple was submerged by the sea and another temple built. The latter is attributed to a Pandya king, who was wandering around in misery after killing a Brahmin. He felt a great sense of peace when he reached Varkala. A sage who had his hermitage nearby told him of the glory of the place. The king decided to stay on. One night he had a dream where Lord Janardhana told him that the next day, he would find an idol of the Lord in the sea at a spot marked by floating flowers. The king found the idol and installed it in a new temple.

Like Varanasi and Rameswaram, Varkala is a temple important to those who want to propitiate their ancestors. Every day a rite called *Kshetra Pindara Shraddham* is performed. A ball of rice is offered to the departed souls. The ritual is performed on the beachfront. Apart from this, a special day for carrying out this obeisance is New Moon day in the twelfth month of the Malayalam calendar, Karkadakom (July-August).

There are three *pujas* everyday and two *abhisekhams*. Every month on the star Thiruvonam or Sravanam, considered the presiding deity's birth star, a procession is taken out on *Garuda Vahanam*. The annual festival takes place over 10 days in the month of Meenam (March-April). The deities are given a ceremonial dip in the sea at the conclusion of the festival.

FAST FACTS

How to reach

Air	:	Thiruvananthapuram is the nearest airport and is 46 km away
Rail	:	Varkala railway station lies on the Thiruvananthapuram-Quilon route. It is 42 km from Thiruvananthapuram.
Road	:	Varkala can be easily accessed from Thiruvananthapuram, which is 40 km away. It is on NH 47.
Local Transport	:	Tourist taxis and auto rickshaws.
Season	:	Throughout the year.
Clothing	:	Light tropical cottons. An umbrella is a must in rainy season (June-July).
Languages Spoken	:	Malayalam and English.

Accommodation

	Tariff Range (INR)	*Phone*
Taj Garden Retreat	2900-4000	0473-2603000
Hill top	350-700	0473-2601237
Sea Pearl	400	0473-2660105
Preeth	600-2500	0473-2600942
Thiruvambadi	500-650	0473-2601028

PLACES OF INTEREST NEARBY

Thiruvananthapuram: The capital of Kerala, Thiruvananthapuram, is just 40 km away from Varkala, and is rich in art galleries, museums and temples. The Kovalam beach resort can be accessed via the city.

Samadhi of Sree Narayana Guru: The *samadhi* or final resting place of Kerala's great social reformer Sree Narayana Guru, is located in Varkala. It can be found atop a hill called Sivagiri.

VADAKKUNATHA TEMPLE
in Thrissur

The Vadakkunatha temple in the heart of Thrissur is the oldest temple in Kerala. As per lore it is said to be as old as the landmass itself. Thrissur, also called Trichur, is the shortened version of the ancient name for the place. That was *Thiru Siva Perur* – the great abode of Lord Siva.

As you approach the sanctum sanctorum of the Vadakkunatha temple in Thrissur, you are all prepared to pay obeisance to Siva in the form of a majestic *lingam*. What you see through a window, however, is a light brown granular mass that appears somewhat like the trunk of a massive tree with an uneven and undulating surface. As you squint to see the *lingam*, a helpful Namboodiri (priest) reveals that its appearance is because of the thick coat of ghee that has formed over the *lingam*. Ghee is used regularly for ablating the main deity Vadakkunatha.

There is a story behind this practice. Once the Namboodiris found that the *lingam* was bleeding. Enquiries revealed that a wooden piece had fallen on the *lingam*, during construction work nearby. The frightened Namboodiris tried to stem the flow of blood but they could not. At the time Pakkanar, a great devotee, told the priests to perform an *abhishekam* (oblation) with ghee and coconut water. When that was done the bleeding stopped! Ever since this *abhishekam* is done as a daily ritual.

The other aspect that has made this temple world-renowned is the *Pooram* festival that takes place in April-May every year. The unique feature of this festival is the grand assembly of caparisoned elephants, the most colourful and glittering parasols and spectacular firework displays. You can see one row of elephants donning splendid caparisons facing another equally splendid row arrayed opposite. The burst of colour when the parasols unfurl in a competition between two groups of men and elephants, is a sight that attracts tourists from the farthest corners of the globe. The fireworks that follow are no less impressive.

The essence of *Pooram* is paying obeisance by the deity of the Paramelkavu Bhagavathi temple to Lord Vadakkunnatha along with the Krishna deities of Thiruvambadi Temple. A grand procession starts from Paramelkavu temple and proceeds to the Vadakkunatha temple with full accompaniment of *panchavadyam* and *pandi melom* (style of music unique to Kerala). The two temples vie with each other along with their 15 majestic caparisoned elephants to outdo each other in their colourful obeisance to Lord Vadakkunatha.

Prince Ramavarma, popularly known as Sakthan Thampuran (1750-1805), introduced the *Pooram* celebrations to spread religion and worship among the people of the erstwhile Cochin state. An unwavering devotee of Lord Siva, he renovated the temple by creating a massive edifice in a ten-acre complex and built lofty masonry walls. He erected 4 stately *gopurams* at the crest of a seven acre, evenly sloping *maidan* (ground).

According to a story found in the *Brahmanda Purana*, Parasurama is believed to have founded the temple. It is a universally accepted legend with shades of differences on some minor detail or the other between scholars.

Parasurama, after the extermination of the Kshatriyas, wanted to expiate his sins and performed a *yagna* during which he gave away all his lands. He then requested Lord Varuna to give him a piece of land to retire to and continue his penance.

Varuna gave him a winnow, which turned into a land mass. The other version is that Varuna asked Parasurama to hurl his axe into the sea and that turned into a land mass. This is present day Kerala, as per legend.

Having got land, Parasurama approached his guru Lord Siva, and asked him to make Kerala his abode and bless it. Siva obliged his beloved pupil by appearing with Parvathy, Ganapathy and Subramania on his vehicle Vrushabha (bull). When Vrushabha (also called Vithabha) became a *Kunru* (hillock), the God came to be known as Vithabhakunrunathar, which in the efflux of time became Vadakkunathar. The other explanation is that Siva, who came from the direction of *vadakku* (north), took the title of Vadakkunatha.

After a while, Siva returned to Mount Kailash leaving a bright *lingam* under a Banyan tree. The Namboodiris brought by Parasurama looked after the temple and their chief was called the Yogathiripad.

The king of the area wanted the *lingam* to be moved to a better place and a temple built over it. How to move it was the question. For this, the Banyan had to be cut and cutting the tree might endanger the *lingam*. To solve this problem, the Yogathiripad protected the *lingam* with his own body and the tree was cut. The *lingam* was then moved to its present location and a beautiful temple built.

Architecturally, the temple has huge ramparts and resembles a fortress from inside. Of the 4 *gopurams* only 2 of the portals are open, the east and the west, which form the entry to and exit from the temple. The first thing that strikes the eye about the temple is its massive pagoda-shaped east *gopuram*. Unlike the *shikaras* of the temples of Tamil Nadu, the temples of Kerala have a shape that is broader and less pyramidal. The stress is on width rather than height. The temple itself is situated on a small plateau, which adds to the impact that the squat tower makes. It has a stucco and mortar base over which elaborate woodwork of rafters and supports form the base for a three-tiered tiled awning, finally ending in a triangular tile-paved summit.

You enter the temple through a small gate, and pass through a number of low-ceiling *prakarams* called *chuttambalam* in Malayalam, to come on to a vast courtyard. You can have a panoramic view of the other temple *gopuram* and the shrines from here.

The temple has a spacious and pleasant atmosphere and is one of the finest examples of Kerala temple architecture. Expansive use of wood and stucco and tiles mark the edifice. Low ceilings, sharp turnouts and well-paved walkways characterise the structure. The entire temple is well ventilated and breezy. The cleanliness is striking.

There are a large number of shrines in the compound. The temple has shrines to Goddess Parvathy, Lord Ganapathy, Lord Sankaranarayana, Lord Rama, Lord Goshala Krishna, Nandikeswara, Simhodhara, Sastha and Adi Sankara.

Adi Sankara, the great exponent of Advaita, has a close association with this temple, as it was here that his parents had a vision of Siva. Siva asked the childless couple to choose between a brilliant child who would have a short life and an idiot with longevity. The couple chose the former and were blessed with Sankara.

There is a painting of Nruthanatha (Siva) in the temple, which was done by a Namboodiri. It is believed that after the painting was completed it came to life and the Lord danced and the earth shook. Even to this day a lamp is lit before this painting.

There are numerous stories about this temple that illustrate the compassionate nature of the deity. While one tells of how Vadakkunatha saved a devotee from demons, another tells of how the marks of injury on a devotee were reflected on the divine *lingam*.

A visit to Vadakkunatha is indeed an ennobling experience.

FAST FACTS

How to reach

Air	:	The nearest airport is Nedumbassery (58 km). It is well connected to major cities by all airlines.
Rail	:	Thrissur is well connected by rail to all parts of India and is an important junction of Southern Railway.
Road	:	It is well connected to all major cities and towns in Kerala, Tamil Nadu and Karnataka.

Accommodation

Thrissur	Tariff (INR)	Phone Nos:
Sidharth Residency	Rs.600-1200	0487 2424773
Casino Hotel	Rs.400-1500	0487 2424699
Luciya Palace	Rs.350-1250	0487 2424731
Manappuram	Rs.275-1000	0487 2440933

NEARBY ATTRACTIONS

Guruvayur: The famous temple town of Guruvayur is 29 km from Thrissur. Look for details on the Sri Krishna temple under the chapter on Guruvayur.

Irinjalakuda Koodal Manickam Temple: This ancient temple is situated 10 km from Irinjalakuda railway station and 21 km from Thrissur. The presiding deity is Bharatha, the brother of Sri Rama. This is the unique feature of the temple.

Cheruthuruthy: The Kerala Kala Mandalam is located here. It trains people in Kerala's famous dance forms – Kathakali, Mohini Attam and Thullal. It is 32 km north of Thrissur.

Zoo: There is a zoo, 2 km from Thrissur town. It is open on all days between 9 am and 5 pm except Mondays. An art museum is located in the zoo complex.

Vilangankunnu: This is a nice picnic spot located on a hill, 7 km from Thrissur.

Peechi Dam: This dam, which has boating facilities, is 20 km east of Thrissur.

Adhirapalli: There is a scenic waterfall here, tumbling down from a height of 80 feet. It is 63 km from Thrissur.

KALADI
Birthplace of Adi Sankara

The story of Adi Sankara is a fount of inspiration for its enunciation of Hindu philosophy, commitment to service and establishment of mutts in different parts of India. Kaladi is the place most closely associated with him, apart from the locations where he established mutts or *peetas*. This is because this small town on the banks of the river Periyar (or Purna) in Kerala was his birthplace.

Sankara was born in the 8th century A D to a Namboodiri Brahmin couple, Sivaguru and Aryamba. The story goes that the couple, who were issueless, prayed to Lord Vadakkunatha of Thrissur for offspring. Lord Siva asked them in a vision whether they wanted many children who would have longevity but poor intellect, or one child who would have a short life but would be brilliant and pious. The couple chose the latter, and Sankara was born. Astrologers, even at the time of his birth, predicted that he would become a *sarvajna* or an enlightened sage.

A precocious lad, he mastered his studies at a young age. His father died early and it was his mother who brought him up. Once she fell seriously ill and Sankara took care of her till she recovered. He even prayed to the Lord that the river Purna should change its course so that his mother could bathe in it every day, and so it did!

In another instance, while bathing in the river, a crocodile caught him by the leg. His mother heard his screams and ran to the riverside. Sankara told her that there was only one way for him to survive – he had to become a *sanyasi*. Only when she agreed, did the crocodile let go. Sankara left home after promising her that he would return for her funeral rites. He kept the promise and came to Kaladi when she passed away. He performed her funeral rites, despite the people objecting on the grounds that an ascetic should not perform such rites.

In the course of Sankara's life, many important things happened. He met his guru Govinda on the banks of the river Narmadha and gained mastery over Vedanta, Yoga and other branches of Hinduism. He went from temple to temple and got himself many students in the process. He wrote commentaries on learned Hindu texts like the *Brahmasutras*, the *Upanishads*, the *Vishnu Sahasranama* and the *Bhagavad Gita*. He formulated his philosophy of *Advaita*. Called Monism, this school states that the *Jivatman* (soul) and the *Brahman* (Godhead) are one.

One day, Sankara learnt a philosophical truth from none other than Lord Siva. A *chandala* asked him for water, and Sankara refused because of his caste. He asked the *chandala* to move out of his way. The latter is then said to have asked him, "Who are you to ask me to get away, the body or the soul? The soul is pure and omnipresent. Is there any difference in the reflection of the moon as seen in the Ganges or in a wine cup?" Sankara immediately realized that it was no ordinary person who was before him. He was none other than Lord Siva! Sankara wrote the famous *Manishapanchakam* after his experience. Adi Sankara attained *mahasamadhi* at the age of 32.

Kaladi is now a sacred memorial to Adi Sankara. The 33rd *acharya* (pontiff) of the Sringeri Sarada Peetam, Sri Narasimha Bharati Theertha Swami, installed the idols of Adi Sankara and Goddess Saradamba early in the 20th century. In the middle is the *samadhi* to the saint's mother. To it's west is a

Sri Krishna Temple, which is said to have been built by Sankara, and a shrine to Lord Ganapathi. The next *peetadipathi* of Sringeri, Sri Chandrasekhara Bharati Swami, constructed a bathing *ghat* and a *patashala* (educational institution). The Sankara Memorial Trust has also been set up, which carries out service-oriented activities.

There is also a Sri Ramakrishna Advaita Ashram at Kaladi, which is involved in dissemination of spiritual knowledge and charitable activities. Here, there is a statue of Sri Ramakrishna in white marble.

Recently, another memorial to Adi Sankara was built. A tall, circular structure, one has to climb up the steps in concentric circles to see the paintings depicting scenes from the saint's life. The entrance, marked by two elephants, takes the visitor to the *Paduka Mandapa*, which has two silver knobs representing the footwear of Adi Sankara.

The important festivals at Kaladi are *Sankara Jayanti*, celebrated in April-May and *Navarathri* in September-October.

FAST FACTS

How to reach

Air	:	Kochi is the nearest airport, 35 km away.
Rail	:	The railhead for Kaladi is Angamali, which is 10 km away.
Road	:	Kaladi can be approached from Angamali, Alwaye (10 km) or Kochi.
Local Transport	:	As there is no local transport, it is advisable to take a tourist taxi or a public bus to Kaladi.
Season	:	Apart from the monsoon months of June to August, all other months.
Clothing	:	Tropical, light cottons. Carry an umbrella.
Languages Spoken	:	English and Malayalam.

Accommodation

Kochi	Tariff (INR)	Phone Nos:
Luxury		
Taj Residency	3200-5500 (+15% tax)	0484-2371471
Quality Inn Residency	1495-2500	0484-2394300
Moderate		
Woodlands	500-1500 (+tax)	0484-2368900
Budget		
Good Shepherd Tourist Home	390-490	0484-2381143

PLACES OF INTEREST NEARBY

The Hill Palace Museum, Thirupunithura: The official residence of the erstwhile Cochin Royal Family, it was built in 1865. The traditional Kerala style of architecture can be seen in the 49 buildings of the palace complex. It is surrounded by 52 acres of terraced land with a deer park and horse riding facilities. There is an ethno-archaeological museum at this spot, which is 10 km from Kochi. It is open from 9 a.m to 12.30 p.m and 2 p.m to 4.30 p.m on all days except Monday.

Malayatoor: This hill, 609 m high, has a Catholic church. St. Thomas is said to have prayed here. Thousands of devotees come here to participate in the annual festival in March-April. It is 2 km from Kaladi.

Thattekkadu: This is a bird sanctuary 20 km from Kothamangalam, on the Kochi-Munnar route. It is named after renowned ornithologist, Dr Salim Ali, and is noted for indigenous birds like the Malabar Grey-Hornbill, the Woodpecker, Rose-Ringed and Blue-Winged Parakeet. Rare birds like Ceylon Grog-Moth and Rosebilled Roller can also be seen.

Tirumala, Tirupati Gopuram

Temples of
ANDHRA PRADESH

Aakasaganga

Sila Toranam

Kapilateertham

Bhadrachalam

Footsteps of Lord Venkateswara

Mantralayam

Sri Kalahasti Temple

Simhachalam Temple

RAGHAVENDRA
the saint of Mantralayam

The concept of preordination is fascinating. It gives spectacular evidence of divine planning and inscrutable execution, often too subtle for human grasp. What life holds for an individual, just as what course a river will follow, seems to be ordained much ahead. It is only as events unfold that the hand of destiny is seen playing over the strings of the instrument that is Man. Few events illustrate this concept better than the life of the great saint of Mantralayam, Swami Raghavendra.

Mantralayam, on the Chennai-Mumbai broad gauge rail route, is a famous pilgrimage centre in South India. Mantralayam Road is a small wayside station with just one platform. The station has its share of taxi drivers who will take travellers to the mutt, 16 km away, for a fee.

Mantralayam town was unbelievably peaceful. At a comfortable guesthouse built by the mutt and run by a franchisee, rooms are available from Rs.150 onwards. A spacious air-conditioned room with an attached dining room can be had for Rs. 650. Food is not served here, but there is a caretaker available to run out and get cups of tea or coffee or a south Indian meal from a good (read clean!) hotel.

The mutt is a short distance from the guesthouse. There, we learnt of the life of Saint Raghavendra, who was – and still continues to be – a source of great inspiration and strength to his myriad devotees. He lived in the 16th century and was a proponent of the *Dwaita* (Dualism) school of philosophy, which holds that God and Man are distinct entities.

Surprisingly, the mutt is not built in the *gopuram* style of architecture common in South India. What we see is the *Raghavendra Brindavanam*, which houses the *jeeva samadhi* (when a holy person decides voluntarily to shed his mortal coils) of Swamy Raghavendra. He is said to have entered alive the masonry structures we can still see at Mantralayam.

On that day, the Saint, after completing all his morning rituals and granting a final benediction to his assembled devotees, said to them, "Though I cast off my mortal frame, I shall always be here and protect *Sanatana Dharma* (Hinduism) according to the command of Lord Hari. I will abide here in my subtle body and protect all my devotees". So saying, he directed his tearful devotees to raise a structure of holy stones and seal it with 1200 *Laxminarayana Saligramams* (holy stones found in the river Ganges).

Indeed, Saint Raghavendra spent his entire life to spread the worship of Hari or Vishnu. We hear of many a miracle that he performed, reinforcing the faith of the people in him and in the Supreme Lord. According to his chroniclers, Raghavendra made the poor rich, brought the dead to life and cured the incurable of disease!

How did all this transpire? Born in Bhuvanagiri in Tamil Nadu and named Venkatanath by his parents, he was leading the life of a householder, earning his livelihood as a teacher. His preceptor was Sudhindra Tirtha. One day his guru told him that he wanted Venkatanath to take over from him as head of the Vibhudendra mutt in Kumbakonam. But he refused, because he had never thought of himself as an ascetic, and said he could not abandon his wife and young son. But divine will could not be set aside!

Venkatanath soon had a vision in which an effulgent being called Vidyadhare told him that guru Sudhindra would pass away soon and that it was the disciple's duty to perpetuate his noble deeds and continue *pujas* to the deity of *Moola Rama*. The celestial being urged him to become an ascetic and promised that he would attain great glory. Venkatanath finally believed that it was preordained that he would become the mutt head.

After travelling far and wide in his role as an ascetic preacher, Swami Raghavendra, as he was renamed, realized the need to set up a seat where all his devotees could converge and pray. He chose Mantralayam on the banks of the river Tunga. This place was a gift given to him by Siddi Masood Khan, a minor king of the times. People were surprised that the saint had asked for the gift of Mantralayam, which was a barren village, when the Muslim ruler was ready to gift him the most fertile of lands. But Raghavendra knew of the sacred greatness of Mantralayam. We will come back to that later.

Many are the miracles he is said to have performed. One of them relates how Masood Khan himself, who was a non-vegetarian, offered the vegetarian saint a dish of fruit and nuts mixed with meat. Miracle of miracles, the flesh vanished and only the fruits and nuts were left! The stunned ruler took the Saint's pardon and immediately offered him a gift of the most fertile lands in his control.

Raghavendra's blessings also made Venkanna, a devout cowherd, rise to the position of a Diwan in Masood Khan's court. The Saint is also said to have brought to life a young boy given up for dead by his parents.

Another miracle occurred after the *samadhi* of the Saint, involving the Collector of Bellary, Thomas Monroe, and is recorded by the Superintendent of the Madras Printing Press in the Gazette of 1861. As per the Reception of Endowments Act, the mutt at Mantralayam was to lapse to the ruling British, as the then pontiff was resident at Nanjangud near Mysore. The people of Mantralayam represented to the Collector that

Mantralayam was a gift given by Masood Khan to the saint and that act was inviolable. To resolve the issue, as it involved religious faith, Munroe paid a visit to the holy site. As he entered the *Brindavanam,* people could see him conversing in English with someone inside but could not see that person. The Collector later asked the people "Is this the saint you have so extolled?" He was quite amazed to hear that Saint Raghavendra had actually attained *samadhi*!

No wonder then, that on returning to Bellary, Monroe recommended to the Governor of the Madras Presidency that *status quo* on Mantralayam should be maintained. He expressed himself fully convinced that it was the legal property of the *Mantralayam Peetha.* But owing to personal reasons the Governor of Madras had to leave for England before he even received the letter. And it so happened that Thomas Monroe, who was directed to assume charge as Governor, received the same letter he himself had written to the Governor's office for approval! The request was immediately sanctioned.

In the sanctum sanctorum, devotees can have the satisfaction of performing *arathi* (worship with a camphor flame) themselves. The approach to the shrine has a low ceiling with wooden lintel painted in red. From the longish corridor, one can have a clear view of the crypt the saint entered. The priests hand out the *prasadam,* coloured rice, to all the devotees. After a *darshan* of the Saint's resting place, you come to a spacious hall with paintings illustrating major events in Swami Raghavendra's life.

A visit to Mantralayam is not complete without a bath in the sacred Tunga river. In November, the waters are cold but gentle. From one spot, you can see the Hanuman Rock where the saint used to go everyday to perform his evening prayers. Local lore has it that he can still be seen every evening walking to the rock.

Devotees worship the *padukai* (sandals) of Sri Raghavendra, which are kept in the house of a priest. They also pray at the Venkateshwara shrine, to which Raghavendra used to perform *puja*. Lunch is provided free to all visitors by the mutt authorities, a repast replete with the spices of the region.

Another nearby temple is associated with Saint Raghavendra. While Mantralayam is located in Andhra Pradesh, the Panchamukha Anjaneya temple is just across the inter-state border in Karnataka at a place called Galandala. The road to this temple is dusty and riddled with potholes. The hot breeze blowing from the arid stone-stacked hillocks of the Deccan plateau makes the journey more difficult. You cross the placid Tungabhadra River across the Andhra Pradesh border to Karnataka. The turning to Galandala village is to the right, off the Mantralayam-Raichur road. But for local advice, visitors will find it difficult to access this unique Anjaneya temple.

It is in the setting of the Panchamukha Anjaneya temple at Galandhala that Sri Raghavendra did arduous penance for 12 years. The cave is dark and deep and the steps leading up to it take you on a journey towards a highly symbolic representation of the combined powers of the devotee and the divine. The devotees are Anjaneya and Garuda, and the divine the forms of Lord Vishnu. Of course, Raghavendra represents the true devotee.

This vision of Anjaneya with 5 faces – Anjaneya in the centre, surrounded by Garuda, Hayagreeva, Narasimha and Varaha, was revealed to Sri Raghavendra. Hayagreeva is the horse form of Lord Vishnu, Narasimha the lion and Varaha the boar. Hanuman or Anjaneya is the monkey god who is the most famous of Lord Rama's devotees while Garuda the eagle is Lord Vishnu's *vahana* or vehicle. Altogether, surely, a most mighty manifestation of the godly.

The rocky structure of the temple has been retained in the slanting cave-shrine, and levelled only in the entrance hall. The cave also contains idols of Goddess Lakshmi and Lord Srinivasa. The penance, says a notice, was undertaken by the saint in the 16th century A D.

The outer façade is white in colour and can be seen from a distance as it is at a height. The rough terrain is more suitable to heavy vehicles and there is a quaint sight of devotees travelling in tractors to the temple. The village *shandy* (fair) *en route* is replicated in miniature at the foot of the shrine, where there are numerous small shops selling pictures of Anjaneya, Raghavendra, devotional cassettes and bric-a-brac. Small *lingams* and other objects made of ceramic are a unique craft belonging to this area.

The priests are friendly and eager to explain the spiritual significance of the venue. The *prasadam* in this temple is not the customary *kumkum* but a black-coloured ash derived from the performance of a *yagna* called the *pavana*. *Pavana*, meaning wind, is one of the names of Anjaneya, who is the son of Vayu or the wind god.

Near the main cave-temple are two small shrines where the *padukai* (footwear) of Anjaneya can be seen. The priests swear that the footwear shrinks in size every year. Lord Anjaneya, one is told, is wearing them out every night while going on rounds to protect His devotees! In keeping with the legend, a stone in the natural form of a mace is found nearby. It was in Galandala that Sri Raghavendra was instructed to settle down in Mantralayam and preach his message of devotion to Lord Venkateshwara.

It is no exaggeration to say that the air at Mantralayam is different. It is pure, not only in physical terms, but in the spiritual too!

FAST FACTS

How to reach

Air	:	The nearest airport is Hyderabad, 240 km away.
Rail	:	Mantralayam Road is on the Chennai-Mumbai line. Trains from Bangalore to Mumbai also stop here. Mantralayam is 16 km away.
Road	:	It is 595 km from Chennai, 690 km from Mumbai and 360 km from Hyderabad.
Local Transport	:	Tourist taxis, tourist buses and public buses.
Season	:	Very hot in summer. Cool in December-January.
Languages spoken	:	English, Telugu, Kannada and Hindi.

Accommodation

Mantralayam : The following are guesthouses attached to the Mutt. Room rent varies from Rs.50 to Rs.700.
Sri Sarvjna Mandiram
Sri Panchamukhi Darshan
Brindavan Gardens
Sujayeendra Guest house
Sri Vyasa Mandiram
Sujayeendra Guest House Block I
Jayatheerth Mandiram
Sujayeendra Vishranthi Griham
Cottages of the Mutt

For all the above contact Mutt authorities on Phone: 91-8512-279429 and 279459. After ascertaining the room rent a demand draft has to be sent to the Sri Raghavendra Swamy Mutt, Mantralayam, Kurnool District, Andhra Pradesh. Pin Code: 518345

RESERVATIONS CAN ALSO BE MADE AT

Manager, NSRS Mutt, 5th block Jayanagar, Bangalore 080-26343962

Manager, NSRS Mutt, T.P. Koil Street, Triplicane, Chennai 044-28440582

Manager, SRS Mutt, Bharkatpur, Hyderabad 040-27560170.

The true devotion of
BHADRACHALA RAMDAS

It is considered auspicious to worship Lord Rama in the company of Sita, and preferably with his brothers Lakshmana, Bharata and Shatrugna, and devotee Anjaneya – the way Valmiki envisaged Rama during his *pattabhishekam* or coronation. How heart-warming is a visit to the temple at Bhadrachalam, where Sita is seen sitting on the lap of Rama. A concept more common to idols of Lakshmi Narayana or Lakshmi Narasimha, this idol is indeed unique!

While Sita is seated on Sri Rama's left thigh, Lakshmana is by his side. Rama holds the *chakra* in his left hand and *shankhu* in the right hand. In his other two hands, he holds the bow and arrow. This temple is said to be on the exact spot where Rama crossed the river Godavari on his way to rescue Sita, who had been abducted by the demon king of Sri Lanka, Ravana. He also spent a part of his exile from the kingdom of Ayodhya along with Sita at a spot called Parnashala, about 30 km away from Bhadrachalam. It is from here that Sita was taken away by Ravana (some say that this took place at Panchavati).

The *Ramayana* has two predominant themes. While one is the victory of good over evil, the other is the separation of Rama from Sita, and their subsequent reunion. Rama is a human manifestation of Vishnu while Sita is his consort Lakshmi. In that sense, the whole poem by Sage Valmiki and the several translations and reworking thereof are allegory.

The *Ramayana* is about how an ideal human being ought to conduct himself, depicted through story as well as sermon.

The account of the separation is tragic – Rama's immeasurable grief while having to act to rescue Sita; and her bottomless fount of sorrow, having to ward off Ravana while keeping alive her hopes. The *Ramayana* culminates in the reunion of Rama and Sita and the coronation of Rama (accounts which proceed further are not very popular and are considered of later vintage by some scholars.)

At the spot near Bhadrachalam where Sita lived with Rama, there are two stones called *Pasupu Rallu* and *Kumkuma Rallu*, as they yield powder of yellow and red colours respectively. Sita is said to have used these powder pastes for bathing in the river Godavary. There is also a tree nearby, which the locals refer to as Surpanaka, Ravana's sister, who desired to marry Rama. Lakshmana is said to have cut off her nose in anger, increasing Ravana's fury against Rama. Pilgrims symbolically throw a stone at the tree.

The name Bhadrachalam is said to be derived from *rishi* Bhadra, who, after severe penance, got *darshan* of Lord Rama here. As per mythology, Rama was unable to fulfil Bhadra's wish during *Ramavatara* as he was preoccupied with various matters. He left *Vaikunta* after *Ramavatara* had concluded, only to keep his promise to sage Bhadra and came to this location. Rama at Bhadrachalam is also known as *Vaikunta Rama*.

The idols of Rama, Sita and Lakshmana in the temple are believed to be self-manifested. The story goes that they were present in the jungle and this was revealed to a pious lady, Pokala Dhammakka, in a dream. A descendant of Rama's great devotee Sabari, she rushed to the jungle, cleared the place and did *puja* to the deities.

When Gopanna, who later came to be known as Bhadrachala Ramdas, came to hear of this, he decided to build a temple for the idols. Local funds were first collected, and when he found that they were not enough, he delved into the government tax revenues. This was possible because Gopanna was the *tahsildar* of Palvoncha *pargana* (area division).

Gopanna was born in 1620 A D in Nelakondapalli. He was the son-in-law of Akkaanna, a minister under Abul Hassan Taneshah, the ruler of Golconda. Not only did he build the temple using government funds, he also decorated the idols with jewels, conducted festivals and fed the poor. This came to the knowledge of Taneshah. Gopanna was arrested and brought to the capital. He was incarcerated in a room on the Golconda Fort for 12 long years. Visitors who climb the fort can see this spot even now.

Gopanna was called *Bandekhana* after his incarceration. From prison, he cried out in his now famous song, 'Ishvaku Kula Tilaka', his anger and anguish at the treatment meted out to him. Sri Rama responded to his devotee's call and came along with Lakshmana to the ruler's court in disguise. He repaid the money taken by Gopanna, got a receipt for the money and papers to get him released! So goes the legend.

It further adds that the Lord in disguise returned six lakh *mohurs* (gold coins) to the ruler and the ruler in turn gave them back to Gopanna realising his true merit and stature as a beloved devotee of the God. Gopanna took only two coins as a token of the Almighty's compassion towards him and as evidence of the vindication of faith. The golden coins are called *Rama Tanaka* coins. The coins on view in the temple today are said to be these very same coins. They have *Rama Pattabhishekham* imprinted on one side and Lord Anjaneya on the other.

The king, moved by Gopanna's devotion, granted him land around Bhadrachalam. Ramadas, as he came to be known, spent the rest of his life there and composed many more divine *kritis* and *divyanamas*. They are popular inclusions in Carnatic

music concerts. Ramadas' famous work is the *Dasarathi Satakam*. Saint Thyagaraja himself has acknowledged the incomparable devotion of Bhadrachala Ramdras in many of his *kritis*. For instance in the popular *Kshira sagara sayana* in Devagandhari raga, Thyagaraja asks Lord Rama,
"*Dhirudau Ramadasuni
Bandhamu dirchinadi Vinnanura Rama*"?
("O Rama! I have heard
Of your having released from bondage the firm Ramadas")

The temple in its present form is attributed to the 18th century. Though falling well after the Vijayanagara dynasty ended, it has some features of this style of architecture, especially in its graceful aesthetics. It also bears features of the Chola style.

The first sight of the temple is an impressive multi-tiered *gopuram* with finials adorning the crest. The temple is surrounded by high walls, which are part of the enclosing corridors with dome like roofs conforming to the Dravidian style of temple architecture. The approach to the temple, which is situated on a hill, is through a flight of 100 steps.

The first *mandapam* has 4 pillars with sculptures of the 8 Lakshmis, various forms of Siva, 10 incarnations of Vishnu and his devotees, the Azhwars. Exquisite depictions of celestial beings adorn the inner walls of the *mukha mandapam*. On the ceilings, the zodiac signs are sculpted. This is a feature of the Chola style of temple architecture.

The sanctum sanctorum, which is shielded by a *vimanam* of three tiers is made of granite, and reminds you of the Chola temples. It is studded with images of Gods and Goddesses from the Hindu pantheon. The dome or final covering is made of one block of granite weighing 36 tonnes, reminiscent of the dome in the Brihadeeswara temple in Thanjavur, built by the Chola emperor Raja Raja Chola. The rare sight of a *Sudarshana Chakra* at the apex of the *vimanam* is awe-inspiring. Bhadrachala Ramdas found it in the river Godavari. The *chakra* is eight-faced, with a thousand corners. An image of *Sudarshana* is engraved at the centre.

The temple is remarkable for its kindly treatment of devotees. There is a festive atmosphere as most visitors have travelled some distance to reach the temple and go on to spend the day there. They either bring picnic lunches or buy the delicious Andhra style *Puliyogarai* (tamarind rice), curd rice and *Chakkarai Pongal* (sweet rice) made by the temple cooks and sold at reasonable rates.

Many people also take a boat ride on the Godavari river. Of course, this is possible only when there is enough water in the river. Scenes from the *Ramayana* are depicted all along the picturesque approach to the temple in the form of statues.

The most important festival at Bhadrachalam is *Sri Rama Navami*, Lord Rama's birthday. As part of the celebrations, the divine marriage between Rama and Sita is conducted. On this occasion the Lord is sent a gift of pearls by the Government, continuing a tradition initiated by Abul Hassan Taneshah and unbroken by the Nizams. The festivities attract over three lakh people.

Of Bhadrachala Ramadas' songs, let us quote just one. He appeals to Goddess Sita, in the kriti *Nannu Brova Mani Chepavae Sitamma Talli* in Raga Kalyani,

"Oh Mother, My mother! When you are alone with your Lord and my Father after the day's events, please speak to him on my behalf and create a compassionate mood in him. Please remind him of my sufferings and ask him to cast his merciful glances at me."

FAST FACTS

How to reach

Air : Hyderabad Begumpet airport is the nearest and is 325 km away.

Rail	:	The nearest main line railhead is Kothagudem (40 km). One can also detrain at Mehmoobabad on the Secunderabad-Warangal route and take connecting bus or taxi. There is a branch line to Bhadrachalam road that takes off at Dornakal. Most people detrain at Khammam, the district headquarters (120 km) as good bus facilities are available to reach Bhadrachalam. It is advisable to check if the direct train is operating before planning this route.
Road	:	It is linked to Khammam (120 km) and Hyderabad (325 km).
Local Transport	:	Rickshaws.
Season	:	It is very hot in May and June when the mercury touches 50°. Otherwise, through the year.
Clothing	:	Tropical, light cottons.
Languages Spoken	:	Telugu, Hindi and English.

Accommodation

	Tariff (INR)	Phone nos:
Yatrika Sadanam	20	08743-232428
Yatrika Sadanam (DR)	90	(Common phone for all guest houses)
TTD choultry	45	
Vemulavada	45	
Veera Reddy sadan	50	
Sita Nilayam AC	400	
Sharda Nilayam AC	400	
Nandi Nilayam AC	500	

A number of private hotels with tariff ranging from Rs 80 to Rs 450 are available.
Some of the names are:
Ramakrishna Lodge
Apsara Lodge
Samrat Lodge
Kakatiya Lodge

Places of interest nearby

Parnashala: This was the hermitage set up by Rama to spend his *Vanvas* (time in the forest) with Sita and Lakshmana. It was from here that Sita was abducted by Ravana. One can see the idol of *Soka Rama* (sad Rama) here. It is 25 km from Bhadrachalam. (Another version says that this happened at Panchvati).

Jatayu Pakha: The great eagle Jatayu, after being wounded mortally by Ravana, lay here to tell Rama what had transpired in his absence.

Gundala: This is a hot spring in which the Trinity of the Hindu pantheon are said to bathe every winter. It is 5 km from Bhadrachalam.

The spider, the serpent and the elephant —
SRIKALAHASTHI

The Srikalahasthi temple in Chittoor district of Andhra Pradesh is an important shrine for Rahu and Kethu, who form part of the *navagrahams* or 9 planets. Hindus believe that these planets can be malefic, and their position in a horoscope at the time of birth determines many things like health, prosperity, marriage and progeny. There are many *pujas* and *pariharams*, which are offerings one can do or make to alleviate the ill effects of these planets at the birth position or even later on in life.

Mythology says that Rahu was a demon, who stole some *amirtham,* the divine ambrosia, and drank it. He was cut into two halves by Vishnu, who was in the form of Mohini. As he had drunk of the divine potion, his head was still alive. He did penance to Vishnu and got the status of a *graham*. The body became Rahu. The duration of Godhood for Rahu is for one and a half hours a day, called *Rahukala*.

While the body of the demon became Rahu in the form of a snake, the head became Kethu, in the form of a snakehead. Rahu and Kethu are believed to 'swallow' the sun and the moon for a while because the latter alerted Lord Vishnu when *amirtham* was being stolen. This is the mythological explanation for the solar and lunar eclipses. It has to be mentioned here that the *navagrahams* do not conform to the modern Solar system and planets and are an ancient interpretation of the bright objects seen in the sky. It is said that in Srikalahasthi temple, Lord Siva and Goddess Parvathy have themselves taken the form of Rahu and Kethu respectively, to alleviate devotees' problems.

There are many legends associated with this temple. Let us begin with that of Kannappa Nayanar, a hunter who attained the status of a *Nayanmar* (Saivite saint). Adi Sankara tells the story of Kannappa Nayanar in his famous *Sivananda Lahari*. The *Periya Puranam* written by Sekkizhar in the 12th century too describes it. Sundarar also sings of him.

Kannappa Nayanar, whose given name was Thinna, used to worship Siva at this temple by offering him raw meat. He used to taste the meat himself first, to make sure it was edible. He would also bring water in his mouth to offer to the Lord. Another devotee who saw this was horrified and purified the temple, as he thought fit. Lord Siva then appeared in a dream to the latter and asked him to hide behind his idol the next day and watch what happened. The 'pure' devotee did so.

Thinna appeared and carried on with his worship. Blood suddenly began to flow from the eyes of Siva's idol. Thinna tried to stem the blood but could not. Distraught, he gouged out one of his eyes and offered it to Siva. Bleeding from that eye stopped, but started from the other eye. As he began removing his second eye, Siva stopped him. As Thinna had offered his very eyes to him, he would hence be called Kannappa (*Kannu* – eye, in Tamil). The God then bade him to be with Him always. The figure of Kannappa is seen inside the sanctorum, standing by the side of the *lingam*.

Two other legends revolve around a spider and the conflict between a serpent and an elephant, all devotees of Lord Siva. The Lord, Srikalahasthiswara, is believed to have got his name from these legends (*Sri* – spider, *Kala* – serpent and *Hasthi* – elephant).

The spider, cursed by the Creator Brahma, had to come to earth. In its original form, it was Urnaabha, the son of the divine architect Viswakarma. Brahma was angry with him for trying to replicate his own work. The spider lived in the temple and used to spin its web everyday, decorating the temple as it were! The Lord wanted to test the spider's devotion and one day the cobwebs were burnt by the flame from a lamp. The spider prayed to Siva and attacked the lamp and was burnt to death. The Lord blessed the spider with salvation.

The snake, which used to adorn Lord Siva's neck, angered him and so had to leave him. The elephant used to serve Siva and was cursed by Parvathy when it once disturbed her moment of intimacy with Siva. The second legend revolves around the serpent and the elephant. The serpent used to pray at the shrine everyday, by offering gems. Soon, an elephant started coming to the place. It used to brush the gems aside and replace them with flowers and leaves of the *bilva* (Bengal Quince) tree, sacred to Siva – its own form of worship. This went on till the inevitable clash occurred. The serpent, which hid itself one day to see who or what was removing the gems, slithered into the elephant's trunk and bit it. The elephant, unable to bear the terrible pain, hit itself against a rock. Both died and were given salvation by Siva. It is said the spider, the serpent and the elephant are portrayed on the surface of the main *lingam*.

In *Temples of South India*, N S Ramaswamy says over 200 inscription can be found in this temple. They range from 989 A D, the 4th year of Raja Raja Chola I's reign, to 1565 A D, the rule of Vijayanagara king Sadasiva. That the temple is very ancient can also be determined, as a poet of the Tamil Sangam age, Nakkeeran, has sung of it. Some credit the Yadava Kings of Devagiri with having built the temple.

Kalahasthi lies on one of the road routes between Chennai and Tirupati, and is in fact just 30 km from Tirupati town. It lies on the banks of the river Swarnamukhi, which is mostly dry now. The temple is west facing and has been built adjoining a hill. The poet Dhurjati has described the story of Srikalahasthi in Telugu. The magnum opus is in four cantos, with 756 poems. The narrator of the story is Siva himself disguised as a wandering ascetic. The poet, who lived during the end of Krishnadeva Raya's reign, says Sage Agastya found the *lingam* of Srikalahasthiswara and did severe penance for a river to flow nearby, as the *Kshetra Theertham* (water source). The Swarnamukhi river was the result.

Do not miss the *Padalavinayaka* shrine while visiting the temple. This shrine has to be accessed by going slowly down a flight of steep stairs. Worship at the Siva shrine first and then at the Goddess's shrine. There is a tradition that devotees should not look back at either of these idols as they leave the shrines. Only then will they be rid of any problem associated with Rahu and Kethu.

The *puja* believed most efficacious is the *Naga puja* (snake worship). Those who are single and finding it difficult to wed, couples who want children and others too perform the *puja*. Devotees sit in two lines and do a *puja* to a small silver serpent with turmeric powder, vermilion and flowers. The serpent is then dropped into the *hundi* (offertory or box for offerings of cash and kind).

As for architecture, there is a large *gopuram* followed by a smaller one, through which you enter the temple. Krishnadeva Raya built this in the early 16th century. The shrines of Kasi Visveswara and his consort are found in the first *prakaram*. The second *prakaram* has the underground shrine of Vinayaka and a *mandapam* named after Krishnadeva Raya. The third *prakaram* has the shrines to the presiding deities, Kalahasthiswara and Gnana Prasannambika. It is said that she got this name after receiving the *Panchakshara Mantra* from Lord Siva himself. Staying in this place as a human being, she did strict penance for long before the *mantra* was imparted. She then attained her original form.

This temple, spread over five acres, is one of the *Pancha bhuta sthalas* of Lord Siva and represents Him as *Vayu* or air. Miraculously, the lamp in the sanctorum keeps flickering despite the total absence of air. The atmosphere in the sanctum sanctorum is awe-inspiring. The priests point out that the *lingam* is never touched by human hand. There is a hill nearby, called *Dakshina Kailasam* (Kailash of the south). It has fine Pallava period carvings.

Maha Shivarathri in the Tamil month of Masi (February 16th – March 15th) is a very important festival here. The deities are taken out in procession. The *Navaratri* festival is also celebrated in the September-October months.

FAST FACTS

How to reach

Air	:	Tirupati is the nearest airport with services to Hyderabad only. It is 37 km away.
Road	:	It is a four-hour drive from Chennai. There are plenty of buses plying to Tirupati and Chennai. It is 37 km from Tirupathi.
Rail	:	It is on the Renigunta-Gudur line.
Local Transport	:	None. Better to take a tourist taxi.
Season	:	Very hot in summer. Otherwise through the year.
Clothing	:	Light tropical cottons.
Languages spoken	:	Telugu.

Accommodation Better to visit from Tirupati or Chennai.
Chennai:

Luxury:	Tariff (INR)	Phone
Chola Sheraton :	5500-6500(+12.5%)	28110101
Budget:		
Ramaprasad	130-650	28523251

Tirupathi (Tirumala Tirupathi Devasthanam accommodation)

Sri Venkateswara Guest House	150	0877-2225144

Sri Padmavati Guest House	200-500	0877-2249629
TTD Alipiri Guest House	100	0877-2230080
Sri Venkateswara Dharamshala	50-100	0877-2225144

No advance reservations.

Bhimas Paradise	475-900+tax	0877-2225747
Mayura	635-975+tax	0877-2225925

PLACES OF INTEREST NEARBY

Manikanteswarar temple: This temple dates back to Raja Raja Chola I's period, the 11th century. Kulottunga Chola III reconstructed it in the 12th century. The name of Siva here is Manikkengauyudaiya. This temple also has a Vishnu shrine.

Lord Srinivasa of
TIRUMALA

How does one undertake to describe the temple of Lord Srinivasa at Tirumala? Saint Thyagaraja is said to have burst out in agonised song when the screen at the sanctum sanctorum closed just as he approached it. *'Teratiyagaradha...* - 'Remove the veil of pride and envy, which, so firm within me, keeps me out of the reach of dharma and moksha'— he sang, and the screen miraculously opened! Annamayya devoted his entire life to composing hundreds of songs steeped in devotion, in praise of Lord Venkateshwara. M S Subbulakshmi, singing Rajaji's *'Kurai Ondrum Illai Govinda,'* infuses a feeling of intense fervour in her listeners. Devotees stand for hours in a queue for a split second *darshan* of the Lord.

The silent yet resounding *Suprabhata Darshan,* the serene *Archana Seva,* the bright *Kalyana Utsavam* and the bustling *Brahmotsavam,* these are some of the highpoints of a visit to Tirupathi. It is said that witnessing the Temple Car (Chariot) festival of Lord Srinivasa confers *moksham.* Thousands line the streets surrounding the temple as the Lord comes out in his various chariots. 'Govinda, Govinda', they cry in an immutable chant.

They pray to the Lord on the hill, to the Seven Hills themselves and to the Goddess who abides in Tiruchanoor on the plains. Padmavathy astride the *Garuda Vahana* in Tiruchanoor is an awesome sight, as is Lord Govindaraja in recumbent posture in crowded Tirupathi. Srinivasamangapuram, on the Chittoor road, is quiet and peaceful.

Once past the Alipiri tollgate and after obeisance to the Garuda statue there, the climb up the hill begins. The first stop is usually at the Vinayaka shrine close to the foothills. Soon the ensign of the Lord comes into view. The morning *sevas* start with the *Suprabhata* – the ritual awakening of the Lord to the recitation of Valmiki's poem *Kausalya Supraja Rama,* uttered by Viswamitra to awaken the young Rama. The *Thomala* and *Archana sevas* are particularly serene and beautiful.

Entry for *sevas* is through the Vaikuntam complex, to finally reach the entrance of the *rajagopuram*. There is a thorough security check at this point, which includes surrender of cell phones, rummaging through handbags and going through metal detectors. The water that flows continuously through the entrance steps cleanses the feet. To the left, you can get a brief glimpse of the *thulabharam* (weighing oneself against various commodities or precious metals). You then pass the *Ranga Mandapam* and impressive stone canopies with exquisite carvings on the pillars come into view. On the right is the *bali peetam* and *dwajasthambam* (flagstaff), fully gold-plated. Through the inner *gopuram,* one enters the *vimanam pradakshinam.* A small *mandapam* decorated with chandeliers, precedes the sanctum sanctorum. The narrow entrance leads to a passage, which ends with the holy form of Lord Srinivasa.

Devotees pray to the idol of Garuda, which faces the Lord and sit down for the *Thomala Seva.* As the name implies, in this *seva* the Lord is adorned with garlands or *malas,* which have been strung with fresh flowers. The true dimensions of the *vigraham* can be seen only before the garlands are put up, to fill the eye so that all else recedes. To the accompaniment of rituals and chanting of Tamil *pasurams,* the priests adorn the deity with *malas* made of myriad flowers and *thoranas* (festoons) of *tulsi* leaves. The sacred feet have fragrant rose petals showered on them while a huge garland, which must weigh several kilogrammes, is dexterously placed above the crown and frames the entire *vigraham*. The diamond encrusted *shanku* and *chakra* throw out brilliant rays of light as the *deeparadhanai* (illuminating the idol with lamps) is performed. The flame of the lamps ignites the burning devotion in the hearts of the devotees, as they chant 'Govinda Govinda'.

The *Sevarthis* (those who perform the *seva*) are then allowed to enter the sanctum sanctorum. They come within a few feet of the Lord and receive the *satari*, which symbolises the *padam* or feet of the Lord, on their heads. It is said that focussing on the feet of the Lord, which is indicated by His right hand, is the path to *moksham*. The left hand is poised to hug the devotee, protecting him against the sea of troubles in worldly life.

After *darshan*, devotees leave the sanctum sanctorum with a feeling of fullness blended with an intense desire to spend a few more moments with the Lord. This quality of Srinivasa is described in the *Venkatesa Mangala Sasanam* as *'athrupthyamrutharupaya'* or 'One whose beautiful form generates a feeling of dissatisfaction at not having had enough' (of viewing).

Devotees exit the precincts of the sanctum sanctorum and enter the inner *prakaram*. On the left is a shrine of Varadaraja of Kanchipuram (this shrine can be seen to the right when one comes in the normal *seva* queue). From the *prakaram*, steps lead to the elevated corridor on the outer edge. The first shrine is that of Vakula Devi, the mother of the Lord. The adjoining *madapalli* or kitchen has a window through which she can supervise the preparation of food for the Lord!

After coming out of the Vakula Devi shrine, they go along the same corridor and have *darshan* of the idols of Angadha, Sugriva, Anjaneya, Ananth, Viswaksena and Garudu in two rows. This is also the point where priests give holy water (*theertham*) to the devotees.

Devotees walk around the *prakaram* in the ceremonial *pradakshinam*. On the way is the enclosure where coins dropped into the *hundi* (repository for offerings) are counted and the enclosure where currency notes are counted. A small flight of steps leads to the spot where you can and pray to *Vimana Venkateshwara*. This idol carved on the golden *vimanam* is outlined in silver for easy identification. Devotees then pray at the shrines of Bhashyakarla (Ramanuja) and Yoga Narasimha. The shrines are closed, but one can look through openings in the doors. The three-tiered *vimanam* is a delicate work of art. In 1958, it was rebuilt and gilded with 12,000 *tolas* of gold.

Next, devotees go to the *Srivari Hundi*. After dropping their offerings into the *hundi*, they go to the gold-plated bas-relief of Goddess Mahalakshmi on one of the temple walls. She is depicted as showering wealth on the devotee. They reach up to touch her feet. They then come to the eastern face of the quadrangle and prostrate before the etching of Lord Ranganatha, which is covered by a glass panel. Earlier, it was possible to go near the idol and place the head on the *pada peetam,* signifying the feet of the Lord, but now, this has been barricaded. On the way out, you can see the statues of King Krishnadeva Raya and his consorts, Thirumala Devi and Chinnamma Devi, who face the *garba griham.*

After this, you come to the spot where all devotees are given free *prasadam*. Apart from this, each ticket bought for entry into the temple brings with it the famous Tirupathi *laddu*. The number depends on the denomination of the ticket or the *seva* performed. The distribution has now been reorganised so that there is no over-crowding. Renovation is being carried out at the temple. A huge *Mahaprakaram* is being built for the convenience of pilgrims.

Let us now look at the legend, history, architecture and customs, unique to this temple. Some scholars believe that the idol of Lord Venkateshwara could be either Siva, Shakthi, or Muruga. Whether these contentions are true or not, today the Lord is worshipped here as Venkateshwara.

Maharishi Suta narrates the story of Sri Venkateshwara to Sownaka and other sages in the *Varaha Purana*. According to this legend, the Earth had been taken away to the netherworld by the demon Hiranyaksha. Lord Vishnu incarnated as Varaha, the boar, to rescue Her. He defeated Hiranyaksha and restored the Earth to her rightful place. As chaos had ruled in Earth's absence, he marked out the 7 *lokas* (worlds) and the 7 seas and asked Brahma, the Creator, to regenerate life on Earth. He decided to stay on Earth and asked his divine vehicle Garuda, to bring his heavenly abode, *Kriddhachala* from *Vaikunta* (Heaven).

The divine hill resembled Adi Sesha and was therefore also called Seshadri. Seshadri is actually 'Seven Hills', or *Ezhu Malai* in Tamil. Tirumala is said to be the head of the serpent, Srikahalahasthi, the mouth, Ahobilam, the body, and Srisailam, the tail. As this hill was once in Heaven, it is also known as Vaikuntadri. Brahma got a promise from Vishnu that all those who came to the hill and temple would be redeemed of sin. The hills therefore are known as Venkatadri, meaning 'Destroyer of sin'.

Varaha's abode was on the western side of the sacred tank called the *Swami Pushkarani*. The devotee is supposed to worship at this Varaha temple first before approaching the sanctum sanctorum of Lord Venkateshwara. With his tusks and fearsome appearance, Varaha provoked fear and so Brahma, the Gods and the *Saptarishis* (the seven sages), asked

Lord Vishnu to manifest himself in a kindly and peaceful form in the place. The Supreme Lord therefore came to Seshadri Hill in a beneficent form, with his conch, discus and mace. With him were his consorts Sreedevi and Bhoodevi. His abode is called *Divya Vimanam*. He was variously given the names Venkateshwara, Venkatachalapathy, Balaji, Perumal, Malaiappa, Govinda, Narayana and Srinivasa. The Vaishnavite saint Nammazhwar, describes the Lord of the Seven Hills as *Alarmelmangai urai marba*, which translates literally to 'The Divine Being on whose chest Goddess Alarmelmangai resides'. In Sanskrit this would be 'Srinivasa'. Arguably, the name Srinivasa, which means, 'One in whom Lakshmi abides', is his most popular name today!

Let us now narrate some of the legends attached to Lord Srinivasa himself. It is said that at the end of *Dwapara Yugam*, Lord Vishnu returned to Heaven. When Brahma learnt of this through Sage Narada, he asked the latter to somehow bring Vishnu back to Earth. To facilitate this, Brahma raised a tamarind tree under which was an anthill. He chose this as the resting spot for Lord Vishnu. Narada went to the banks of the river Ganga, where sages were performing rituals. When asked whom they were dedicating the rites to, the sages were puzzled. They sent Sage Brighu to Heaven to take a decision on whether to dedicate the prayers to Brahma, Siva or Vishnu.

Brighu first went to Brahma. The Creator, in a playful mood, did not offer a seat and the sage left in anger. Siva was next. He was with his consort Parvathi and did not receive the sage properly. Brighu moved on to Vishnu. The Lord was lying on Adi Sesha, with Mahalakshmi at his feet. Angered at Vishnu too seemingly ignoring him, Brighu kicked Vishnu in the chest. Despite the insult, Vishnu offered *Argyam* and *Padyam* (honours) to Brighu as a mark of respect. Brighu was pacified and decided to offer the fruits of the penance to Vishnu. Mahalakshmi, angered that Brighu had kicked Vishnu in the chest where she resided, and that Vishnu had not remonstrated with him, left Heaven and came down to Earth. Vishnu, who could not bear to be separated from her, returned to the Seshadri Hill and entered the anthill. He lived there for thousands of years. In the meantime *Kali Yuga* began.

Mahalaksmi, feeling remorseful, took the form of a milkmaid and asked Brahma and Siva to assume the forms of a cow and a calf respectively. She sold them to a Chola Queen who ruled over the region where the anthill was located. The Queen was looking for a cow to feed her own baby. She got a cowherd to look after the animals, but the cow yielded no milk. The cowherd, to discover why, followed the cow one day. He saw that the cow was emptying its udders on an anthill. Angrily he tried to hit the cow, but Lord Vishnu emerged from the anthill and took the blow on himself. The cowherd fell dead. Vishnu was badly injured. The Chola king came to the spot looking for the cowherd. Vishnu cursed the king, saying he would have to suffer through *Kali Yuga* in various lives. The king pleaded that it was not his fault. Vishnu relented and said a curse could not be retracted, but the king would experience joy when he was born as Akasha Raja and his daughter Padmavathy would marry Vishnu in the form of Lord Venkateshwara.

Vishnu then took human form and searched for curative herbs. Varaha Swamy encountered him, and not recognizing him, attacked him. Lord Vishnu showed him His divine form. Varaha then asked him why he was without Mahalakshmi. Vishnu explained to him what had happened and requested him for a place to reside on the south bank of the *Swami Pushkarini*. Vishnu also told him that without Lakshmi, all his prosperity had left him. Therefore, he would be unable to pay any rent. To compensate, he told Varaha that all divine offerings made to him would first be placed at Varaha's shrine. Varaha granted the land and also sent Vakulamalika to care for Vishnu and treat his wounds. She was actually none other than Krishna's mother Yashodha. Her role was to care for Vishnu in his *archavataram* as Venkateswara and see him as a *Kalyanamoorthy* (in the married state).

Akasha Raja was born and ruled over Thondaimandalam. Childless, he performed a great sacrifice. While ploughing the land, he discovered a 1000-petalled lotus cradling a baby. This was Padmavathi, who soon grew up into a beautiful young girl. One day, Narada went to the king's court and read Padmavathy's hand. He predicted that she would be Vishnu's bride. The same day, Srinivasa was chasing a white elephant and entered the royal garden. Padmavathi saw him and fell in love with him. He asked Padmavathi to marry him. She told him that he should not approach her directly, but should speak to her father.

Srinivasa went home and explained his predicament to Vakulamalika. She requested an audience with Padmavathi's mother. Meanwhile, Srinivasa went to the capital disguised as a female astrologer and told the queen that her daughter had fallen in love with a handsome youth called Srinivasa, who was none other than the Lord of Venkatadri. He said the marriage should take place immediately. Otherwise, Padmavathi would collapse in three days. He told the queen that a woman would arrive to discuss the wedding.

Vakulamalika came to the queen and obtained consent for the marriage. The divine architect Viswakarma constructed a wonderful city and Lord Indra, a *mandapam*. Grand celebrations were held for four days with all the Gods, Goddesses and sages attending. As Venkateshwara had no money with him, he had to take a loan from the God of Wealth, Kubera, for the festivities and promised to repay him within 1000 years.

Meanwhile, Narada, known for his *kalagam* (trouble-making), informed Lakshmi of the marriage. Furious, she rushed to the marriage venue and fought with Padmavathi.

Venkateshwara convinced her that Padmavathi was none other than Lakshmi herself, but irritated at the quarrel, he went away alone to the top of the Tirumala Hill. This is where we see him today. It is in Tiruchanoor that He is with his consorts. (The festival idol in Tirumala is complete with his consorts Sreedevi and Bhoodevi).

The history of this temple is traceable using both literature and inscriptions. The earliest mention in literature is in the Tamil grammar text, *Tolkappiam*, written some time in 200 B C. It mentions *Ven Kadan*, which translates to 'debts', in an allusion to the loan Kubera granted to Lord Venkatesa to defray his marriage expenses. It also could have meant *Ven-Kadam*, which means 'burning slopes'- a reference to the fires which were a frequent occurrence in the deciduous forests of the hill range.

The first reference to the deity is found in the Tamil literary work *Silappadikaram* (8th century A D), which talks of Vishnu as 'the Lord with lotus eyes', standing atop the Vengadam hill. The poems of the Azhwars are replete with references to Vengadam.

The construction of the temple was begun by Thondaiman, the ruler of Narayana Vanam, who was of the lineage of Kulottunga Chola of Thanjavur. He discovered the idol half buried in an anthill and cleared the forests to establish a temple for the Lord in the mid-6th century A D. This was the beginning of the edifice that exists today.

The Bana dynasty in the 9th century, the Pallavas, the Cholas and the Pandyas, all in their turn, endowed the temple with lavish gifts. The Yadava Rayas, the feudatories of the Cholas, contributed most to the development of the temple between 1184–1355. During this period, Saint Ramanuja visited the shrine and established it firmly as a Vishnu temple. During the Muslim invasion by Malik Kafur, the festival idol of the Srirangam temple was brought to Vengadam for safe keeping, as the hill shrine was inaccessible to the invading armies. A mention of this is found in the Srirangam temple chronicles.

In the 14th century, the region came under the Sangama dynasty of Vijayanagar and received huge benefactions from the rulers in the form of new structures and jewels. The Saluva, Tuluva and Aravidu dynasties followed the Sangamas. Krishna Deva Raya and his brother Achyuta Raya of the Tuluva dynasty made sizeable contributions.

Following the fall of the Hindu dynasties, the region and the temple came under the Sultan of Golconda and the Nawab of Carnatic from 1650–1800. In 1753, an attempt to pillage the temple by a Muslim chief was foiled by the British, who then took over the region where the temple lay. The temple revenues went into the coffers of the East India Company till 1843, when it was handed over to the priests of Tirupati, called *Mahants*.

Two Englishmen, Sir Thomas Munroe, Governor of Madras and Lord Williams were devotees of Venkatesa and both prompted charitable activities to be undertaken at the temple from endowments made by them. In 1933, the temple administration was brought under a Board of Trustees appointed by the Madras Presidency. After independence, when the state of Andhra Pradesh was formed, the state government constituted the Tirumala Tirupati Devasthanam and appointed trustees to look after the temple.

Architecture: The outer *prakaram* is a rectangle measuring 129 m x 82 m. While the idol is pre-Pallava (6th century), the sanctum sanctorum dates to the Yadava Raya period (12th century). All other structures date from the 15th to the 17th centuries, corresponding to Vijayanagar and· Muslim rules. The architecture is predominantly Vijayanagara.

The temple has an entry facing east with a *gopuram* much smaller than the *rajagopurams* one usually finds in the Chola and Pandya temples of south India. The *gopurams* on the pathway to the temple, culminating in the *gali gopuram,* are taller and larger.

There are a series of pillared halls before the *prakaram,* surrounding the sanctum sanctorum. The *mandapams* are called *Ranga mandapam, Pratima mandapam, Thirumala Raya mandapam, Dwajasthambha mandapam, Kalyana mandapam, Thirumamani mandapam, Snapana mandapam* and *Sayana mandapam.* They are based on *adhistanas* or platforms and are elaborately decorated with sculptural motifs. They serve a specific purpose in the daily scheme of temple programmes and activities.

There are a number of customs associated with the Hill shrine. The most popular is the tonsuring of the head at the complexes called *kalyanakatta* on the Thirumala Hill. Here, barbers shave the heads of men and women in a couple of minutes. The tonsuring is a symbolic process of humbling oneself before the Lord. The hair collected is auctioned by the TTD and proceeds go to the temple. These complexes work round-the-clock. All measures are taken to ensure hygiene here.

The other popular custom is walking up the hill. The walk involves a distance of 7 km from Alipiri or the foothills. One has to cross six hills — Seshachala, Garudachala, Venkatadri, Narayanadri, Vrushabadri and Vrushadri (Simhachalam is considered the seventh hill) to reach the summit. Devotees can deposit their luggage at the foothills and collect it at the top. The usual time taken is 4 – 5 hours, depending on the devotee's physical condition. It is a wonder to see the aged and the handicapped achieving the climb. The popular belief is that it is the Lord who climbs and not the devotee!

The third most important custom is *angapradakshina*. Here, devotees have a bath in the *Swami Pushkarini* and with wet clothes, roll around the *pradakshina prakaram*. They then pray at the sanctum sanctorum.

Another custom is to offer small metal sheets embossed with body parts or the whole body to the Lord. These are called *prathamai*. This is usually done when the devotee or a relative has some ailment. The embossed images are dropped into the *hundi*.

Kalyana Utsavam is usually performed after a couple gets married. This involves sitting before the festival idols of Lord Srinivasa, Sreedevi and Bhoodevi and watching the divine marriage, after which the couple receive the blessings.

There are many other special *sevas* like *Vasanthotsava, Abhishekam, Thiruppavadai Seva, Sahasrakalasabhishekham, Vastraalankara Seva, Pulangi Seva, Dolotsava* and *Ashtadala-padapadmaradhanaseva*. The most important festival of the year is the 11-day Brahmotsavam in the month of Purattasi (September-October), when the decorated idols of the *utsavars* are taken around the streets abutting the temple in different *vahanams* or vehicles. Lakhs of devotees assemble for this festival. The entire hill town is lit up so brightly that you feel you are in heavenly realms.

What is different about Tirupathi? There are many shrines to Lord Srinivasa, but here He is different. It is in the Lord Venkateshwara shrine on Tirumala that the devotee and the deity come closest to each other. The utter yearning of the *bhakta* to get a glimpse of Govinda, if only for a few seconds, cannot be witnessed in any other temple.

Most people go to Tirupati repeatedly. Families make it a point to make at least an annual pilgrimage to the hill. Special *sevas* are booked months in advance, and despite every effort by the TTD authorities to manage crowds, the numbers are on the rise. Despite the constant crowds, the hill is kept remarkably clean and every devotee bar one in a lakh or so gets *darshan*.

Lord Srinivasa is called *'Kaliyugathu Perumal.'* In this *Kali Yuga*, when *adharma* is on the rise, He is the God who forgives easily, is accessible to all and offers salvation on surrender. This is perhaps why He is the most sought after deity. Call Him Balaji, Govinda, Venkateswara, Srinivasa or what you will; the thought that reverberates in the mind of every devotee, while leaving the hill shrine is that the Lord should grant another opportunity to have *darshan* – '*Punah darshana prapti rastu*'.

'*Om Sri Venkatesaya Namaha*'

FAST FACTS

How to reach

Air	:	Air services are available from Tirupathi airport to Hyderabad.
Rail	:	Tirupathi is 152 km from Chennai and 10 km from Renigunta. It is now an important station with links to all over the country.
Road	:	Chennai is 160 km away. From Tirupathi one has to take a 16 km ghat road to Tirumala. There are two ghat roads, one for vehicles going up and the other for those coming down. The downward road has a number of hairpin bends.
Local Transport	:	On Tirumala free buses run by the TTD and taxis are available.
Season	:	Throughout the year.
Clothing	:	Winter nights are cold. Cottons for day and light woollens for the night.
Accommodation	:	The TTD has built a number of cottages. Rents range from Rs 100 to Rs 2500 per day. There are free choultries too. Devotees can reserve paid rooms for Rs.100 a day category rooms 30 days in advance by writing to: AEO (Reception 1).
		TTD, Tirumala 517504, enclosing a Demand Draft for Rs. 100 favouring EO/TTD drawn on a nationalised bank payable at Tirupati. Stay can

also be reserved 30 days in advance at Delhi, Mumbai, Chennai, Hyderabad Bangalore, Pondicherry, Visakhapatnam and District Headquarters in Andhra Pradesh. Other types of accommodation can be reserved only at the CRO/Tirumala. *For further details contact* **www.tirumala.org**. It is advisable to book accommodation well in advance.

Places of interest nearby

Tirumala

Papavinasam: A low waterfall, 5 km from the temple, is said to be sacred. A bath on the 7th or 12th day of the *shukla paksha* (waxing phase) of the moon in the month of Ashad (July-August) is said to free one of the sins of the previous birth.

Akasha Gangai: This water source on the northern side of the temple is said to be the place where Anjana Devi, the mother of Hanuman, did penance for 12 years. Water from here, collected in silver pots, is used for the ablutions of the Lord.

Tirupathi

Tiruchanoor: This is the famous temple of Padmavathi, the consort of Srinivasa. As per lore, the Lord, unable to bear the quarrel between Mahalakshmi and Padmavati, went away to Tirumala. Padmavati resides in the temple at Tiruchanoor, which is also called Alamelumangapuram. The goddess here is four-armed. She bears lotuses in two hands while the other two are the *abhaya* and *varada hastams* – offering protection and boons. It is traditional to pray here before going up to the hill shrine.

Govindaraja Perumal: This huge temple is characterised by a towering *rajagopuram* and a number of *gopurams* and *vimanams,* Vishnu can be seen in the recumbent posture as Govindaraja. This temple was established by Saint Ramanuja and was mainly built in the 14th and 15th centuries by the Saluva kings.

The unique idol of
VARAHA NARASIMHA

In *Kali Yugam*, it is said that worship of the Lord in his *Vyuha* (idol) form is the easy way of approach for a devotee. Some idols draw the devotee more than others, a phenomenon that can be attributed more to what is inherent in the idol than the skill of the sculptor. A remarkable illustration of this is the idol of Varaha Narasimha at Simhachalam in Andhra Pradesh. No matter that the idol — which is part boar, part lion and part man — is swathed in white cloth every day of the year bar one, so that its contours cannot be seen, it still commands awe among devotees!

Simhachalam literally means 'Hill of the Lion'. The abode of Sri Varaha Lakshmi Narasimha Swamy is situated 16 km to the north of Visakhapatnam at a height of 800 m above sea level. A short ride by car or bus from Visakhapatnam up the small hillock takes you to the temple.

The legend goes that owing to certain misdeeds, the gatekeepers of Heaven, Jaya and Vijaya, were cursed to be born as demons. One was born as Hiranyaksha and the other as Hiranyakasipu, to sage Kasyapa. When Hiranyaksha with his demonic powers carried the Earth to the nether regions, Vishnu assumed the form of a boar (Varaha) and rescued the Earth after slaying him.

Hiranyakasipu, aggrieved by the death of his brother, wished to vanquish the Lord. Performing penance, he attained many boons, which made his death by man or beast, by day or night or inside or outdoors impossible. He then became a scourge to the followers of Vishnu.

The celestials prayed to Lord Vishnu to rid the earth of the demon. The Lord ensured that one of his faithful servants Sumukha, was born as the son of Hiranyakasipu. The child, Prahlada, grew up to be a great devotee of Lord Vishnu. Aghast, the demon tried his best to persuade him to decry Vishnu. When all his attempts were rebuffed, the demon decided to do away with the life of his own son.

When Hiranyakasipu's agents threw Prahlada into the sea and tried to place a mountain on top of him, the Lord tipped the mountain and saved the child. Taking the form of Narasimha, the man-lion, he slew the demon. At that time, his ardent devotee expressed his desire to see both the aspects of the Lord, while slaying Hiranyaksha and Hiranyakasipu.

Acceding to this wish, Lord Vishnu appeared in the Varaha Narasimha form where the three aspects of Boar-Man-Lion are seen. An ecstatic Prahlada built a shrine to this form on the very Simhadri Hill, which his demon father sought to place on him. He continued worship here for long.

At the end of *Krita Yugam*, the temple fell into disuse, and the idol was covered with dust and soil. Some years later King Pururava of the lunar dynasty discovered the temple while travelling on an aerial chariot with his spouse Urvasi. He was magically drawn towards the location of this ancient shrine. As he removed the soil coating the idol, he heard an ethereal voice, which bade him not to expose the idol as it was too *ugra* (fierce), but to cover it with sandal paste. The voice also said that the Lord should be worshipped only in this form. Only once a year, on the third day in the month of Visakha, should the original form be revealed. Obeying the dictates of the heavenly voice, the king covered the *vigraham* with sandal paste and built a new temple over it.

Going by epigraphic evidence, of which this temple has plenty, Kulottunga Chola I gave donations to this temple in the late 11th century. The Chalukyas are also credited with having carried out work on the temple.

It was the Eastern Gangas, chiefly Narasimha I (1234 – 1263), who constructed the temple in its present form. Its simple façade makes the intricate and rich architecture in the interiors a pleasant surprise. With ornately carved pillars and large *mandapams*, it has a five-tiered *rajagopuram* and a white coloured *shikara*. The corners of the base of the *shikara* have lions symbolising Lord Narasimha. The eastern face of the *shikara* has a sculpture of Indra on his mount Airavata. Lower down there is Gajalakshmi. The *shikara* is crowned by a gold-plated dome.

There is another entrance in the north. Steps lead to a three-tiered *gopuram*, through which one can access the *ardha mandapam*. There is a metal *dhwajasthambham* in front of the *maha mandapam*.

The sanctum sanctorum is cube-shaped and the Hoysala style is evident in the fine sculptures in niches on the walls of the *garba griham*. In the entire temple, there is a combination of architectural styles. Apart from Hoysala, Chalukya and Chola, some parts bear a marked resemblance to the Konark temple. This is particularly seen in the ornate three-tiered *shikara* shaped like a step-pyramid. This influence can be attributed to the fact that coastal Andhra Pradesh was under the Gajapathis of Orissa in the late 15th and early 16th century.

There is an intricately chiselled circular stone pillar in the *mandapam* just outside the sanctum sanctorum. It is said that encircling this pillar with the arms will bring all prosperity and well being to the devotee. In the inner enclosure, there is a *kalyana mandapam* with 96 pillars. The *natya mandapam* is to the right of the northern entrance and has 16 pillars. The *kalyana mandapam* contains numerous bas-reliefs portraying Lord Vishnu's *avataras* on pillars. Depictions of Lord Narasimha, in particular, can be seen everywhere. Another feature worth mentioning is a beautiful stone chariot with well carved horses. Numerous inscriptions recording the munificence of royal patrons and the commemoration of their victories are also found.

The most important festival is on the third day of the month of Visakha (April-May), when the idol is divested of its cover of sandal paste and huge crowds come to witness this once-in-a-year event.

FAST FACTS

How to reach

Air	:	Vishakapatnam airport is 10 km away.
Rail	:	The Vishakapatnam rail station is on the Chennai-Howrah B.G line. There are also trains running in the Hyderabad direction.
Road	:	Good road services to major cities and towns of Andhra Pradesh are there from Vishakapatnam.
Local Transport	:	Cars, Taxis, and buses.
Season	:	Throughout the year.
Clothing	:	Light tropical cottons. The humidity is high as the city on the coast.
Languages spoken	:	English, Telugu

Accommodation	*Tariff Range (INR)*	*Phone*
Hotel Taj Residency	2200-4600+5%	0891 2567756
Hotel Daspalla	1100-1800+5%	0891-2564825
Hotel Dolphin	1295-2495+5%	0891-2554488
Hotel Grand Bay	2400-5000+5%	0891-2560101

Railway Retiring Rooms.

PLACES OF INTEREST NEARBY

Kali Temple: This temple on the beach road was built in 1984, with a Siva temple following in 1987. The unique feature is the *Siva lingam,* made of a single stone of 10 kg weight. It is called *Rasa lingam*. Several festivals are celebrated here.

Ross Hill: Named after Ross, a local authority, this place is famed for its shrines for three religions–Iashique Darga, Venkateswara temple and Velangannimata Church.

Kailasgiri: This is a nearby hill with numerous attractions such as viewpoints, children's park and a floral clock. There are statues of Siva, Parvathi and Vishnu. There is also a jungle trail. The view of the sea from atop is breath taking.

Dolphin's Nose: It is a striking landmark in Vishakhapatnam. A massive rock, 358 m above sea level, juts out from the blue waters, resembling a dolphin. One can have a nice view from the beachfront. This rock makes Visakhapatnam Port a natural harbour. There is a temple to goddess Kanakadurga.

Ramakrishna Beach: An enchanting stretch of beach right in the heart of the city, it derives its name from the nearby temple of Lord Rama and Krishna. RK beach has well-landscaped parks.

Rishikonda Beach: Eight km from the city, this beach is ideal for swimming, water skiing and wind surfing. The Andhra Pradesh Tourism Development Corporation has built cottages here.

Bheemili Beach: Drive through one of the longest beach side roads in India, 25 km long to reach Bheemunipatnam. Apart from water sports, this spot is noted for a 17th century Dutch settlement with a ruined fort, armoury and cemetery. On the way is a place called Erramatti Dibbalu, which, with its red sand dunes and ravines is a favourite with film makers.

Submarine museum: A decommissioned submarine called Kurusura is one of the big attractions on the sands of RK beach. Not too far away is War Memorial. It was built in 1971 by the Eastern Naval Command to commemorate the Indian Navy's victory in 1971. The entry fee is Rs. 25.

Araku Valley (120 km): This hill station is unique for its green lands and water falls. Located at an altitude of 3400 ft, it can be reached by road or rail. The tribals who live here have kept their culture alive and perform the Dhimsa dance regularly for the benefit of tourists. There is a tribal museum and a landscaped garden. Local crafts are bamboo, pottery, terracotta and lacquer.

Borra Caves: These are fascinating natural caves in the Eastern Ghats. Borra is 90 km from Visakhapatnam en route to Arakku. The perennial river Gosthani, has its origin in these caves. One can see stalactites and stalagmites of limestone here. Some of the formations look like various religious figures and have been so named. Deep inside the caves, there is a small Siva temple, where Sivarathri is celebrated every year. The caves have been illuminated. There is a small admission fee.

Panchanarasimha Sthala
YADAGIRIGUTTA

Just two hours drive from Secunderabad is the fascinating cave temple of Yadagirigutta, dedicated to Lord Narasimha, the fourth incarnation of Lord Vishnu. Located near Bhongir (Bhuvanagiri) on the Secunderabad-Kazipet route is the Yadagiri hill, housing 5 forms of Narasimha. This *Pancha Narasimha Sthala* has in worship Jwala Narasimha, Yoga Narasimha, Lakshmi Narasimha, Ugra Narasimha and Ghandabheranda Narasimha.

Three rock formations in the natural cave are revered as the first three forms. The *Jwala Narasimha* image looks somewhat like a serpent, while the Yoga Narasimha shows the Lord seated in meditation. *Ghandabheranda Narasimha,* a formless manifestation of *Narasimha,* is acknowledged by the presence of a lamp that burns continuously within a crevice underneath the Hanuman shrine. *Ugra Narasimha* is the entrance to the cave itself, opening His mouth in His fierce manifestation.

The festival image is Lakshmi Narasimha, who is in *Kalyana* (wedding) and *Vaidya* (doctor) form here. This large silver *vigraham,* where the god and goddess are together in the idol, is heart – warming and most people visit Yadagirigutta to get their grace. There are also shrines to Goddess Andal and to the Vaishnavite saint poets, the Azhwars, Hanuman and Sudarshana, the discus of Lord Vishnu.

The temple with a majestic five-storeyed *gopuram* is situated at a height of 300 ft on the Yadigiri Hill, which also has a temple to Lord Siva. The entrance at the foothills is called *Vaikunta Dwara*. There is a shrine to Hanuman, who is an extremely popular deity in Andhra Pradesh, at the entrance.

First time visitors to Yadagirigutta will be attracted by the bright colours of the shrine. The deities are draped in dazzling attire and the priests make it a point to highlight the contours of the images. Worship is conducted according to the *Pancharatra Agama* (mode of worship).

According to legend, Yadava, the son of sage Rishyashringa meditated on Lord Vishnu in this area, seeking a vision of three forms of Lord Narasimha. Lord Hanuman was sent to direct Yadava to a particular spot on the plains where there was a temple. Here, Vishnu granted him his wish. This was in *Tretha Yugam*. Since this spot was at the base of a hillock, the hill came to be known as Yadavagiri, later abbreviated to Yadagiri.

Yadava attained salvation here. Hearing of the presence of a temple, a number of tribal people were said to have come to worship here. But owing to ignorance, they indulged in some improper practices. As a result, the Lord moved up to the hills, and the tribal people searched in vain for him, says the legend.

After many years, Lord Narasimha appeared in the dream of a devout lady among the tribals, and directed her to a large cavern where He revealed Himself to all of them in five forms. It is believed that worshipping at this temple for a continuous period of 40 days will cure devotees of incurable ailments.

The temple *Brahmotsavam* is held in March-April. The belief is that Brahma himself presides over the festival. The deities are taken out in procession everyday. The festival begins with the hoisting of the temple flag and concludes with the lowering of the temple flag. The *garuda vahanam* and taking out of the temple chariot are usually the highlights.

FAST FACTS

How to reach

Air	:	The nearest airport is Hyderabad, 69 km away.
Rail	:	The nearest railhead is Bhongir, which is 48 km from Secunderabad.
Road	:	The temple is 69 km from Hyderabad.
Local Transport	:	It is best to take a tourist taxi or public bus from Secunderabad.
Season	:	Throughout the year, except peak summer.
Clothing	:	Tropical, light cottons.
Languages Spoken	:	English and Telugu.

Accommodation

	Tariff range (INR)	Phone
Luxury		
Taj Residency	3900-14000	04023393939
Moderate		
Hotel Baseraa	1650-3500	04027703200
Budget		
Jaya International	400-495	04024752929

PROPITIATING LORD SANEESWARA
at Tirunallar

The passenger train from Thanjavur to Nagore passes through lush, green paddy fields, irrigated by the waters of the river Cauvery. The train is virtually empty and there is plenty of time to drink in the scenery and absorb the quiet and peace. In contrast, the town of Nagore is busy and crowded. Visitors come in large numbers to the Nagore Dargah and the nearby shrine of Velankanni. Most people make it a triple pilgrimage, worshipping at the Saneeswara shrine at Thirunallar too. The unique aspect of these three shrines is that people come to pray whatever caste or creed they belong to.

The dominant mood in Thirunallar, just a few kilometres from Karaikal, a pocket of Pondicherry in Tamil Nadu, is one of hope. It is usually the sick and the needy who come here, apart from the inveterate temple enthusiasts. The legends revolving around this temple are so many and so varied that people come here for a solution to any type of problem.

Of all the 9 planets, Saneeswara, the offspring of Surya and Chaaya, inspires the most awe. This is because he is said to hold sway over a person's fortunes throughout his or her life. Starting from the position of this planet in the horoscope to the corresponding placements of other planets, Lord Sani is believed to influence the course of one's life.

Among the Saneeswara shrines, Thirunallar is believed to be the most sacred and the most efficacious, a belief that has come about because of the various miracles which are believed to have happened here. The most popular among them is that of King Nala, of the Nala-Damayanti legend. Afflicted by numerous problems because of the adverse effects of Sani, he was at the end of his tether. A bath in the temple tank is said to have cured him of all his problems and he felt as though a great weight had been lifted off him! The pond is called *Nala Theertham* and Thirunallar itself derives its name from Nala.

Kalinga Raja is also said to have got deliverance here. Once when Bhargava *Munivar* (sage) visited him he did not heed the sage's words properly. Bhargava cursed him to become an elephant and roam around in the forest. The king was essentially a good man and Sage Narada took pity on him. He asked him to pray to Lord Siva at Thirunallar, who removed the effects of the curse.

The main deity here is Darbaranyeeswarar, a manifestation of Lord Siva, who is also called Nallatreeswarar. The goddess is called Ambigai. There is also a unique idol of Swarna Vinayakar here. At the entrance is Karpaga Vinayakar, who bestows all good. To the right of the main shrine is the Saneeswara shrine. Since Lord Sani has a separate shrine to himself here, he is believed to be in a kindly mood. He is an *anugraha murthy*, a granter of boons. Though the interior is dark, the flames from a thousand oil and ghee lamps lit by devotees dance brightly.

Many poets have sung of Lord Siva and of Lord Sani here, among them being Thirugnanasambandar, Thirunavukkarasar and Sundaramurthy Swamigal. *Nanniya Kulirpunal Puguthu Nallaru* (The place with refreshing, cool waters) sang Thirugnanasambandar, the child saint of Saivism.

These and other literature tell us that the place where the temple is situated was originally a forest of *Darba* grass or coarse grass. The idol of Darbaranyeeswarar (the God who dwells in the forest of coarse grass) appeared in *swayambhu* form. *Darba* grass is used for many Hindu rites and rituals, such as marriage, *yagnas*, death ceremonies, etc. Tying the grass around the finger authorizes a person to commence a *puja* or austerity.

A place where this grass grows in plenty is, therefore, naturally considered the holiest of holy places.

FAST FACTS

How to reach

Air	:	The nearest airport is Tiruchirapalli, 156 km away.
Rail	:	The nearest railhead is Nagapattinam, 18 km away.
Road	:	Thirunallar is 18 km from Nagapattinam, 101 km from Thanjavur and 5 km west of Karaikal.
Local Transport	:	Tourist taxis; auto rickshaws and cycle rickshaws are available.
Season	:	Through the year.
Clothing	:	Tropical, light cottons.
Languages spoken	:	English and Tamil.

Accommodation

Nagapattinam:	Tariff(INR)	Phone
Hotel Sea Horse	150-690	04365-263910
Hotel Tamil Nadu	500-1000	04365-224389

NEARBY ATTRACTIONS

Velankanni Shrine: The Shrine of Our Lady of Health at Velankanni is one of the most popular among all Christian shrines in India. This is particularly true in September, when a special festival is celebrated to commemorate the birth of Mary, Mother of Jesus. Pope John XXIII elevated the shrine to the status of a Basilica in 1962. Located on the shores of the Bay of Bengal, the shrine is known in Tamil as the *Velankanni Matha Koil.* It is 11 km from Nagapattinam and has excellent access by road and rail. Legends abound about this shrine. How the Holy Mother appeared as an apparition to many devotees and provided succour and solace to them. The gifts lavished by the grateful devotees are stored in a museum.

Nagore Dargah: The Nagore Dargah of Meeran Sahib Abdul Qadir Shahul Hamid Badshah is a popular pilgrim centre. With its beautiful domed arches and minarets, it is a pleasure to the eye as well as a balm to the soul to visit the Dargah. There are actually three shrines – Nagore, Vanjur and Silladi – with the main centre being at Nagore. The latter has four entrances, with the one on the west, 131 ft tall, being the most impressive. It is called *Periya Minara* in Tamil. This was built by the Tanjore King Pratap Singh around 1760 A D, 200 years after the death of Meeran Sahib, as a thanksgiving for grace received from him. Under the golden dome lie three tombs, with silver entrance doors. They contain the mortal remains of Meeran Sahib, his son Syed Mohammed Yusuf and his daughter-in-law Saeeda Sultana Biwi. Many legends abound on the miracles wrought by Meeran Sahib, particularly his cures of the sick and the ailing. The link with the Hindu religion is strong in the adoption of certain Hindu rituals such as applying sandalwood paste, offering of holy water and other *prasad* and tonsure of the head. The most important festival is *Kanduri Urs* in the lunar month of Jumada al-Thani, which marks the death anniversary of Meeran Sahib. The Nagore Dargah is 4 km from Nagapattinam and 12 km from Karaikal.

MANARKULA VINAYAKA
in Pondicherry

The Manarkula Vinayaka temple is one of the numerous tourist attractions that the Union Territory of Pondicherry offers. This coastal area of Pondicherry has many temples in its different enclaves – Karaikal (in Tamil Nadu), Yanam (in Andhra Pradesh) and Mahe (in Kerala), apart from those in the capital.

The ancient name of Pondicherry was Vedapuri. Two reasons exist for this. First, there is an ancient Vedapureeswarar temple in Pondicherry. Second, this used to be a favourite spot for Vedic scholars to live and explore the depths of knowledge. The Vedapureeswarar Temple, and another famous temple, the Arya Vaisya Temple, were ruined, according to historical accounts. The Vedapureeswarar Temple has now been renovated.

The Manarkula Vinayaka temple was also destroyed, in this case by the French rulers of Pondicherry, but the idol was so powerful that it rose again like a phoenix, say legends. It is believed that the Vinayaka idol was thrown into the sea, but reappeared miraculously!

Undoubtedly, the history of the 300-year-old temple is chequered. The French banned the annual temple festival from taking place in the streets of Pondicherry. They wanted to propagate French culture in this area, which was under their control. The people revolted and about 15,000 of them gathered. All workers in local textile mills, they were about to begin a march to Chennai (Madras), when the French relented, worried about the adverse effect on the mills. This incident was not a stray one and kept repeating till the God had his way. Dupleix, the French governor, became fond of Lord Vinayaka! Things went smoothly, thereafter.

The original name of the temple was 'Manarkula Vinayaka'. This translates to 'Vinayaka who lives in an area bounded by sand'. The sea and the sands are to the eastern precincts of the temple. There is also a small pond inside the temple. The priest has to be requested to show it to devotees with the help of light from lit camphor. The water in the pond is clear, though the sea is nearby. It is said that anything put into the pond will turn black. The *mandapam* abutting the sanctum sanctorum is replete with paintings of Lord Vinayaka in his numerous forms. *Pujas* are performed as per the Rig Veda.

For long, there was no festival idol in the temple. This was installed and a *kumbabhisekham* was performed in 1966 in the presence of the Kanchi Sankaracharya. The *vigraham* is taken out in procession in a golden chariot on *Karthigai Deepam* day.

The name of the temple has changed over time to 'Manakkula Vinayaka'. It is a popular custom to get newly purchased vehicles blessed by this Lord. The temple and its deity have inspired many a poet to sing its praises. Visitors to Pondicherry (called Puducherry in Tamil) should make it a point to visit this temple.

FAST FACTS

How to reach

Air	:	The nearest airport is Chennai, 162 km away.
Rail	:	Pondicherry is a BG railhead with link to Chennai and Tirupathi.

Road	:	Pondicherry can be easily accessed from Chennai by the East Coast Road. The distance is 162 km.
Local Transport	:	Tourist taxis, taxis, auto rickshaws, cycle rickshaws, horse carts, and bicycles.
Season	:	Throughout the year.
Clothing	:	Tropical, light cottons.
Languages Spoken	:	English, French and Tamil.

Accommodation

Guest Houses of the Ashram:	*Tariff (INR)*	*Phone No:*
Park Guest House:	200 to 600	0413-2334412
International Guest House	150 to 450	0413-2336699
Beach Resorts:		
Pondicherry Ashok	1600-2400	0413-2655160
St.James Beach Resort	1195	0413-2655174
Hotels:		
Mass	600-1650	0413-2204001
Seaside Guest House	350-850	0413-2336494

PLACES OF INTEREST NEARBY

Aurobindo Ashram: Established by the poet and philosopher, Sri Aurobindo in 1926, the Ashram is now the centre of attraction in Pondicherry. It houses the marble *samadhis* of Sri Aurobindo and The Mother. The Ashram conducts myriad activities in Pondicherry, including educational and social. It is also a centre for yoga and meditation.

Auroville: Called 'Universal Town' or 'City of Dawn', Auroville is 10 km north of Pondicherry town. It is a self-contained township where people of different nationalities live and work. There is a beautiful dome-shaped building called Matri Mandir, which serves as a wonderful venue for meditation.

Sacred Heart Church: The Gothic architecture and stained glass panels, which tell the story of the life of Christ, make this an interesting church to visit. It is dedicated to the Sacred Heart of Jesus.

Jamia Mosque: This mosque has some distinctive architectural features. It is located in the Muslim quarter.

Beachfront: The Rue de Rampart, Cours de Chabrol or Gouber Salai is the beachfront in Pondicherry. The promenade is 1.5 km long and people come here to experience the cool sea breeze. The statues of Mahatma Gandhi and Dupleix, the War Memorial and the lighthouse are other attractions here.

Museums: Pondicherry has a number of museums worth visiting. The house of the famous poet Subramania Bharathiar has been converted into a museum. So has the house of the poet Bharathidasan, who was born in Pondicherry. The mansion of Ananda Rangapillai, who was a courtier to Dupleix, was built in 1773 and is a good example of Indo-French architecture. The diary he maintained from 1736 to 1760 can be seen here and is an invaluable source of information on the history of French rule in Pondicherry.

Chunnambar: The backwaters of the Bay of Bengal provide an ideal location for water sports at Chunnambar, 8 km from Pondicherry. One can go for an adventurous speed boat ride or go canoeing.

CAUTIONS

All visitors to temples should take certain precautions. Some are particularly applicable to foreign tourists. They are listed serially

- ❖ Beware of touts, hangers on and beggars. Most famous temples will abound with this group of people, who will try to make a fast buck by promising quick entry for a special price or by offering to put in a word with the temple priests for a *darshan* that is already full or not available on that particular day. Tickets should be bought only from authorised temple counters or their agents. Where beggars are concerned, while it is tempting to drop a few coins into pleading hands, this will result in a melee. Therefore, avoid giving alms.
- ❖ In crowded temples beware of pickpockets. Some pushing and shoving is bound to happen, so it is best to keep a watch on purses and handbags. In addition, unless unavoidable, large amounts of cash need not be carried to temples.
- ❖ Third, keep a very close watch on children. Children below the age of 12 should be escorted always by an adult. Temple festivals are the most common places where parents and children get separated, often because the child sees something it wants to get closer to. In case of a mishap and anyone in the family goes missing, contact the temple authorities and the police immediately and arrange for announcements to be made through loudspeakers. Do not panic.
- ❖ Do not buy food or water from wayside sellers. Carry water from home or buy mineral water with certification. As for

food, temple *prasad* is usually hygienic and the less spicy items should suit even delicate stomachs. If you are going to a restaurant, find a clean one, with no flies flying around, and eat only freshly made food – steamed rice pancakes (*idlis*) are usually a safe bet. Avoid *chutney*. Eat the *sambar* only if hot. Avoid deep fried food and non-vegetarian food, as the latter is more prone to contamination. The other alternative is to buy bread, a bottle of jam or some cheese and make your snack with fresh fruits to go along.

- Be careful with the transport you use. Hire tourist taxis from authorized agencies, which are listed in the telephone directory, or from a tourist taxi stand. The local railway stationmaster will often be of help in picking out a good taxi, as these vehicles tend to congregate near the railway station and public bus stands. Settle the fare in advance, but do not pay in advance unless it is a big agency and it is their practice. Taxi drivers often stop to fill up petrol as soon as the journey starts. If they ask you to pay for the petrol, remember to deduct this amount when the final settlement is made. A 10% tip is acceptable for the driver.
- If you are travelling by auto rickshaw, try your best to get the driver to put on the fare meter. If this fails, settle the fare in advance.
- Hassles over payment will not usually arise if you are using public or tourist buses. The latter are usually more comfortable.
- Most people near temples will speak some English. Guides who speak English may also be available. Fix the payment in advance. Helpful guidebooks are also available in many languages.
- Keep a list of emergency phone numbers with you – family member to be contacted in case of need, doctor and place of stay in the area and in your base.

- Carry a basic first aid kit with you – some over-the-counter medicines for minor ailments, antiseptic solution and plaster. If you are feeling very unwell, contact a doctor or hospital immediately.

Happy Travelling!

BIBLIOGRAPHY
English

1. A History of South India, Neelakanta Sastri K., Madras 1958
2. Temples of South India, Srinivasan K R, National Book Trust, New Delhi 1998
3. Hampi Ruins, Longhurst A H, Asian Educational Services, New Delhi 2002
4. Thulasi Garland, Aswathi Thirunal Gouri Lakshmi Bayi, Bharatiya Vidya Bhavan, Mumbai 1998
5. Temples of South India, Ramaswami N S, Vasan Publications, Bangalore 1998
6. The Royal city -Mysore, Issar T P, Issar T P, Bangalore 1991
7. Spell of the South, South Zone Cultural Centre, Thanjavur 1987
8. Hindu Symbology and other essays, Swami Swahananda, Sri Ramakrishna Math Publications, Chennai
9. Spiritual Heritage of India, Swami Prabhavananda, Sri Ramakrishna Math Publications, Chennai
10. Hindu Gods and Goddesses, Swami Harshananda, Sri Ramakrishna Math Publications, Chennai 1987
11. The essentials of Hinduism, Swami Bhaskarananda, Sri Ramakrishna Math Publications, Chennai 1998
12. Srimad Bhagavad Gita, Swami Paramananda, Sri Ramakrishna Math Publications, Chennai

13. The spiritual Heritage of Tyagaraja, C.Ramanujachari and B.Raghavan, Sri Ramakrishna Math Publications, Chennai
14. Life of Sri Ramanuja, Swami Ramakrishnananda, Sri Ramakrishna Math Publications, Chennai
15. Life and miracles of Sri Raghavendra, Ramandas, Shree Veeresh Prakashan, Hubli
16. Sree Ranganathaswami, Jeannine Auboyer, Srirangam Temple Publication, Trichy 2000
17. Srirangam, S.Aruniappan, Srirangam Devasthanam Publication, Srirangam
18. Sree Simhachala Kshetra Mahatyam, Late Pulipaka Ramachandra Rao Pantulu, Simhachalam Temple Publication, Simhachalam
19. Guruvayur Bhooloka Vaikundham, P V Subramanian, Guruvayur Dewaswom Publication, Guruvayur 2003
20. Chidambaram Temple, Meyyappan S, Manivasagar Publications, Chennai 1996
21. Thai Mookambika, Shankar Kumar V, Shankar Kumar V, Bangalore 1995
22. Sixteen Saiva Temples of Tamil Nadu, Rajagopalan M, Rajagopalan M, Chennai 1995
23. Know your Tirupathi, Sundaracharlu R and Kalyani Sundaracharlu, Kalyani Sundaracharlu, Chennai
24. Tirupathi Sree Venkateswara Balaji, Muniswany Chetty P M, Chukkula Singaiah Chetty, Tirupati
25. Balaji-Venkateshwara Lord of Tirumala- Tirupati, Nanditha Krishna, Vakils, Feffer and Simons Ltd., Mumbai 2000
26. Encyclopaedia Brittanica

TAMIL AND OTHER INDIAN LANGUAGES

1. Vinayaka, Swami Kripananda Variar
2. Ganapathi Cult in Tamil Nadu, N Kalyana Sundaram, Thirukumaran Publications, Tiruchendur 1994
3. Sree Vishnu Puranam, Swamy S K, Prema Publications, Chennai
4. Arubathumoovar Kadhaigal, Prema Publications, Chennai 1967
5. 108 Sree Vaishnava Divya Desas, LIFCO Publications, Chennai
6. Arultharum Thamizhaga Aalayangal, Uma Sankaran, Narmada Publications, Chennai 1992
7. Azhwargal Varalaru, A Ethirajan, Vaishnava Siddhanta Book Publishers, Karaikkudi 1998
8. Chozhanattu Sivalayangal, S Bhaskar, Umamaheswari Publications, Chennai 1999
9. Aalayangalin Arputh Varalaru, P Narayanan, Arivalayam, Chennai 1990
10. Arulmigu Dandayuthapani Thirukkoil, Devasthanam Publication, Palani
11. Mylai Arulmigu Kabaleeswarar Aalaya Thala Varalaru, publication of HR&CE department of Tamil Nadu, 1993
12. Thirukadaiyur Sthala Varalaru, A V Ramasamy, Kumari Publications, Nagapattinam 2001

13. Srivilliputthur Mannin Thiruvizhakkal, S S Maniam, Mazhalai Publications,Srivilliputhur 2002
14. Sree Mookambika Devi, Srivatsa Rajan, Chitramoola Publications,Kollur
15. Suchindram, V Prasanna
16. Varkala Sree Janardhana temple, Temple Publication/ Malayalam
17. SreeVadakkunatha Temple, Temple Publication/ Malayalam and English
18. Anegudde Vinayaka Temple, Temple Publication/ Kannada
19. Sree Vinayaka Thiruthalangal 108, Nagercoil Krishnan, Kumaran Publications,Chennai. 1996